R. W. Church

Occanational Papers

R. W. Church

Occanational Papers

ISBN/EAN: 9783742839497

Manufactured in Europe, USA, Canada, Australia, Japa

Cover: Foto ©Andreas Hilbeck / pixelio.de

Manufactured and distributed by brebook publishing software (www.brebook.com)

R. W. Church

Occanational Papers

OCCASIONAL PAPERS

SELECTED FROM

THE GUARDIAN, THE TIMES, AND
THE SATURDAY REVIEW

1846–1890

BY THE LATE

R. W. CHURCH, M.A., D.C.L.

SOMETIME RECTOR OF WHATLEY, DEAN OF ST. PAUL'S
HONORARY FELLOW OF ORIEL COLLEGE

IN TWO VOLS.—VOL. II

London

MACMILLAN AND CO., Limited
NEW YORK: THE MACMILLAN COMPANY

1897

First Edition February 1897
Reprinted April 1897

CONTENTS

I
                                                                PAGE
MR. GLADSTONE ON THE ROYAL SUPREMACY   .   1

II
JOYCE ON COURTS OF SPIRITUAL APPEAL   .   21

III
PRIVY COUNCIL JUDGMENTS   .   .   32

IV
SIR JOHN COLERIDGE ON THE PURCHAS CASE   .   48

V
MR. GLADSTONE'S LETTER ON THE ENGLISH CHURCH   63

VI
DISENDOWMENT   70

VII
The New Court

VIII
Mozley's Bampton Lectures

IX
Ecce Homo

X
The Author of "Robert Elsmere" on a [?] Reformation

XI
Renan's "Vie de Jésus"

XII
Renan's "Les Apôtres"

XIII
Renan's Hibbert Lectures

XIV
Renan's "Souvenirs d'Enfance"

VII

THE NEW COURT

VIII

MOZLEY'S BAMPTON LECTURES

IX

ECCE HOMO

X

THE AUTHOR OF "ROBERT ELSMERE" ON A NEW REFORMATION

XI

RENAN'S "VIE DE JÉSUS"

XII

RENAN'S "LES APÔTRES"

XIII

RENAN'S HIBBERT LECTURES

XIV

RENAN'S "SOUVENIRS D'ENFANCE"

CONTENTS

XV
LIFE OF FREDERICK ROBERTSON ... 253

XVI
LIFE OF BARON BUNSEN ... 273

XVII
COLERIDGE'S MEMOIR OF KEBLE ... 292

XVIII
MAURICE'S THEOLOGICAL ESSAYS ... 309

XIX
FREDERICK DENISON MAURICE ... 320

XX
SIR RICHARD CHURCH ... 327

XXI
DEATH OF BISHOP WILBERFORCE ... 334

XXII
RETIREMENT OF THE PROVOST OF ORIEL ... 343

XXIII
MARK PATTISON ... 351

XXIV
	PAGE
Pattison's Essays	357

XXV
Bishop Frazer 373

XXVI
Newman's "Apologia" 379

XXVII
Dr. Newman on the "Eirenicon" . . 398

XXVIII
Newman's Parochial Sermons . . . 441

XXIX
Cardinal Newman 463

XXX
Cardinal Newman's Course . . 470

XXXI
Cardinal Newman's Naturalness . . . 479

XXXII
Lord Blachford . . . 483

MR. GLADSTONE ON THE ROYAL SUPREMACY[1]

Mr. Gladstone has not disappointed the confidence of those who have believed of him that when great occasions presented themselves, of interest to the Church, he would not be found wanting. A statesman has a right to reserve himself and bide his time, and in doubtful circumstances may fairly ask us to trust his discretion as to when is his time. But there are critical seasons about whose seriousness there can be no doubt. One of these is now passing over the English Church. And Mr. Gladstone has recognised it, and borne himself in it with a manliness, earnestness, and temper which justify those who have never despaired of his doing worthy service to the Church, with whose cause he so early identified himself.

The pamphlet before us, to which he has put his

[1] *Remarks on the Royal Supremacy, as it is Defined by Reason, History, and the Constitution.* A Letter to the Lord Bishop of London, by the Right Hon. W. E. Gladstone, M.P. for the University of Oxford. *Guardian*, 10th July 1850.

name, is the most important, perhaps, of all that have been elicited by the deep interest felt in the matter on which it treats. Besides its importance as the expression of the opinion, and, it must be added, the anxieties of a leading statesman, it has two intrinsic advantages. It undertakes to deal closely and strictly with those facts in the case mainly belonging to the period of the Reformation, on which the great stress has been laid in the arguments both against our liberty and our very being as a Church. And, further, it gives us on these facts, and, in connection with them, on the events of the crisis itself, the judgment and the anticipations of a mind at once deeply imbued with religious philosophy, and also familiar with the consideration of constitutional questions, and accustomed to view them in their practical entanglements as well as in their abstract and ideal forms. It is, indeed, thus only that the magnitude and the true extent of the relations of the present contest can be appreciated. The intrinsic greatness, indeed, of religious interests cannot receive addition of dignity here. But the manner of treating them may. And Mr. Gladstone has done what was both due to the question at issue, and in the highest degree important for its serious consideration and full elucidation, in raising it from a discussion of abstract principles to what it is no less—a real problem of English constitutional law.

The following passage will show briefly the ground over which the discussion travels :—

The questions, then, that I seek to examine will be as follow :—

1. Did the statutes of the Reformation involve the abandonment of the duty of the Church to be the guardian of her faith?

2. Is the present composition of the appellate tribunal conformable either to reason or to the statutes of the Reformation, and the spirit of the Constitution as expressed in them?

3. Is the Royal Supremacy, according to the Constitution, any bar to the adjustment of the appellate jurisdiction in such a manner as that it shall convey the sense of the Church in questions of doctrine?

All these questions I humbly propose to answer in the negative, and so to answer them in conformity with what I understand to be the principles of our history and law. My endeavour will be to show that the powers of the State so determined, in regard to the legislative office of the Church (setting aside for the moment any question as to the right of assent in the laity), are powers of restraint; that the jurisdictions united and annexed to the Crown are corrective jurisdictions; and that their exercise is subject to the general maxim, that the laws ecclesiastical are to be administered by ecclesiastical judges.

Mr. Gladstone first goes into the question—What was done, and what was the understanding at the Reformation? All agree that this was a time of great changes, and that in the settlement resulting from them the State took, and the Church yielded, a great deal. And on the strength of this broad general fact, the details of the settlement have been treated with an *a priori* boldness, not deficient often in that kind of precision which can be gained by totally putting aside inconvenient or perplexing elements, and having both its intellectual and moral recommendations to many minds; but highly undesirable where a great issue has been raised for the religion of millions, and the political constitution of a great nation. Men who are not lawyers seem to have thought that, by taking a lawyer's view, or what they considered such, of the Reformation Acts, they had disposed of the question for ever. It was, indeed, time for a statesman to step in, and protest, if only in the name of constitutional and political philosophy, against so narrow and unreal an abuse of law-texts—documents of the highest importance in right hands, and in their proper place, but capable, as all must know, of leading to inconceivable absurdity in speculation, and not impossibly fatal confusion in fact.

The bulk of this pamphlet is devoted to the consideration of the language and effect, legal and constitutional, of those famous statutes with the titles of which recent controversy has made us so familiar. Mr. Gladstone makes it clear that it does not at all follow that because the Church conceded a great deal, she conceded, or even was expected to concede, indefinitely, whatever might be claimed. She conceded, but she conceded by compact;—a compact which supposed her power to concede, and secured to her untouched whatever was not conceded. And she did not concede, nor was asked for, her highest power, her legislative power. She did not concede, nor was asked to concede, that any but her own ministers—by the avowal of all drawing their spiritual authority from a source which nothing human could touch—should declare her doctrine, or should be employed in administering her laws. What she did concede was, not original powers of direction and guidance, but powers of restraint and correction;—under securities greater, both in form and in working, than those possessed at the time by any other body in England, for their rights and liberties—greater far than might have been expected, when the consequences of a long foreign supremacy—not righteously maintained and exercised, because at the moment unrighteously thrown off—increased the control which the Civil Government always must claim over the Church, by the sudden abstraction of a power which, though usurping, was spiritual; and presented to the ambition of a despotic King a number of unwarrantable prerogatives which the separation from the Pope had left without an owner.

On the trite saying, meant at first to represent, roughly and invidiously, the effect of the Reformation, and lately urged as technically and literally true—" The assertion that in the time of Henry VIII. the See of Rome was both 'the source and centre of ecclesiastical jurisdiction,' and therefore the supreme judge of doctrine; and that this power of the Pope was transferred in its entireness to the Crown "—Mr. Gladstone remarks as follows:—

I will not ask whether the Pope was indeed at that time the supreme judge of doctrine ; it is enough for me that not very long before the Council of Constance had solemnly said otherwise, in words which, though they may be forgotten, cannot be annulled. . . .

That the Pope was the source of ecclesiastical jurisdiction in the English Church before the Reformation is an assertion of the gravest import, which ought not to have been thus taken for granted. . . . The fact really is this :—A modern opinion, which, by force of modern circumstances, has of late gained great favour in the Church of Rome, is here dated back and fastened upon ages to whose fixed principles it was unknown and alien ; and the case of the Church of England is truly hard when the Papal authority of the Middle Ages is exaggerated far beyond its real and historical scope, with the effect only of fastening that visionary exaggeration, through the medium of another fictitious notion of wholesale transfer of the Papal privileges to the Crown, upon us, as the true and legal measure of the Royal Supremacy.

It appears to me that he who alleges in the gross that the Papal prerogatives were carried over to the Crown at the Reformation, greatly belies the laws and the people of that era. Their unvarying doctrine was, that they were restoring the ancient regal jurisdiction, and abolishing one that had been usurped. But there is no evidence to show that these were identical in themselves, or co-extensive in their range. In some respects the Crown obtained at that period more than the Pope had ever had ; for I am not aware that the Convocation required his license to deliberate upon canons, or his assent to their promulgation. In other respects the Crown acquired less; for not the Crown, but the Archbishop of Canterbury was appointed to exercise the power of dispensation in things lawful, and to confirm Episcopal elections. Neither the Crown nor the Archbishop succeeded to such Papal prerogatives as were contrary to the law of the land; for neither the 26th of Henry VIII. nor the 2nd of Elizabeth annexed to the Crown all the powers of correction and reformation which had been actually claimed by the Pope, but only such as "hath heretofore been or may lawfully be exercised or used." . . . The "ancient jurisdiction," and not the then recently claimed or exercised powers, was the measure and the substance of what the Crown received from the Legislature; and, with those ancient rights for his rule, no impartial man would say that the Crown was the source of ecclesiastical jurisdiction according to the statutes of the Reformation. But the statutes of the Reformation era relating to jurisdiction, having as statutes the assent of the laity, and accepted by the canons of the clergy, are the standard to which the Church has bound herself as a religious society to conform.

The word "jurisdiction" has played an important part in the recent discussions; whether its meaning, with its various involved and associated ideas, by no means free from intricacy and confusion, have been duly unravelled and made clear, we may be permitted to doubt. A distinction of the canonists has been assumed by those who have used the word with most precision—*assumed*, though it is by no means a simple and indisputable one. Mr. Gladstone draws attention to this, when, after noticing that nowhere in the ecclesiastical legislation of Elizabeth is the claim made on behalf of the Crown to be the source of ecclesiastical jurisdiction, he admits that this *is* the language of the school of English law, and offers an explanation of the fact. That which Acts of Parliament do not say, which is negatived in actual practice by contradictory and irreconcilable facts, is yet wanted by lawyers for the theoretic completeness of their idea and system of law. The fact is important as a reminder that what is one real aspect, or, perhaps, the most complete and consistent representation of a system on paper, may be inadequate and untrue as an exhibition of its real working and appearance in the world.

To sum up the whole, then, I contend that the Crown did not claim by statute, either to be of right, or to become by convention, the *source* of that kind of action, which was committed by the Saviour to the Apostolic Church, whether for the enactment of laws, or for the administration of its discipline; but the claim was, that all the canons of the Church, and all its judicial proceedings, inasmuch as they were to form parts respectively of the laws and of the legal administration of justice in the kingdom, should run only with the assent and sanction of the Crown. They were to carry with them a double force—a force of coercion, visible and palpable; a force addressed to conscience, neither visible nor palpable, and in its nature only capable of being inwardly appreciated. Was it then unreasonable that they should bear outwardly the tokens of that power to which they were to be indebted for their outward observance, and should work only within by that wholly different influence that governs the kingdom which is not of this world, and flows immediately from its King? . . . But while, according to the letter and spirit of the law, such appear to be the limits of the Royal Supremacy in regard to the *legislative*, which is the highest, action of the Church, I do not deny that in other branches it goes farther, and will now assume that the supremacy in all causes, which is at least a claim to control at every point the jurisdiction of the Church, may also be construed to mean as much as that the Crown is the ultimate source of jurisdiction of whatever kind.

Here, however, I must commence by stating that, as it appears to me, Lord Coke and others attach to the very word jurisdiction a narrower sense than it bears in popular acceptation, or in the works of canonists—a sense which excludes altogether that of the canonists; and also a sense which appears to be the genuine and legitimate sense of the word in its first intention. Now, when we are endeavouring to appreciate the force and scope of the legal doctrine concerning ecclesiastical and spiritual jurisdiction, it is plain that we must take the term employed in the sense of our own law, and not in the different and derivative sense in which it has been used by canonists and theologians. But canonists themselves bear witness to the distinction which I have now pointed out. The one kind is *Jurisdictio coactiva proprie dicta, principibus data;* the other is *Jurisdictio improprié dicta ac mere spiritualis, Ecclesiæ ejusque Episcopis a Christo data.* . . .

Properly speaking, I submit that there is no such thing as jurisdiction in any private association of men, or anywhere else than under the authority of the State. *Jus* is the scheme of rights subsisting between men in the relations, not of all, but of civil society; and *jurisdictio* is the authority to determine and enunciate those rights from time to time. Church authority, therefore, so long as it stands alone, is not in strictness of speech, or according to history, jurisdiction, because it is not essentially bound up with civil law.

But when the State and the Church came to be united, by the conversion of nations, and the submission of the private conscience to Christianity—when the Church placed her power of self-regulation under the guardianship of the State, and the State annexed its own potent sanction to rules, which without it would have been matter of mere private contract, then *jus* or civil right soon found its way into the Church, and the respective interests and obligations of its various orders, and of the individuals composing them, were regulated by provisions forming part of the law of the land. Matter ecclesiastical or spiritual moulded in the forms of civil law, became the proper subject of ecclesiastical or spiritual jurisdiction, properly so called.

Now, inasmuch as laws are abstractions until they are put into execution, through the medium of executive and judicial authority, it is evident that the cogency of the reasons for welding together, so to speak, civil and ecclesiastical authority is much more full with regard to these latter branches of power than with regard to legislation. There had been in the Church, from its first existence as a spiritual society, a right to govern, to decide, to adjudge for spiritual purposes; that was a true, self-governing authority; but it was not properly jurisdiction. It naturally came to be included, or rather enfolded, in the term, when for many centuries the secular arm had been in perpetual co-operation with the tribunals of the Church. The thing to be done, and the means by which it was done, were bound together; the authority and the power being always united in fact, were treated as an unity for the purposes of law. As the potentate possessing not the head but the mouth or issue of a river, has the right to determine what shall pass to or from the sea, so the State, standing between an injunction of the Church and its execution, had a right to refer that execution wholly to its own authority.

There was not contained or implied in such a doctrine any denial of the original and proper authority of the Church for its own self-government, or any assertion that it had passed to and become the property of the Crown. But that authority, though not in its source, yet in its exercise, had immersed itself in the forms of law; had invoked and obtained the aid of certain elements of external power, which belonged exclusively to the State, and for the right and just use of which the State had a separate and independent responsibility, so that it could not, without breach of duty, allow them to be parted from itself. It was, therefore, I submit, an intelligible and, under given circumstances, a warrantable scheme of action, under which the State virtually said: Church decrees, taking the form of law, and obtaining their full and certain effect only in that form, can be executed only as law, and while they are in process of being put into practice can only be regarded as law, and therefore the whole power of their execution, that is to say, all jurisdiction in matters ecclesiastical and spiritual, must, according to the doctrine of law, proceed from the fountain-head of law, namely, from the Crown. In the last legal resort there can be but one origin for all which is to be done in societies of men by force of legal power; nor, if so, can doubt arise what that origin must be.

If you allege that the Church has a spiritual authority to regulate doctrines and discipline, still, as you choose to back that authority with the force of temporal law, and as the State is exclusively responsible for the use of that force, you must be content to fold up the authority of the Church in that exterior form through which you desire it to take effect. From whatsoever source it may come originally, it comes to the subject as law; it therefore comes to him from the fountain of law. . . . The faith of Christendom has been received in England; the discipline of the Christian Church, cast into its local form, modified by statutes of the realm, and by the common law and prerogative, has from time immemorial been received in England; but we can view them only as law, although you may look further back to the divine and spiritual sanction, in virtue of which they acquired that social position, which made it expedient that they should associate with law and should therefore become law.

But as to the doctrine itself, it is most obvious to notice that it is not more strange, and not necessarily more literally real, than those other legal views of royal prerogative and perfection, which are the received theory of all our great jurists—accepted by them for very good reasons, but not the less astounding when presented as naked and independent truths. It was natural enough that they should claim for the Crown the origination of ecclesiastical jurisdiction, considering what else they claimed for it. Mr. Allen can present us with a more than Chinese idea of royal power, when he draws it only from Blackstone :—

They may have heard [he says, speaking of the "unlearned in the law"] that the law of England is founded in reason and wisdom. The first lesson they are taught will inform them, that the law of England attributes to the King absolute perfection, absolute immortality, and legal ubiquity. They will be told that the King of England is not only incapable of doing wrong, but of thinking wrong. They will be informed that he never dies, that he is invisible as well as immortal, and that in the eye of the law he is present at one and the same instant in every court of justice within his dominions. . . . They may have been told that the royal prerogative in England is limited; but when they consult the sages of the law, they will be assured that the legal authority of the King of England is absolute and irresistible . . . that all are under him, while he is under none but God. . . .

If they have had the benefit of a liberal education, they have been taught that to obtain security for persons and property was the great end for which men submitted to the restraints of civil government; and they may have heard of the indispensable necessity of an independent magistracy for the due administration of justice; but when they direct their inquiries to the laws and constitution of England, they will find it an established maxim in that country that all jurisdiction emanates from the Crown. They will be told that the King is not only the chief, but the sole magistrate of the nation; and that all others act by his commission, and in subordination to him.[1]

"In the most limited monarchy," as he says truly the "King is represented in law books, as in theory an absolute sovereign." "Even now," says Mr. Gladstone, "after three centuries of progress toward democratic sway, the Crown has prerogatives by acting upon which, within their strict and unquestioned bounds, it might at any time throw the country into confusion. And so has each House of Parliament." But if the absolute supremacy of the Crown *in the legal point of view exactly the same over temporal matters and causes as over spiritual*, is taken by no sane man to be a literal fact in temporal matters, it is violating the analogy of the Constitution, and dealing with the most important subjects in a mere spirit of narrow perverseness, to insist that it can have none but a literal meaning in ecclesiastical matters; and that the Church *did* mean, though the State *did not*, to accept a despotic prerogative, unbounded by custom, convention, or law, and unchecked by acknowledged and active powers in herself. Yet such is the assumption, made in bitterness and vexation of spirit by some of those who have lately so hastily given up her

[1] *Allen on the Royal Prerogative*, pp. 1-3.

cause; made with singular assurance by others, who, Liberals in all their political doctrines, have, for want of better arguments, invoked prerogative against the Church.

What the securities and checks were that the Church, not less than the nation, contemplated and possessed, are not expressed in the theory itself of the royal prerogative; and, as in the case of the nation, we might presume beforehand, that they would be found in practice rather than on paper. They were, however, real ones. "With the same theoretical laxity and practical security," as in the case of Parliaments and temporal judges, "was provision made for the conduct of Church affairs." Making allowance for the never absent disturbances arising out of political trouble and of personal character, the Church had very important means of making her own power felt in the administration of her laws, as well as in the making of them.

The real question, I apprehend, is this:—When the Church assented to those great concessions which were embodied in our permanent law at the Reformation, had she *adequate securities* that the powers so conveyed would be exercised, upon the whole, with a due regard to the integrity of her faith, and of her office, which was and has ever been a part of that faith? I do not ask whether these securities were all on parchment or not —whether they were written or unwritten—whether they were in statute, or in common law, or in fixed usage, or in the spirit of the Constitution and in the habits of the people—I ask the one vital question, whether, whatever they were in form, they were in substance sufficient?

The securities which the Church had were these: First, that the assembling of the Convocation was obviously necessary for the purposes of taxation; secondly and mainly, that the very solemn and fundamental laws by which the jurisdiction of the See of Rome was cut off, assigned to the spiritualty of the realm the care of matters spiritual, as distinctly and formally as to the temporalty the care of matters temporal; and that it was an understood principle, and (as long as it continued) a regular usage of the Constitution, that ecclesiastical laws should be administered by ecclesiastical judges. These were the securities on which the Church relied; on which she had a right to rely; and on which, for a long series of years, her alliance was justified by the results.

And further:—

The Church had this great and special security on which to rely, that the Sovereigns of this country were, for a century after the Reformation, amongst her best instructed, and even in some instances her most devoted children: that all who made up the governing body (with an insignificant exception) owned personal allegiance to her, and that she might well rest on that personal allegiance as warranting beforehand the expectation, which after experience made good, that the office of the State towards her would be discharged in a friendly and kindly spirit, and that the principles of constitutional law and civil order would not be strained against her, but fairly and fully applied in her behalf.

These securities she now finds herself deprived of. This is the great change made in her position—made insensibly, and in a great measure, undesignedly—which has altered altogether the understanding on which she stood towards the Crown at the Reformation. It now turns out that that understanding, though it might have been deemed sufficient for the time, was not precise enough; and further, was not sufficiently looked after in the times which followed. And on us comes the duty of taking care that it be not finally extinguished; thrown off by the despair of one side, and assumed by the other as at length abandoned to their aggression.

Mr. Gladstone comes to the question with the feelings of a statesman, conscious of the greatness and excellence of the State, and anxious that the Church should not provoke its jealousy, and in urging her claims should "take her stand, as to all matters of substance and principle, on the firm ground of history and law." It makes his judgment on the present state of things more solemn, and his conviction of the necessity of amending it more striking, when they are those of one so earnest for conciliation and peace. But on constitutional not less than on other grounds, he pronounces the strongest condemnation on the present formation of the Court of Appeal, which, working in a way which even its framers did not contemplate, has brought so much distress into the Church, and which yet, in defiance of principle, of consistency, and of the admission of its faultiness, is so recklessly maintained. Feeling and stating very strongly the evil sustained by the Church, from the suspension of her legislative powers,—"that loss of command over her work, and over the heart of the nation, which it has brought upon her,"—so strongly indeed that his words, coming from one familiar with the chances and hazards of a deliberative assembly, give new weight to the argument for the resumption of those powers,—feeling all this, he is ready to acquiesce in the measure beyond which the Bishops did not feel authorised to go, and which Mr. Gladstone regards as "representing the extremest point up to which the love of peace might properly carry the concessions of the Church":—

That which she is entitled in the spirit of the Constitution to demand would be that the Queen's ecclesiastical laws shall be administered by the Queen's ecclesiastical judges, of whom the Bishops are the chief; and this, too, under the checks which the sitting of a body appointed for ecclesiastical legislation would impose.

But if it is not of vital necessity that a Church Legislature should sit at the present time—if it is not of vital necessity that all causes termed ecclesiastical should be treated under special safeguards—if it is not of vital necessity that the function of judgment should be taken out of the hands of the existing court—let the Church frankly and at once subscribe to every one of these great concessions, and reduce her demands to a *minimum* at the outset.

Laws ecclesiastical by ecclesiastical judges, let this be her principle; it plants her on the ground of ancient times, of the Reformation, of our continuous history, of reason and of right. The utmost moderation, in the application of the principle, let this be her temper, and then her case will be strong in the face of God and man, and, come what may, she will conquer. . . . If, my Lord, it be felt by the rulers of the Church, that a scheme like this will meet sufficiently the necessities of her case, it must be no small additional comfort to them to feel that their demand is every way within the spirit of the Constitution, and short of the terms which the great compact of the Reformation would authorise you to seek. You, and not those who are against you, will take your stand with Coke and Blackstone; you, and not they, will wield the weapons of constitutional principle and law; you, and not they, will be entitled to claim the honour of securing the peace of the State no less than the faith of the Church; you, and not they, will justly point the admonitory finger to those remarkable words of the Institutes:—

"And certain it is, that this Kingdom hath been best governed, and peace and quiet preserved, when both parties, that is, when the justices of the temporal courts and the ecclesiastical judges have kept themselves within their proper jurisdiction, without encroaching or usurping one upon another; and where such encroachments or usurpations have been made, they have been the seeds of great trouble and inconvenience."

Because none can resist the principle of your proposal, who admit that the Church has a sphere of proper jurisdiction at all, or any duty beyond that of taking the rule of her doctrine and her practice from the lips of ministers or parliaments. If it shall be deliberately refused to adopt a proposition so moderate, so guarded and restrained in the particular instance, and so sustained by history, by analogy, and by common reason, in the case of the faith of the Church, and if no preferable measure be substituted, it can only be in consequence of a latent intention that the voice of the Civil Power should be henceforward supreme in the determination of Christian doctrine.

We trust that such an assurance, backed as it is by the solemn and earnest warnings of one who is not an enthusiast or an agitator, but one of the leading men in the Parliament of England, will not be without its full weight with those on whom devolves the duty of guiding and leading us in this crisis. The Bishops of England have a great responsibility on them. Reason, not less than Christian loyalty and Christian charity, requires the fairest interpretation of their acts, and it may be of their hesitation,—the utmost consideration of their difficulties. But reason, not less than Christian loyalty and charity, expects that, having accepted the responsibilities of the Episcopate, they should not withdraw from them when they arrive; and that there should be neither shrinking nor rest nor compromise till the creed and the rights of the Church entrusted to their fidelity be placed, as far as depends on them, beyond danger.

II

JOYCE ON COURTS OF SPIRITUAL APPEAL[1]

NOTHING can be more natural than the extreme dissatisfaction felt by a large body of persons in the Church of England at the present Court of Final Appeal in matters of doctrine. The grievance, and its effect, may have been exaggerated; and the expressions of feeling about it certainly have not always been the wisest and most becoming. But as the Church of England *is* acknowledged to hold certain doctrines on matters of the highest importance, and, in common with all other religious bodies, claims the right of saying what are her own doctrines, it is not surprising that an arrangement which seems likely to end in handing over to indifferent or unfriendly judges the power of saying what those doctrines are, or even whether she has any doctrines at all, should create irritation and impatience. There is nothing peculiar to the English Church in the assumption, either that

[1] *Ecclesia Vindicata; a Treatise on Appeals in Matters Spiritual.* By James Wayland Joyce. *Saturday Review,* 22nd October 1864.

outsiders should not meddle with and govern what she professes to believe and teach, or that the proper and natural persons to deal with theological questions are the class set apart to teach and maintain her characteristic belief. Whatever may ultimately become of these assumptions, they unquestionably represent the ideas which have been derived from the earliest and the uniform practice of the Christian Church, and are held by most even of the sects which have separated from it. To any one who does not look upon the English Church as simply a legally constituted department of the State, like the army or navy or the department of revenue, and believes it to have a basis and authority of its own, antecedent to its rights by statute, there cannot but be a great anomaly in an arrangement which, when doctrinal questions are pushed to their final issues, seems to deprive her of any voice or control in the matters in which she is most interested, and commits them to the decision, not merely of a lay, but of a secular and not necessarily even Christian court, where the feeling about them is not unlikely to be that represented by the story, told by Mr. Joyce, of the eminent lawyer who said of some theological debate that he could only decide it "by tossing up a coin of the realm." The anomaly of such a court can hardly be denied, both as a matter of theory and —supposing it to matter at all what Church doctrine really is—as illustrated in some late results of its action. It is still more provoking to observe, as Mr.

Joyce brings out in his historical sketch, that simple carelessness and blundering have conspired with the evident tendency of things to cripple and narrow the jurisdiction of the Church in what seems to be her proper sphere. The ecclesiastical appeals, before the Reformation, were to the ecclesiastical jurisdiction alone. They were given to the civil power by the Tudor legislation, but to the civil power acting, if not by the obligation of law, yet by usage and in fact, through ecclesiastical organs and judges. Lastly, by a recent change, of which its authors have admitted that they did not contemplate the effect, these appeals are now to the civil jurisdiction acting through purely civil courts. It is an aggravation of this, when the change which seems so formidable has become firmly established, to be told that it was, after all, the result of accident and inadvertence, and a "careless use of terms in drafting an Act of Parliament"; and that difficult and perilous theological questions have come, by "a haphazard chance," before a court which was never meant to decide them. It cannot be doubted that those who are most interested in the Church of England feel deeply and strongly about keeping up what they believe to be the soundness and purity of her professed doctrine; and they think that, under fair conditions, they have clear and firm ground for making good their position. But it seems by no means unlikely that in the working of the Court of Final Appeal there will be found a means of evading the substance of questions, and of disposing of very important issues by a side wind, to the prejudice of what have hitherto been recognised as rightful claims. An arrangement which bears hard upon the Church theoretically, as a controversial argument in the hands of Dr. Manning or Mr. Binney, and as an additional proof of its Erastian subjection to the State, and which also works ill and threatens serious mischief, may fairly be regarded by Churchmen with jealousy and dislike, and be denounced as injurious to interests for which they have a right to claim respect. The complaint that the State is going to force new senses on theological terms, or to change by an unavowed process the meaning of acknowledged formularies in such a body as the English Church, is at least as deserving of attention as the reluctance of conscientious Dissenters to pay Church-rates.

Mr. Joyce's book shows comprehensively and succinctly the history of the changes which have brought matters to their present point, and the look which they wear in the eyes of a zealous Churchman, disturbed both by the shock given to his ideas of fitness and consistency, and by the prospect of practical evils. It is a clergyman's view of the subject, but it is not disposed of by saying that it is a clergyman's view. It is incomplete and one-sided, and leaves out considerations of great importance which ought to be attended to in forming a judgment on the whole question; but it is difficult to say that, regarded simply in itself, the claim that the Church should settle her own controversies, and that Church doctrine should be judged of in Church courts, is not a reasonable one. The truth is that the present arrangement, if we think only of its abstract suitableness and its direct and ostensible claims to our respect, would need Swift himself to do justice to its exquisite unreasonableness. It is absurd to assume, as it is assumed in the whole of our ecclesiastical legislation, that the Church is bound to watch most jealously over doctrine, and then at the last moment to refuse her the natural means of guarding it. It is absurd to assume that the "spiritualty" are the only proper persons to teach doctrine, and then to act as if they were unfit to judge of doctrine. It is not easy, in the abstract, to see why articles which were trusted to clergymen to draw up may not be trusted to clergymen to explain, and why what there was learning and wisdom enough to do in the violent party times and comparative inexperience of the Reformation, cannot be safely left to the learning and wisdom of our day for correction or completion. If Churchmen and ecclesiastics may care too much for the things about which they dispute, it seems undeniable that lawyers who need not even be Christians, may care for them too little; and if the Churchmen make a mistake in the matter, at least it is their own affair, and they may be more fairly made to take the consequences of their own acts than of other people's. A strong case, if a strong case were all that was wanted, might be made out for a change in the authority which at present pronounces in the last resort on Church of England doctrine.

But the difficulty is, not to see that the present state of things, which has come about almost by accident, is irregular and unsatisfactory, and that in it the civil power has stolen a march on the privileges which even Tudors and Hanoverians left to the Church, but to suggest what would be more just and more promising. A mixed tribunal, composed of laymen and ecclesiastics, would be in effect, as Mr Joyce perceives, simply the present court with a sham colour of Church authority added to it; and he describes with candid force the confusion which might arise if the lawyers and divines took different sides, and how, in the unequal struggle, the latter might "find themselves hopelessly prostrate in the stronger grasp of their more powerful associates." His own scheme of a theological and ecclesiastical committee of reference, to which a purely legal tribunal might send down questions of doctrine to be answered, as "experts" or juries give answers about matters of science or matters of fact, is hardly more hopeful; for even he would not bind the legal court, as of course it could not be bound, to accept the doctrine of the ecclesiastical committee. He promises, indeed, on the authority of Lord Derby, that in ninety-nine cases out of a hundred the lawyers would accept the answer of the divines; but whatever the scandal is now, it would be far greater if an unorthodox judgment were given in flat contradiction to the report of the committee of reference.

As to a purely ecclesiastical Court of Appeal,

in the present state of the Church both in England and all over the world, it ought to console those who must be well aware that here at least it is hardly to be looked for, to reflect how such courts act, after all, where they have the power to act, and how far things would have gone in a better or happier fashion among us if, instead of the Privy Council, there had been a tribunal of divines to give final judgment. The history of appeals to Rome, from the days of the Jansenists and Fénelon to those of Lamennais, may be no doubt satisfactory to those who believe it necessary to ascribe to the Pope the highest wisdom and the most consummate justice; but to those who venture to notice the real steps of the process, and the collateral considerations, political and local, which influenced the decision, the review is hardly calculated to make those who are debarred from it regret the loss of this unalloyed purity of ecclesiastical jurisdiction. And, as regards ourselves, it is true that an ecclesiastical tribunal would hardly have been ingenious enough to find the means of saying that Messrs. Wilson and Williams had not taught in contradiction to the doctrines of the English Church, and that they actually, under its present constitution, possessed the liberty which, under a different—and, as some people think, a better—constitution, they might possess. But it ought also to be borne in mind what other judgments ecclesiastical tribunals might have given. An ecclesiastical tribunal, unless it had been packed or accidentally one-sided, would probably have condemned Mr. Gorham. An ecclesiastical tribunal would almost certainly have expelled Archdeacon Denison from his preferments. Indeed, the judgment of the Six Doctors on Dr. Pusey, arbitrary and unconstitutional as it may be considered, was by no means a doubtful foreshadowing of what a verdict upon him would have been from any court that we can imagine formed of the high ecclesiastical authorities of the time. It undoubtedly seems the most natural thing in the world that a great religious body should settle, without hindrance, its own doctrines and control its own ministers ; but it is also some compensation for the perversity with which the course of things has interfered with ideal completeness, that our condition, if it had been theoretically perfect, would have been perfectly intolerable.

It would be highly unwise in those who direct the counsels of the Church of England to accept a practical disadvantage for the gain of a greater simplicity and consistency of system. The true moral to be deduced from the anomalies of ecclesiastical appeals seems to be, to have as little to do with them as possible. The idea of seeking a remedy for the perplexities of theology in judicial rulings, and the rage for having recourse to law courts, are of recent date in our controversies. They were revived among us as one of the results of the violent panic caused by the Oxford movement, and of the inconsiderate impatience of surprised ignorance which dictated extreme and forcible measures ; and as this is a kind of game at which, when once started, both parties can play, the policy of setting the law in motion to silence theological opponents has become a natural and favourite one. But it may be some excuse for the legislators who, in 1833, in constructing a new Court of Appeal, so completely forgot or underrated the functions which it would be called to discharge in the decision of momentous doctrinal questions, that at the time no one thought much of carrying theological controversies to legal arbitrament. The experiment is a natural one to have been made in times of strong and earnest religious contention; but, now that it has had its course, it is not difficult to see that it was a mistaken one. There seems something almost ludicrously incongruous in bringing a theological question into the atmosphere and within the technical handling of a law court, and in submitting delicate and subtle attempts to grasp the mysteries of the unseen and the infinite, of God and the soul, of grace and redemption, to the hard logic and intentionally confined and limited view of forensic debate. Theological truth, in the view of all who believe in it, must always remain independent of a legal decision ; and, therefore, as regards any real settlement, a theological question must come out of a legal sentence in a totally different condition from any others where the true and indisputable law of the case is, for the time at least, what the supreme tribunal has pronounced it to be. People chafed at not getting what they thought the plain broad conclusions from facts and documents accepted; they appealed to law from the uncertainty of controversy, and found law still more uncertain, and a good deal more dangerous. They thought that they were going to condemn crimes and expel wrongdoers; they found that these prosecutions inevitably assumed the character of the old political trials, which were but an indirect and very mischievous form of the struggle between two avowed parties, and in which, though the technical question was whether the accused had committed the crime, the real one was whether the alleged crime were a crime at all. Accordingly, wider considerations than those arising out of the strict merits of the case told upon the decision; and the negative judgment, and resolute evasion of a condemnation, in each of the cases which were of wide and serious importance, were proofs of the same tendency in English opinion which has made political trials, except in the most extreme cases, almost inconceivable. They mean that the questions raised must be fought out and settled in a different and more genuine way, and that law feels itself out of place when called to interfere in them. As all parties have failed in turning the law into a weapon, and yet as all parties have really gained much more than they have lost by the odd anomalies of our ecclesiastical jurisprudence, the wisest course would seem to be for those who feel the deep importance of doctrinal questions to leave the law alone, either as to employing it or attempting to change it. Controversy, argument, the display of the intrinsic and inherent strength of a great and varied system, are what all causes must in the last resort trust to. Lord Westbury will have done the Church of England more good than perhaps he thought of doing, if his *dicta* make theologians see that they can be much better and more hopefully employed than in trying legal conclusions with unorthodox theorisers, or in busying themselves with inventing imaginary improvements for a Final Court of Appeal.

III

PRIVY COUNCIL JUDGMENTS[1]

THE Bishop of London has done a useful service in causing the various decisions of the present Court of Appeal to be collected into a volume. There is such an obvious convenience about the plan that it hardly needed the conventional reason given for it, that "the knowledge generally possessed on the subject of the Court is vague, and the sources from which accurate information can be obtained are little understood; and that people who discuss it ought in the first place to know what the Court is, and what it does." This is the mere customary formula of a preface turned into a rhetorical insinuation which would have been better away; most of those who care about the subject, and have expressed opinions about it, know pretty well the

[1] *A Collection of the Judgments of the Judicial Committee of the Privy Council in Ecclesiastical Cases relating to Doctrine and Discipline; with a Preface by the Lord Bishop of London, and an Historical Introduction.* Edited by the Hon. G. Brodrick, Barrister-at-Law, and Rev. the Hon. W. H. Fremantle, Chaplain to the Bishop of London. *Guardian*, 15th February 1865.

nature of the Court and the result of its working, and whatever variations there may be in the judgment passed upon it arise not from any serious imperfection of knowledge but from differences of principle. It was hardly suitable in a work like this to assume a mystery and obscurity about the subject where there is really none, and to claim superior exactness and authenticity of information about a matter which in all its substantial points is open to all the world. And we could conceive the design, well-intentioned as it is, carried out in a way more fitting to the gravity of the occasion which has suggested it. The Bishop says truly enough that the questions involved in the constitution of such a court are some of the most difficult with which statesmen have to deal. Therefore it seems to us that a collection of the decisions of such a court, put forth for the use of the Church and nation under the authority of the Bishop of London, ought to have had the dignity and the reserve of a work meant for permanence and for the use of men of various opinions, and ought not to have had even the semblance, as this book has, of an *ex parte* pamphlet. The Bishop of London is, of course, quite right to let the Church know what he thinks about the Court of Final Appeal; and he is perfectly justified in recommending us, in forming our opinion, to study carefully the facts of the existing state of things; but it seems hardly becoming to make the facts a vehicle for indirectly forcing on us, in the shape of comments, a very definite and one-sided view of them, which is the very subject of vehement contradiction and dispute. It would have been better to have committed what was necessary in the way of explanation and illustration to some one of greater weight and experience than two clever young men of strong bias and manifest indisposition to respect or attend to, or even to be patient with, any aspect of the subject but their own in this complicated and eventful question, and who, partly from overlooking great and material elements in it, and partly from an imperfect apprehension of what they had to do, have failed to present even the matters of fact with which they deal with the necessary exactness and even-handedness. It seems to us that in a work intended for the general use of the Church and addressed to men of all opinions, they only remember to be thoroughgoing advocates and justifiers of the Court which happens to have grown into such important consequence to the English Church. The position is a perfectly legitimate one; but we think it had better not have been connected with a documentary work like the present, set forth by the direction and under the sanction of a Bishop of London.

In looking over the cases which have been brought together into a connected series, the first point which is suggested by the review is the great and important change in the aspect and bearing of doctrinal controversies, and in the situation of the Church, as affected by them, which the creation and action of this Court have made. From making it almost a matter of principle and boast to dispense with any living judge of controversies, the Church has passed to having a very energetic one. Up to the Gorham judgment, it can hardly be said that the ruling of courts of law had had the slightest influence on the doctrinal position and character of the Church. Keen and fierce as had been the controversies in the Church up to that judgment, how often had a legal testing of her standards been seriously sought for or seriously appealed to? There had been accusations of heresy, trials, condemnations, especially in the times following the Reformation and preceding the Civil War; there had been appeals and final judgments given in such final courts as existed; but all without making any mark on the public mind or the received meaning of doctrines and formularies, and without leaving a trace except in law reports. They seem to have been forgotten as soon as the particular case was disposed of. The limits of supposed orthodox belief revived; but it was not the action of judicial decisions which either narrowed or enlarged them. Bishop Marsh's Calvinists never thought of having recourse to law. If the Church did not do entirely without a Court of Final Appeal, it is simply a matter of fact that the same weight and authority were not attached to the proceedings of such a court which are attached to them now. But since the Gorham case, the work of settling authoritatively, if not the meaning of doctrines and of formularies, at any rate the methods of interpreting and applying them, has been briskly going on in the courts, and a law laid down by judges without appeal has been insensibly fastening its hold upon us. The action of the courts is extolled as being all in the direction of liberty. Whatever this praise may be worth, it is to be observed that it is, after all, a wooden sort of liberty, and shuts up quite as much as it opens. It may save, in this case or that, individual liberty; but it does so by narrowing artificially the natural and common-sense grounds of argument in religious controversy, and abridging as much as possible the province of theology. Before the Gorham case, the Formularies in general were the standard and test, free to both sides, about baptismal regeneration. Both parties had the ground open to them, to make what they could of them by argument and reason. Discipline was limited by the Articles and Formularies, and in part by the authority of great divines and by the prevailing opinion of the Church, and by nothing else; these were the means which each side had to convince and persuade and silence the other, and each side might hope that in the course of time its sounder and better supported view might prevail. But now upon this state of things comes from without a dry, legal, narrow stereotyping, officially and by authority, of the sense to be put upon part of the documents in the controversy. You appeal to the Prayer-book; your opponent tells you, Oh, the Court of Appeal has ruled against you there: and that part of your case is withdrawn from you, and he need give himself no trouble to argue the matter with you.

Against certain theological positions, perhaps of great weight, and theological evidence, comes, not only the doctrine of theological opponents, but the objection that they are bad law. The interpretation which, it may be, we have assumed all our lives, and which we know to be that of Fathers and divines, is suddenly pronounced not to be legal. The decision does not close the controversy, which goes on as keenly and with perhaps a little more exasperation than before; it simply stops off, by virtue of a legal construction, a portion of the field of argument for one party, which was, perhaps, supposed to have the strongest claim to it. The Gorham case bred others; and now, at last, after fifteen years, we have got, as may be seen in Messrs. Brodrick and Fremantle's book, a body of judicial *dicta*, interpretations, rules of exposition, and theological propositions, which have grown up in the course of these cases, and which in various ways force a meaning and construction on the theological standards and language of the Church, which in some instances they were never thought to have, and which they certainly never had authoritatively before. Besides her Articles and Prayer-book, speaking the language of divines and open to each party to interpret according to the strength and soundness of their theological ground, we are getting a supplementary set of legal limitations and glosses, claiming to regulate theological argument if not teaching, and imposed upon us by the authority not of the Church or even of Parliament but of the Judges of the Privy Council.

This, it strikes us, is a new position of things in the Church, a new understanding and a changed set of conditions on which to carry on controversies of doctrine; and it seems to us to have a serious influence not only on the responsibility of the Church for her own doctrine, but on the freedom and genuineness with which questions as to that doctrine are discussed. The Court is not to blame for this result; to do it justice, it has generally sought to decide as little as it could; and the interference of law with the province of pure theology is to be rather attributed to that mania for deciding, which of late has taken possession pretty equally of all parties. But the indisputable result is seen to be, after the experience of fifteen years, that law is taking a place in our theological disputes and our theological system which is new to it in our theological history; law, not laid down prospectively in general provisions, but emerging indirectly and incidentally out of constructions and judicial rulings on cases of pressing and hazardous exigency; law, applying its technical and deliberately narrow processes to questions which of course it cannot solve, but can only throw into formal and inadequate, if not unreal, terms; and laying down the limits of belief and assertion on matters about which hearts burn and souls tremble, by the mouth of judges whose consummate calmness and ability is only equalled by their profound and avowed want of sympathy for the theology of which their position makes them the expounders and final arbiters. A system has begun with respect to English Church doctrine, analogous to that by which Lord Stowell made the recent law of the sea, or that by which on a larger scale the rescripts and decrees of the Popes moulded the great system of the canon law.

This is the first thing that strikes us on a comparative survey of this set of decisions. The second point is one which at first sight seems greatly to diminish the importance of this new condition of things, but which on further consideration is seen to have a more serious bearing than might have been thought. This is, the odd haphazard way in which points have come up for decision; the sort of apparent chance which has finally governed the issue of the various contentions; and the infinitesimally fine character of the few propositions of doctrine to which the Court has given the sanction of its ruling. Knowing what we all of us cannot help knowing, and seeing things which lawyers and judges are bound not to allow themselves to see or take account of, we find it difficult to repress the feeling of amazement, as we travel through the volume, to see Mr Gorham let off, Mr. Heath deprived, then Dr. Williams and Mr. Wilson let off, and to notice the delicate technical point which brought to nought the laborious and at one time hopeful efforts of the worthy persons who tried to turn out Archdeacon Denison. And as to the matter of the decisions, though undoubtedly *dicta* of great importance are laid down in the course of them, yet it is curious to observe the extremely minute and insignificant statements on which in the more important cases judgment is actually pronounced. The Gorham case was held to affect the position of a great party; but the language and theory actually examined and allowed would hardly, in legal strictness, authorise much more than the very peculiar views of Mr. Gorham himself. And in the last case, the outside lay world has hardly yet done wondering at the consummate feat of legal subtlety by which the issue whether the English Church teaches that the Bible is inspired was transmuted into the question whether it teaches that every single part of every single book is inspired. It might seem that rulings, of which the actual product in the way of doctrinal propositions was so small, were hardly subjects for any keen interest. But it would be short-sighted to regard the matter in this way. In the first place, whatever may have happened as yet, it is manifestly a serious thing for Church of England doctrine to have been thrown, on a scale which is quite new, into the domain of a court of law, to lie at the mercy of the confessed chances and uncertainties of legal interpretation, with nothing really effective to correct and remedy what may possibly be, without any fault in the judges, a fatally mischievous construction of the text and letter of her authoritative documents. In the next place, no one can fail to see, no one in fact affects to deny, that the general result of these recent decisions, capricious as their conclusions look at first sight, has been to make the Formularies mean much less than they were supposed to mean. The tendency of every English court, appealed to not as a court of equity but one of criminal jurisdiction, is naturally to be exacting and even narrow in the interpretation of language. The general impression left by these cases is that the lines of doctrine in the English Church are regarded by the judicial mind as very faint, and not much to be depended upon; and that these judgments may be the first steps in that insensible process by which the unpretending but subtle and powerful engine of interpretation has been applied by the courts to give a certain turn to law and policy; applied, in this instance, to undermine the definiteness and certainty of doctrine, and in the end, the understanding itself which has hitherto existed between the Church and the State, and has kept alive the idea of her distinct basis, functions, and rights.

This is the view of matters which arises from an examination of the proceedings contained in this volume. What is the argument urged in the Historical Introduction to justify or recommend our acquiescence in it? It seems to us to consist mainly in a one-sided and exaggerated statement of the Supremacy claimed and brought in by Henry VIII., and of the effect in theory and fact which it ought to have on our notion of the Church and of Church right. The complaint of the present state of things is, that those who may be taken to represent the interests of the Church in such a matter as the character of her teaching are practically excluded from having any real influence in the decision of questions by which the character of that teaching is affected. The answer is that she has no right to claim a separate interest in the matter, and that the doctrine of the Royal Supremacy was meant to extinguish, and has extinguished, any pretence to such a claim. The *animus* which pervades the work, and which is not obscurely disclosed in such things as footnotes and abridgments of legal arguments, is thus given—more freely, of course, than it would be proper to introduce in a book like this—in some remarks of Mr. Brodrick, one of the editors, at a recent discussion of the question of Ecclesiastical Appeals in a committee of the Social Science Association. He is reported to have spoken as follows :—

The Church of England being established by law, could not be allowed any independence of action; and those who wished for it were like people who wanted to have their cake and eat it. As to the Privy Council, he had never heard its decisions charged with error. What was complained of was that it had declined to take the current opinions of theologians and make them part of the Thirty-nine Articles. There was no need whatever for the Privy Council to possess any special theological knowledge. The only case where that knowledge was necessary was when it was alleged that doctrines had been held in the Church without censure. That was a case in which considerable theological lore was required; but it was within the province of counsel to supply it. Divines had now discovered, what lawyers could have told them long ago, and what he knew some of them had been told —namely, that it would not do to treat the Thirty-nine Articles as penal statutes; because, if that were done, a coach might be easily driven through them. If they had wished to maintain the authority of the Articles, they would have done best to have kept quiet.

The present Court of Appeal is deduced, in the Historical Introduction, as a natural and logical consequence, from Henry VIII.'s Supremacy. Undoubtedly it is scarcely possible to overstate the all-grasping despotism of Henry VIII., and if a precedent for anything reckless of all separate rights and independence should be wanted, it would never be sought in vain if looked for in the policy and legislation of that reign. So far the editors are right; the power over religion claimed by Henry VIII. will carry them wherever they want to go; it will give them, if they need it, as a still more logical and legitimate development of the Supremacy, the Court of High Commission. Only they ought to have remembered, as fair historians, that even in the days of the Supremacy the distinct nature and business of the Church and of Churchmen was never denied. Laymen were given powers over the Church and in the Church which were new; but the distinct province of the Church, if abridged and put under new control, was not abolished. Side by side with the facts showing the Supremacy and its exercise are a set of facts, for those who choose to see them, showing that the Church was still recognised, even by Henry VIII., as a body which he had not created, which he was obliged to take account of, and which filled a place utterly different from every other body in the State. Henry VIII. played the tyrant with his Churchmen as he did with his Parliament and with everybody else; and Churchmen, like everybody else, submitted to him. But the "Imperialism" of Henry VIII., though it went beyond even the Imperialism of Justinian and Charlemagne in its encroachments on the spiritual power, as little denied the fact of that power as they did. He recognised the distinct place and claims of the spiritualty; and, as we suppose that even the editors of this volume hardly feel themselves bound to make out the consistency of Henry, they might have spared themselves the weak and not very fair attempt to get rid of the force of the remarkable words in which this recognition is recorded in the first Statute of Appeals (24 Henry VIII. c. 12). The words would, no doubt, be worth but little, were it not that as a matter of fact a spiritualty did act and judge and lay down doctrine, and even while yielding to unworthy influence did keep up their corporate existence.

But when the ecclesiastical legislation of Henry VIII. is referred to, not merely as the historical beginning of a certain state of things which has undergone great changes in the course of events, but as affording a sort of idea and normal pattern to which our own arrangements ought to conform, as supplying us with a theory of Church and State which holds good at least against the Church, it seems hard that the Church alone should not have the benefit of the entire alteration of circumstances since that theory was a reality. Those who talk about the Supremacy ought to remember what the Supremacy pretended to be. It was over *all* causes and *all* persons, civil as well as ecclesiastical. It held good certainly in theory, and to a great extent in practice, against the temporalty as much as against the spiritualty. Why then are we to invoke the Supremacy as then understood, in a question about courts of spiritual appeals, and not in questions about other courts and other powers in the nation? If the Supremacy, claimed and exercised as Henry claimed and exercised it, is good against the Church, it is good against many other things besides. If the Church inherits bonds and obligations, not merely by virtue of distinct statutes, but by the force of a general vague arbitrary theory of royal power, why has that power been expelled, or transformed into a mere fiction of law, in all other active branches of the national life? Unless the Church is simply, what even Henry VIII. did not regard it, a creation and delegate of the national power, without any roots and constitution of its own, why should the Church be denied the benefit of the common sense, and the change in ideas and usage, which have been so largely appealed to in civil matters? Why are we condemned to a theory which is not only out of date and out of harmony with all the traditions and convictions of modern times, but which was in its own time tyrannous, revolutionary, and intolerable? Arguments in favour of the present Court, drawn from the reason of the thing, and the comparative fitness of the judges for their office, if we do not agree with them, at least we can understand. But precedents and arguments from the Supremacy of Henry VIII. suggest the question whether those who use them are ready to be taken at their word and to have back that Supremacy as it was; and whether the examples of policy of that reign are seemly to quote as adequate measures of the liberty and rights of any set of Englishmen.

The question really calling for solution is—How to reconcile the just freedom of individual teachers in the Church with the maintenance of the right and duty of the Church to uphold the substantial meaning of her body of doctrine? In answering this question we can get no help from this volume. It simply argues that the present is practically the best of all possible courts; that it is a great improvement, which probably it is, on the Courts of Delegates; and that great confidence ought to be felt in its decisions. We are further shown how jealously and carefully the judges have guarded the right of the individual teacher. But it seems to us, according to the views put forward in this book, that as the price of all this—of great learning, weight, and ability in the judges—of great care taken of liberty—the Church is condemned to an interpretation of the Royal Supremacy which floats between the old arbitrary view of it and the modern Liberal one, and which uses each, as it happens to be most convenient, against the claim of the Church to protect her doctrine and exert a real influence on the authoritative declaration of it. We all need liberty, and we all ought to be ready to give the reasonable liberty which we profess to claim for ourselves. But it is a heavy price to pay for it, if the right and the power is to be taken out of the hands of the Church to declare what is the real meaning of what she supposes herself bound to teach.

IV

SIR JOHN COLERIDGE ON THE PURCHAS CASE[1]

No one has more right to speak with authority, or more deserves to be listened to at a difficult and critical moment for the Church, than Sir J. T. Coleridge. An eminent lawyer, and a most earnest and well-informed Churchman, he combines in an unusual way claims on the attention of all who care for the interests of religion, and for those, too, which are so deeply connected with them, the interests of England. The troubles created by the recent judgment have induced him to come forward from his retirement with words of counsel and warning.

The gist of his Letter may be shortly stated. He is inclined to think the decision arrived at by the Judicial Committee a mistaken one. But he thinks that it would be a greater and a worse mistake to make this decision, wrong as it may be, a reason for

[1] *Remarks on Some Parts of the Report of the Judicial Committee in the Case of "Elphinstone against Purchas."* A Letter to Canon Liddon, from the Right Hon. Sir J. T. Coleridge. *Guardian*, 5th April 1871.

looking favourably on disestablishment as a remedy for what is complained of. We are glad to note the judgment of so fair an observer and so distinguished a lawyer, himself a member of the Privy Council, both on the intrinsic suitableness and appropriateness of the position [1] which has been ruled to be illegal, and on the unsatisfactoriness of the interpretation itself, as a matter of judicial reading and construction. A great deal has been said, and it is plain that the topic is inexhaustible, on the unimportance of a position. We agree entirely—on condition that people remember the conditions and consequences of their assertion. Every single outward accompaniment of worship may, if you carry your assertion to its due level, be said to be in itself utterly unimportant; place and time and form and attitude are all things not belonging to the essence of the act itself, and are indefinitely changeable, as, in fact, the changes in them have been countless. Kneeling is not of the essence of prayer, but imagine, first prohibiting the posture of kneeling, and then remonstrating with those who complained of the prohibition, on the ground of postures being unimportant. It is obvious that when you have admitted to the full that a position is in itself unimportant, all kinds of reasons may come in on the further question whether it is right, fitting, natural. There are reasons why the position which has been so largely adopted of late is the natural and

---

[1] The Eastward Position at the celebration of the Holy Communion.

suitable one. Sir John Coleridge states them admirably:—

As to the place of standing at the consecration, my *feeling* is with them. It seems to me not desirable to make it essential or even important that the people should see the breaking of the bread, or the taking the cup into the hands of the priest, and positively mischievous to encourage them in gazing on him, or watching him with critical eyes while so employed. I much prefer the *spirit* of the Rubric of 1549—First Book of Edward VI.—which says, "These words before rehearsed are to be said turning still to the Altar, without any elevation, or showing the Sacraments to the people." The use now enforced, I think, tends to deprive the most solemn rite of our religion of one of its most solemn particulars. Surely, whatever school we belong to, and even if we consider the whole rite merely commemorative, it is a very solemn idea to conceive the priest at the head of his flock, and, as it were, a shepherd leading them on in heart and spirit, imploring for them and with them the greatest blessing which man is capable of receiving on earth; he alone uttering the prayer—they meanwhile kneeling all, and in deep silence listening, not gazing, rather with closed eyes—and with their whole undistracted attention, joining in the prayer with one heart and without sound until the united "Amen" breaks from them at the close, and seals their union and assent.

But, of course, comes the further question, whether an English clergyman is authorised to use it. He is not authorised if the Prayer Book tells him not to.

Of that there is no question. But if the Prayer Book not only seems to give him the liberty, but, by the *prima facie* look of its words, seems to prescribe it, the harshness of a ruling which summarily and under penalties prohibits it is not to be smoothed down by saying that the matter is unimportant. Sir John Coleridge's view of the two points will be read with interest :—

You will understand, of course, that I write in respect of the Report recently made by the Judicial Committee in the Purchas case. I am not about to defend it. No one, however, ought to pronounce a condemnation of the solemn judgment of such a tribunal without much consideration; and this remark applies with special force to myself, well knowing as I do those from whom it proceeded, and having withdrawn from sharing in the labours of the Committee only because age had impaired, with the strength of my body, the faculties also of my mind; and so disabled me from the proper discharge of any judicial duties. With this admission on my part, I yet venture to say that I think Mr. Purchas has not had justice done to him in two main points of the late appeal; I mean the use of the vestments complained of and the side of the communion-table which he faced when consecrating the elements for the Holy Communion. Before I state my reasons, let me premise that I am no Ritualist, in the now conventional use of the term. I do not presume to judge of the motives of those to whom that name is applied. From the information of common but undisputed report as to some of the most conspicuous, I believe them entitled to all praise for their pastoral devotedness and their laborious, self-denying lives; still, I do not shrink from saying that I think them misguided, and the cause of mischief in the Church. So much for my *feeling* in regard to the vestments. I prefer the surplice at all times and in all ministrations.

This is my *feeling*—and I see no word in the sober language of our rubric which interferes with it—but my *feeling* is of no importance in the argument, and I mention it only in candour, to show in what spirit I approach the argument.

Now Mr. Purchas has been tried before the Committee for offences alleged to have been committed against the provisions of the "Act of Uniformity"; of this Act the Common Prayer Book is part and parcel. As to the vestments, his conduct was alleged to be in derogation of the rubric as to the ornaments of the Church and the ministers thereof, which ordains that such shall be retained and be in use as were in the Church of England by the authority of Parliament in the second year of the reign of King Edward VI. The Act of Uniformity is to be construed by the same rules exactly as any Act passed in the last session of Parliament. The clause in question (by which I mean the rubric in question) is perfectly unambiguous in language, free from all difficulty as to construction; it therefore lets in no argument as to intention other than that which the words themselves import. There might be a seeming difficulty in *fact*, because it might not be known what vestments were in use by authority of Parliament in the second year of the reign of King Edward VI.; but this difficulty has been removed. It is conceded in the Report that the vestments, the use of which is now condemned, were in use by authority of Parliament in that year. Having that fact, you are bound to construe the rubric as if those vestments were specifically named in it, instead of being only referred to. If an Act should be passed to-morrow that the uniform of the Guards should henceforth be such as was ordered for them by authority and used by them in the 1st George I., you would first ascertain what that uniform was; and, having ascertained it, you would not inquire into the changes which may have been made, many or few, with or without lawful authority, between the 1st George I. and the passing of the new Act. All these, that Act, specifying the earlier date, would have made wholly immaterial. It would have seemed strange, I suppose, if a commanding officer, disobeying the statute, had said in his defence, "There have been many changes since the reign of George I.; and as to 'retaining,' we put a gloss on that, and thought it might mean only retaining to the Queen's use; so we have put the uniforms safely in store." But I think it would have seemed more strange to punish and mulct him severely if he had obeyed the law and put no gloss on plain words.

This case stands on the same principle. The rubric indeed seems to me to imply with some clearness that in the long interval between Edward VI. and the 14th Charles II. there had been many changes; but it does not stay to specify them, or distinguish between what was mere evasion and what was lawful; it quietly passes them all by, and goes back to the legalised usage of the second year of Edward VI. What had prevailed since, whether by an Archbishop's gloss, by Commissions, or even Statutes, whether, in short, legal or illegal, it makes quite immaterial.

I forbear to go through the long inquiry which these last words remind one of—not, I am sure, out of any disrespectful feeling to the learned and reverend authors of the Report, but because it seems to me wholly irrelevant to the point for decision. This alone I must add, that even were the inquiry relevant, the authorities, on which they rely do not appear to me so clear or cogent, nor the analogies relied on so just, as to warrant the conclusion arrived at. For it should never be forgotten that the defendant in a criminal case, acquitted as to this charge by the learned judge below, was entitled to every presumption in his favour, and could not properly be condemned but by a judgment free from all reasonable doubt. And this remark acquires additional strength because the judgment will be final not only on him but on the whole Church for all time, unless reversed by the Legislature.

On the second point he thus speaks, in terms which for their guarded moderation are all the more worth notice :—

Upon the second point I have less to say, though it is to me much the most important. The Report, I think, cannot be shown conclusively to be wrong here, as it may be on the other; still it does not seem to me to be shown conclusively to be right. You have yourself given no reason in your second letter of the 8th March for doubting at least.

Let me add that, in my opinion, on such a question as this, where a conclusion is to be arrived at upon the true meaning of Rubrics framed more than two centuries since, and certainly not with a view to any such minute criticism as on these occasions is and must be applied to them, and where the evidence of facts is by no means clear, none probably can be arrived at free from reasonable objection. What is the consequence? It will be asked, Is the question to receive no judicial solution? I am not afraid to answer, Better far that it should receive none than that injustice should be done. The principles of English law furnish the practical solution: dismiss the party charged, unless his conviction can be based on grounds on which reasonable and competent minds can rest satisfied and without scruple. And what mighty mischief will result to countervail the application of this rule of justice? For two centuries our Church has subsisted without an answer to the question which alone gives importance to this inquiry, and surely has not been without God's blessing for that time, in spite of all much more serious shortcomings. Let us remember that Charity, or to use perhaps a better word, Love, is the greatest of all; if that prevail there need be little fear for our Faith or our Hope.

Having said this much, Sir John Coleridge proceeds to the second, and indeed the main object of his letter—to remonstrate against exaggeration in complaint, both of the particular decision and of the Court which gave it:—

I now return to your letter. You proceed to attempt to show that the words of Keble to yourself, which you cite, are justified by remarks in this Report and some previous judgments of the same tribunal, which appear to you so inconsistent with each other as to make it difficult to believe that the Court was impartial, or "incapable of regarding the documents before it in the light of a plastic material, which might be made to support conclusions held to be advisable at the moment, and on independent grounds." I wish these words had never been written. They will, I fear, be understood as conveying your formed opinions; and coming from you, and addressed to minds already excited and embittered, they will be readily accepted, though they import the heaviest charges against judges—some of them bishops—all of high and hitherto unimpeached character. A very long experience of judicial life makes me know that judges will often provoke and bitterly disappoint both the suitors before them and the public, when discharging their duty honestly and carefully, and a man is scarcely fit for the station unless he can sit tolerably easy under censures which even these may pass upon him. Yet, imputations of partiality or corruption are somewhat hard to bear when they are made by persons of your station and character. When the Judicial Committee sits on appeals from the Spiritual Courts, it *may* certainly be under God's displeasure, the members *may* be visited with judicial blindness, and deprived of the integrity which in other times and cases they manifest. Against such a supposition there is no direct argument, and I will not enter into such a disputation. I have so much confidence in your generosity and candour, on reflection, as to believe you would not desire I should.

In the individual case I simply protest against the insinuation. I add a word or two by way of general observation.

No doubt you have read the judgments in all the cases you allude to carefully; but have you read the pleadings and arguments of the counsel, so as to know accurately the points raised for the consideration of those who were to decide? To know the offence charged and the judgment pronounced may suffice in some cases for an opinion by a competent person, whether the one warranted the other; but more is required to warrant the imputation of inconsistency, partiality, or indirect motives. He who takes this on himself should know further how the pleadings and the arguments presented the case for judgment, and made this or that particular relevant in the discussion. Every one at all familiar with this matter knows that a judgment not uncommonly fails to reflect the private opinion of the judge on the whole of a great point, because the issues of law or fact actually brought before him, and which alone he was bound to decide, did not bring this before him. And this rule, always binding, is, of course, never more so than in regard to a Court of Final Appeal, which should be careful not to conclude more than is regularly before it. Let me add that a just and considerate person will wholly disregard the gossip which flies about in regard to cases exciting much interest; passing words in the course of an argument, forgotten when the judgment comes to be considered, are too often caught up, as having guided the final determination.

Such words are a just rebuke to much of the inconsiderate talk which follows on any public act which touches the feelings, perhaps the highest and purest feelings of men with deep convictions. Perhaps Mr.

Liddon's words were unguarded ones. But at the same time it is necessary to state without disguise what is the truth in this matter. It is necessary for the sake of justice and historical truth. The Court of Final Appeal is not like other courts. It is not a pure and simple court of law, though it is composed of great lawyers. It is doubtless a court where their high training and high professional honour come in, as they do elsewhere. But great lawyers are men, partisans and politicians, statesmen, if you like; and this is a court where they are not precluded, in the same degree as they are in the regular courts by the habits and prescriptions of the place, from thinking of what comes before them in its relation to public affairs. It is no mere invention of disappointed partisans, it is no idle charge of wilful unfairness, to say that considerations of high policy come into their deliberations; it has been the usual language, ever since the Gorham case, of men who cared little for the subject-matter of the questions debated; it is the language of those who urge the advantages of the Court. "It is a court," as the Bishop of Manchester said the other day, speaking in its praise, "composed of men who look at things not merely with the eyes of lawyers, but also with the eyes of statesmen." Precisely so; and for that reason they must be considered to have the responsibilities, not only of lawyers, but of statesmen, and their acts are proportionably open to discussion. Sir John Coleridge urges the impossibility of any other court; and certainly till we could be induced to trust an ecclesiastical court, composed of bishops or clergymen, in a higher degree than we could do at present, we see no alternative. But to say that a clerical court would be no improvement is not to prove that the present court is a satisfactory one. It may be difficult under our present circumstances to reform it. But though we may have reasons for making the best of it, we may be allowed to say that it is a singularly ill-imagined and ill-constructed court, and one in which the great features of English law and justice are not so conspicuous as they are elsewhere. Suitors do not complain in other courts either of the ruling, or sometimes of the language of judges, as they complain in this. But when this is made a ground for joining with the enemies of all that the English Church holds dear, to bring about a great break-up of the existing state of things, we agree with Sir John Coleridge in thinking that a great mistake is made; and if care is not taken, it may be an irreparable one. He writes:—

I hasten to my conclusion too long delayed, but a word must still be added on a subject of not less consequence than any I have yet touched on. You say, "Churchmen will to a very great extent indeed find relief from the dilemma in a third course, viz. *co-operation with the political forces*, which, year by year, more and more steadily are working towards disestablishment. This is not a menace; it is the statement of a simple fact." I am bound to believe, and I do believe, you do not intend this as a menace; but such a statement of a future course to depend on a contingency cannot but read very much like one—and against your intention it may well be understood as such. You do not say that *you* are one who will co-operate with the political party which now seeks to disestablish the Church in accomplishing its purpose, and I do not suppose you ever will. But on behalf, not so much of the clergy as of the laity —on behalf of the worshippers in our churches, of the sick to be visited at home—of the poor in their cottages, of our children in their schools—of our society in general, I entreat those of the clergy who are now feeling the most acutely in this matter, not to suffer their minds to be so absorbed by the present grievance as to take no thought of the evils of disestablishment. I am not foolishly blind to the faults of the clergy—indeed I fear I am sometimes censorious in regard to them—and some of their faults I do think may be referable to Establishment; the possession of house and land, and a sort of independence of their parishioners, in some cases seems to tend to secularity. I regret sometimes their partisanship at elections, their speeches at public dinners. But what good gift of God is not liable to abuse from men? Taken as a whole, we have owed, and we do owe, under Him, to our Established clergy more than we can ever repay, much of it rendered possible by their Establishment. I may refer, and now with special force, to Education—their services in this respect no one denies —and but for Establishment these, I think, could not have been so effectively and systematically rendered. We are now in a great crisis as to this all-important matter. Concurring, as I do heartily, in the praise which has been bestowed on Mr. Forster, and expecting that his great and arduous office will be discharged with perfect impartiality by him, and with a just sense of how much is due to the clergy in this respect, still it cannot be denied that the powers conferred by the Legislature on the holder of it are alarmingly great, even if necessary; and who shall say in what a spirit they may be exercised by his successor? For the general upholding of religious education, in emergencies not improbable, to whom can we look in general so confidently as to the parochial clergy? I speak now specially in regard to parishes such as I am most familiar with, in agricultural districts, small, not largely endowed, sometimes without resident gentry, and with the land occupied by rack-renting farmers, indifferent or hostile to education.

In what Sir John Coleridge urges against the fatal step of welcoming disestablishment under an impatient sense of injustice we need not say that we concur most earnestly. But it cannot be too seriously considered by those who see the mischief of disestablishment, that as Sir John Coleridge also says, the English Church is, in one sense, a divided one; and that to pursue a policy of humiliating and crippling one of its great parties must at last bring mischief. The position of the High Church party is a remarkable one. It has had more against it than its rivals; yet it is probably the strongest of them all. It is said, probably with reason, to be the unpopular party. It has been the stock object of abuse and sarcasm with a large portion of the press. It has been equally obnoxious to Radical small shopkeepers and "true blue" farmers and their squires. It has been mobbed in churches and censured in Parliament. Things have gone against it, almost uniformly, before the tribunals. And unfortunately it cannot be said that it has been without its full share of folly and extravagance in some of its members. And yet it is the party which has grown; which has drawn some of its antagonists to itself, and has reacted on the ideas and habits of others; its members have gradually, as a matter of course, risen into important post and power. And it is to be noticed that, as a party, it has been the most tolerant. All parties are in their nature intolerant; none more so, where critical points arise, than Liberal ones. But in spite of the Dean of Westminster's surprise at High Churchmen claiming to be tolerant, we still think that, in the first place, they are really much less inclined to meddle with their neighbours than others of equally strong and deep convictions; and further, that they have become so more and more; and they have accepted the lessons of their experience; they have thrown off, more than any strong religious body, the intolerance which was natural to everybody once, and have learned, better than they did at one time, to bear with what they dislike and condemn. If a party like this comes to feel itself dealt with harshly and unfairly, sacrificed to popular clamour or the animosity of inveterate and unscrupulous opponents, it is certain that we shall be in great danger.

V

MR. GLADSTONE'S LETTER ON THE ENGLISH CHURCH [1]

MR. GLADSTONE'S Letter, read at the St. Asaph Diocesan Conference, will not have surprised those who have borne in mind his deep and unintermitted interest in the fortunes and prospects of the Church, and his habit of seeking relief from the pressure of one set of thoughts and anxieties by giving full play to his mental energies in another direction. Its composition and appearance at this moment are quite accounted for; it is a contribution to the business of the conference of his own diocese, and it was promised long before an autumn session on a great question between the two Houses was in view. Still the appearance of such a document from a person in Mr. Gladstone's position must, of course, invite attention and speculation. He may put aside the questions which the word "Disestablishment"—which was in the thesis given him to write upon—is likely to pro-

[1] *Guardian*, 29th October 1884.

voke—"Will it come? ought it to come? must it come? Is it near, or somewhat distant, or indefinitely remote?" On these questions he has not a word to say. But, all the same, people will naturally try to read between the lines, and to find out what was in the writer's thoughts about these questions. We cannot, however, see that there is anything to be gathered from the Letter as to the political aspect of the matter; he simply confines himself to the obvious lesson which passing events sufficiently bring with them, that whatever may come it is our business to be prepared.

His anxieties are characteristic. The paper shows, we think, that it has not escaped him that disestablishment, however compensated as some sanguine people hope, would be a great disaster and ruin. It would be the failure and waste to the country of noble and astonishing efforts; it would be the break-up and collapse of a great and cheap system, by which light and human kindliness and intelligence are carried to vast tracts, that without its presence must soon become as stagnant and hopeless as many of the rural *communes* of France; the blow would at the moment cripple and disorganise the Church for its work even in the towns. But though "happily improbable," it may come; and in such a contingency, what occupies Mr. Gladstone's thoughts is, not the question whether it would be disastrous, but whether it would be disgraceful. That is the point which disturbs and distresses him—the possibility that the end of our later Church history, the end of that wonderful experiment which has been going on from the sixteenth century, with such great vicissitudes, but after every shock with increasing improvement and hope, should at last be not only failure, but failure with dishonour; and this, he says, could only come in one of two ways. It might come from the Church having sunk into sloth and death, without faith, without conscience, without love. This, if it ever was really to be feared, is not the danger before us now. Activity, conviction, energy, self-devotion, these, and not apathetic lethargy, mark the temper of our times; and they are as conspicuous in the Church as anywhere else. But these qualities, as we have had ample experience, may develop into fierce and angry conflicts. It is our internal quarrels, Mr. Gladstone thinks, that create the most serious risk of disestablishment; and it is only our quarrels, which we have not good sense and charity enough to moderate and keep within bounds, which would make it "disgraceful."

The main feature of the Letter is the historical retrospect which Mr. Gladstone gives of the long history, the long travail of the later English Church. Hardly in its first start, under the Tudors, but more and more as time went on, it instinctively, as it were, tried the great and difficult problem of Christian liberty. The Churches of the Continent, Roman and anti-Roman, were simple in their systems; only one sharply defined theology, only the disciples and representatives of one set of religious tendencies, would they allow to dwell within their borders; what was refractory and refused to harmonise was at once cast out; and for a certain time they were unvexed with internal dissensions. This, both in the case of the Roman, the Lutheran, and the Calvinistic Churches of the Continent, requires to be somewhat qualified; still, as compared with the rival schools of the English Church, Puritan and Anglican, the contrast is a true and a sharp one. Mr. Gladstone adopts from a German writer a view which is certainly not new to many in England, that "the Reformation, as a religious movement, took its shape in England, not in the sixteenth century but in the seventeenth." "It seems plain," he says, "that the great bulk of those burned under Mary were Puritans"; and he adds, what is not perhaps so capable of proof, that "under Elizabeth we have to look, with rare exceptions, among the Puritans and Recusants for an active and religious life." It was not till the Restoration, it was not till Puritanism had shown all its intolerance, all its narrowness, and all its helplessness, that the Church was able to settle the real basis and the chief lines of its reformed constitution. It is not, as Mr. Gladstone says, "a heroic history"; there is room enough in the looseness of some of its arrangements, and the incompleteness of others, for diversity of opinion and for polemical criticism. But the result, in fact, of this liberty and this incompleteness has been, not that the Church has declined lower and lower into indifference and negation, but that it has steadily mounted in successive periods to a higher level of purpose, to a higher standard of life and thought, of faith and work. Account for it as we may, with all drawbacks, with great intervals of seeming torpor, with much to be regretted and to be ashamed of, that is literally the history of the English Church since the Restoration settlement. It is not "heroic," but there are no Church annals of the same time more so, and there are none fuller of hope.

But every system has its natural and specific danger, and the specific English danger, as it is the condition of vigorous English life, is that spirit of liberty which allows and attempts to combine very divergent tendencies of opinion. "The Church of England," Mr. Gladstone thinks, "has been peculiarly liable, on the one side and on the other, both to attack and to defection, and the probable cause is to be found in the degree in which, whether for worldly or for religious reasons, it was attempted in her case to combine divergent elements within her borders." She is still, as he says, "working out her system by experience"; and the exclusion of bitterness—even, as he says, of "savagery"—from her debates and controversies is hardly yet accomplished. There is at present, indeed, a remarkable lull, a "truce of God," which, it may be hoped, is of good omen; but we dare not be too sure that it is going to be permanent. In the meantime, those who tremble lest disestablishment should be the signal of a great break up and separation of her different parties cannot do better than meditate on Mr. Gladstone's very solemn words :—

> The great maxim, *in omnibus caritas*, which is so necessary to temper all religious controversy, ought to apply with a tenfold force to the conduct of the members of the Church of England. In respect to differences among themselves they ought, of course, in the first place to remember that their right to differ is limited by the laws of the system to which they belong; but within that limit should they not also, each of them, recollect that his antagonist has something to say; that the Reformation and the counter-Reformation tendencies were, in the order of Providence, placed here in a closer juxtaposition than anywhere else in the Christian world; that a course of destiny so peculiar appears to indicate on the part of the Supreme Orderer a peculiar purpose, that not only no religious but no considerate or prudent man should run the risk of interfering with such a purpose; that the great charity which is a bounden duty everywhere in these matters should here be accompanied and upheld by two ever-striving handmaidens, a great Reverence and a great Patience.

This is true, and of deep moment to those who guide and influence thought and feeling in the Church. But further, those in whose hands the "Supreme Orderer" has placed the springs and the restraints of political movement and of change, if they recognise at all this view of the English Church, ought to feel one duty paramount in regard to it. Never was the Church, they tell us, more active and more hopeful;

well then, what politicians who care for her have to see to is that she shall have *time* to work out effectually the tendencies which are visible in her now more than at any period of her history—that combination which Mr. Gladstone wishes for, of the deepest individual faith and energy, with forbearance and conciliation and the desire for peace. She has a right to claim from English rulers that she should have time to let these things work and bear fruit; if she has lost time before, she never was so manifestly in earnest in trying to make up for it as now. It is not talking, but working together, which brings different minds and tempers to understand one another's divergences; and it is this disposition to work together which shows itself and is growing now. But it needs time. What the Church has a right to ask from the arbiters of her temporal and political position in the country, if that is ultimately and inevitably to be changed, is that nothing precipitate, nothing impatient, should be done; that she should have time adequately to develop and fulfil what she now alone among Christian communities seems in a position to attempt.

VI

DISENDOWMENT[1]

THIS generation has seen no such momentous change as that which has suddenly appeared to be at our very doors, and which people speak of as disestablishment. The word was only invented a few years ago, and was sneered at as a barbarism, worthy of the unpractical folly which it was coined to express. It has been bandied about a good deal lately, sometimes *de cœur léger;* and within the last six months it has assumed the substance and the weight of a formidable probability. Other changes, more or less serious, are awaiting us in the approaching future; but they are encompassed with many uncertainties, and all forecasts of their working are necessarily very doubtful. About this there is an almost brutal clearness and simplicity, as to what it means, as to what is intended by those who have pushed it into prominence, and as to what will follow from their having their way.

Disestablishment has really come to mean, in the

[1] *Guardian*, 14th October 1885.

mouth of friends and foes, simple disendowment. It is well that the question should be set in its true terms, without being confused with vague and less important issues. It is not very easy to say what disestablishment by itself would involve, except the disappearance of Bishops from the Upper House, or the presence of other religious dignitaries, with equal rank and rights, alongside of them. Questions of patronage and ecclesiastical law might be difficult to settle; but otherwise a statute of mere disestablishment, not easy indeed to formulate, would leave the Church in the eyes of the country very much what it found it. Perhaps "My lord" might be more widely dropped in addressing Bishops; but otherwise, the aspect of the Church, its daily work, its organisations, would remain the same, and it would depend on the Church itself whether the consideration paid to it continues what it has been; whether it shall be diminished or increased. The privilege of being publicly recognised with special marks of honour by the State has been dearly paid for by the claim which the State has always, and sometimes unscrupulously, insisted on, of making the true interests of the Church subservient to its own passing necessities.

But there is no haziness about the meaning of disendowment. Property is a tangible thing, and is subject to the four rules of arithmetic, and ultimately to the force of the strong arm. When you talk of disendowment, you talk of taking from the Church, not honour or privilege or influence, but visible things, to be measured and counted and pointed to, which now belong to it and which you want to belong to some one else. They belong to individuals because the individuals belong to a great body. There are, of course, many people who do not believe that such a body exists; or that if it does, it has been called into being and exists simply by the act of the State, like the army, and, like the army, liable to be disbanded by its master. But that is a view resting on a philosophical theory of a purely subjective character; it is as little the historical or legal view as it is the theological view. We have not yet lost our right in the nineteenth century to think of the Church of England as a continuous, historic, religious society, bound by ties which, however strained, are still unbroken with that vast Christendom from which as a matter of fact it sprung, and still, in spite of all differences, external and internal, and by force of its traditions and institutions, as truly one body as anything can be on earth. To this Church, this body, by right which at present is absolutely unquestionable, property belongs; property has been given from time immemorial down to yesterday. This property, in its bulk, with whatever abatements and allowances, it is intended to take from the Church. This is disendowment, and this is what is before us.

It is well to realise as well as we can what is inevitably involved in this vast and, in modern England, unexampled change, which we are sometimes invited to view with philosophic calmness or resignation, as the unavoidable drift of the current of modern thought, or still more cheerfully to welcome, as the beginning of a new era in the prosperity and strength of the Church as a religious institution. We are entreated to be of good cheer. The Church will be more free; it will no longer be mixed up with sordid money matters and unpopular payments; it will no longer have the discredit of State control; the rights of the laity will come up and a blow will be struck at clericalism. With all our machinery shattered and ruined we shall be thrown more on individual energy and spontaneous originality of effort. Our new poverty will spur us into zeal. Above all, the Church will be delivered from the temptation, incident to wealth, of sticking to abuses for the sake of gold; of shrinking from principle and justice and enthusiasm, out of fear of worldly loss. It will no longer be a place for drones and hirelings. It is very kind of the revolutionists to wish all this good to the Church, though if the Church is so bad as to need all these good wishes for its improvement, it would be more consistent, and perhaps less cynical, to wish it ruined altogether. Yet even if the Church were likely to thrive better on no bread, there are reasons of public morality why it should not be robbed. But these prophecies and forecasts really belong to a sphere far removed from the mental activity of those who so easily indulge in them. These excellent persons are hardly fitted by habit and feeling to be judges of the probable course of Divine Providence, or the development of new religious energies and spiritual tendencies in a suddenly impoverished body. What they can foresee, and what we can foresee also is, that these *tabulae novae* will be a great blow to the Church. They mean that, and that we understand.

It is idle to talk as if it was to be no blow to the Church. The confiscation of Wesleyan and Roman Catholic Church property would be a real blow to Wesleyan or Roman Catholic interests; and in proportion as the body is greater the effects of the blow must be heavier and more signal. It is trifling with our patience to pretend to persuade us that such a confiscation scheme as is now recommended to the country would not throw the whole work of the Church into confusion and disaster, not perhaps irreparable, but certainly for the time overwhelming and perilous. People speak sometimes as if such a huge transfer of property was to be done with the stroke of a pen and the aid of a few office clerks; they forget what are the incidents of an institution which has lasted in England for more than a thousand years, and whose business extends to every aspect and degree of our very complex society from the highest to the lowest. Resources may be replaced, but for the time they must be crippled. Life may be rearranged for the new circumstances, but in the meanwhile all the ordinary assumptions have to be changed, all the ordinary channels of activity are stopped up or diverted.

And why should this vast and far-reaching change

be made? Is it unlawful for the Church to hold property? Other religious organisations hold it, and even the Salvation Army knows the importance of funds for its work. Is it State property which the State may resume for other uses? If anything is certain it is that the State, except in an inconsiderable degree, did not endow the Church, but consented in the most solemn way to its being endowed by the gifts of private donors, as it now consents to the endowment in this way of other religious bodies. Does the bigness of the property entitle the State to claim it? This is a formidable doctrine for other religious bodies, as they increase in influence and numbers. Is it vexatious that the Church should be richer and more powerful than the sects? It is not the fault of the Church that it is the largest and the most ancient body in England. There is but one real and adequate reason: it is the wish to disable and paralyse a great religious corporation, the largest and most powerful representative of Christianity in our English society, to exhibit it to the nation after centuries of existence at length defeated and humbled by the new masters' power, to deprive it of the organisation and the resources which it is using daily with increasing effect for impressing religious truth on the people, for winning their interest, their confidence, and their sympathy, for obtaining a hold on the generations which are coming. The Liberation Society might go on for years repeating their dreary catalogue of grievances and misstatements. Doubtless there is much for which they desire to punish the Church; doubtless, too, there are men among them who are persuaded that they would serve religion by discrediting and impoverishing the Church. But they are not the people with whom the Church has to reckon. The Liberationists might have long asked in vain for their pet "emancipation" scheme. They are stronger men than the Liberationists who are going in now for disendowment. They are men—we do them no wrong—who sincerely think Christianity mischievous, and who see in the power and resources of the Church a bulwark and representative of all religion which it is of the first importance to get rid of.

This is the one adequate and consistent reason for the confiscation of the property of the Church. There is no other reason that will bear discussion to be given for what, without it, is a great moral and political wrong. In such a settled society as ours, where men reckon on what is their own, such a sweeping and wholesale transfer of property cannot be justified, on a mere balance of probable expediency in the use of it. Unless it is as a punishment for gross neglect and abuse, as was alleged in the partial confiscations of the sixteenth century, or unless it is called for as a step to break down what can no longer be tolerated, like slavery, there is no other name for it, in the estimate of justice, than that of a deep and irreparable wrong. This is certainly not the time to punish the Church when it never was more improving and more unsparing of sacrifice and effort. But it may be full time to stop a career which may render success more difficult for schemes ahead, which make no secret of their intention to dispense with religion. This, however, is not what most Englishmen wish, whether Liberals or Conservatives, or even Nonconformists; and without this end there is no more justice in disendowing a great religious corporation like the Church, than in disendowing the Duke of Bedford or the Duke of Westminster. Of course no one can deny the competence of Parliament to do either one or the other; but power does not necessarily carry with it justice, and justice means that while there are great and small, rich and poor, the State should equally protect all its members and all its classes, however different. Revolutions have no law; but a great wrong, deliberately inflicted in times of settled order, is more mischievous to the nation than even to those who suffer from it. History has shown us what follows from such gratuitous and wanton wrong in the bitter feeling of defeat and humiliation lasting through generations. But worse than this is the effect on the political morality of the nation; the corrupting and fatal consciousness of having once broken through the restraints of recognised justice, of having acquiesced in a tempting but high-handed wrong. The effects of disendowment concern England and its morality even more deeply than they do the Church.

VII

THE NEW COURT[1]

THE claim maintained by the Archbishop in his Judgment, by virtue of his metropolitical authority and by that alone, to cite, try, and sentence one of his suffragans, is undoubtedly what is called in slang language "a large order." Even by those who may have thought it inevitable, after the Watson case had been so distinctly accepted by the books as a precedent, it is yet felt as a surprise, in the sense in which a thing is often a surprise when, after being only talked about it becomes a reality. We can imagine some people getting up in the morning on last Saturday with one set of feelings, and going to bed with another. Bishops, then, who in spite of the alleged anarchy, are still looked upon with great reverence, as almost irresponsible in what they say and do officially, are, it seems, as much at the mercy of the law as the presbyters and deacons whom they have occasionally sent before the Courts. They, too, at the will of chance accusers who are accountable to no one, are

[1] *Guardian*, 15th May 1889.

liable to the humiliation, worry, and crushing law-bills of an ecclesiastical suit. Whatever may be thought of this now, it would have seemed extravagant and incredible to the older race of Bishops that their actions should be so called in question. They would have thought their dignity gravely assailed, if besides having to incur heavy expense in prosecuting offending clergymen, they had also to incur it in protecting themselves from the charge of being themselves offenders against Church law.

The growth of law is always a mysterious thing; and an outsider and layman is disposed to ask where this great jurisdiction sprung up and grew into shape and power. In the Archbishop's elaborate and able Judgment it is indeed treated as something which had always been; but he was more successful in breaking down the force of alleged authorities, and inferences from them, on the opposite side, than he was in establishing clearly and convincingly his own contention. Considering the dignity and importance of the jurisdiction claimed, it is curious that so little is heard about it till the beginning of the eighteenth century. It is curious that in its two most conspicuous instances it should have been called into activity by those not naturally friendly to large ecclesiastical claims—by Low Churchmen of the Revolution against an offending Jacobite, and by a Puritan association against a High Churchman. There is no such clear and strong case as Bishop Watson's till we come to Bishop Watson. In his argument the Archbishop rested his claim definitely and forcibly on the precedent of Bishop Watson's case, and one or two cases which more or less followed it. That possibly is sufficient for his purpose; but it may still be asked—What did the Watson case itself grow out of? what were the precedents—not merely the analogies and supposed legal necessities, but the precedents—on which this exercise of metropolitical jurisdiction, distinct from the legatine power, rested? For it seems as if a formidable prerogative, not much heard of where we might expect to hear of it, not used by Cranmer and Laud, though approved by Cranmer in the *Reformatio Legum*, had sprung into being and energy in the hands of the mild Archbishop Tenison. Watson's case may be good law and bind the Archbishop. But it would have been more satisfactory if, in reviving a long-disused power, the Archbishop had been able to go behind the Watson case, and to show more certainly that the jurisdiction which he claimed and proposed to exercise in conformity with that case had, like the jurisdiction of other great courts of the Church and realm, been clearly and customarily exercised long before that case.

The appearance of this great tribunal among us, a distinctly spiritual court of the highest dignity, cannot fail to be memorable. It is too early to forecast what its results may be. There may be before it an active and eventful career, or it may fall back into disuse and quiescence. It has jealous and suspicious rivals in the civil courts, never well disposed to the claim of ecclesiastical power or purely spiritual authority; and though its jurisdiction is not likely to be strained at present, it is easy to conceive occasions in the future which may provoke the interference of the civil court.

But there is this interest about the present proceedings, that they illustrate with curious closeness, amid so much that is different, the way in which great spiritual prerogatives grew up in the Church. They may have ended disastrously; but at their first beginnings they were usually inevitable, innocent, blameless. Time after time the necessity arose of some arbiter among those who were themselves arbiters, rulers, judges. Time after time this necessity forced those in the first rank into this position, as being the only persons who could be allowed to take it, and so Archbishops, Metropolitans, Primates appeared, to preside at assemblies, to be the mouthpiece of a general sentiment, to decide between high authorities, to be the centre of appeals. The Papacy itself at its first beginning had no other origin. It interfered because it was asked to interfere; it judged because there was no one else to judge. And so necessities of a very different kind have forced the Archbishop of Canterbury of our day into a position which is new and strange to our experience, and which, however constitutional and reasonable it may be, must give every one who is at all affected by it a good deal to think about.

VIII

MOZLEY'S BAMPTON LECTURES[1]

I

THE way in which the subject of Miracles has been treated, and the place which they have had in our discussions, will remain a characteristic feature of both the religious and philosophical tendencies of thought among us. Miracles, if they are real things, are the most awful and august of realities. But, from various causes, one of which, perhaps, is the very word itself, and the way in which it binds into one vague and technical generality a number of most heterogeneous instances, miracles have lost much of their power to interest those who have thought most in sympathy with their generation. They have been summarily and loosely put aside, sometimes avowedly, more often still by implication. Even by those who accepted and maintained them, they have often been

[1] *Eight Lectures on Miracles: the Bampton Lectures for* 1865. By the Rev. J. B. Mozley, B.D. *The Times*, 5th and 6th June 1866.

touched uncertainly and formally, as if people thought that they were doing a duty, but would like much better to talk about other things which really attracted and filled their minds. In the long course of theological war for the last two centuries, it is hardly too much to say that miracles, as a subject for discussion, have been degraded and worn down from their original significance; vulgarised by passing through the handling of not the highest order of controversialists, who battered and defaced what they bandied about in argument, which was often ingenious and acute, and often mere verbal sophistry, but which, in any case, seldom rose to the true height of the question. Used either as instruments of proof or as fair game for attack, they suffered in the common and popular feeling about them. Taken in a lump, and with little realising of all that they were and implied, they furnished a cheap and tempting material for "short and easy methods" on one side, and on the other side, as it is obvious, a mark for just as easy and tempting objections. They became trite. People got tired of hearing of them, and shy of urging them, and dwelt in preference on other grounds of argument. The more serious feeling and the more profound and original thought of the last half century no longer seemed to give them the value and importance which they had; on both sides a disposition was to be traced to turn aside from them. The deeper religion and the deeper and more enterprising science of the day combined to lower them from their old evidential place. The one threw the moral stress on moral grounds of belief, and seemed inclined to undervalue external proofs. The other more and more yielded to its repugnance to admit the interruption of natural law, and became more and more disinclined even to discuss the supernatural; and, curiously enough, along with this there was in one remarkable school of religious philosophy an increased readiness to believe in miracles as such, without apparently caring much for them as proofs. Of late, indeed, things have taken a different turn. The critical importance of miracles, after for a time having fallen out of prominence behind other questions, has once more made itself felt. Recent controversy has forced them again on men's thoughts, and has made us see that, whether they are accepted or denied, it is idle to ignore them. They mean too much to be evaded. Like all powerful arguments they cut two ways, and of all powerful arguments they are the most clearly two-edged. However we may limit their range, some will remain which we must face; which, according to what is settled about them, either that they are true or not true, will entirely change all that we think of religion. Writers on all sides have begun to be sensible that a decisive point requires their attention, and that its having suffered from an old-fashioned way of handling is no reason why it should not on its own merits engage afresh the interest of serious men, to whom it is certainly of consequence.

The renewed attention of theological writers to the subject of miracles as an element of proof has led to some important discussions upon it, showing in their treatment of a well-worn inquiry that a change in the way of conducting it had become necessary. Of these productions we may place Mr. Mozley's *Bampton Lectures* for last year among the most original and powerful. They are an example, and a very fine one, of a mode of theological writing which is characteristic of the Church of England, and almost peculiar to it. The distinguishing features of it are a combination of intense seriousness with a self-restrained, severe calmness, and of very vigorous and wide-ranging reasoning on the realities of the case with the least amount of care about artificial symmetry or scholastic completeness. Admirers of the Roman style call it cold, indefinite, wanting in dogmatic coherence, comprehensiveness, and grandeur. Admirers of the German style find little to praise in a cautious bit-by-bit method, content with the tests which have most affinity with common sense, incredulous of exhaustive theories, leaving a large margin for the unaccountable or the unexplained. But it has its merits, one of them being that, dealing very solidly and very acutely with large and real matters of experience, the interest of such writings endures as the starting-point and foundation for future work. Butler out of England is hardly known, certainly he is not much valued either as a divine or a philosopher; but in England, though we criticise him freely, it will be a long time before he is out of date. Mr. Mozley's book belongs to that class of writings of which Butler may be taken as the type. It is strong, genuine argument about difficult matters, fairly facing what *is* difficult, fairly trying to grapple, not with what *appears* the gist and strong point of a question, but with what really and at bottom *is* the knot of it. It is a book the reasoning of which may not satisfy every one; but it is a book in which there is nothing plausible, nothing put in to escape the trouble of thinking out what really comes across the writer's path. This will not recommend it to readers who themselves are not fond of trouble; a book of hard thinking cannot be a book of easy reading; nor is it a book for people to go to who only want available arguments, or to see a question apparently settled in a convenient way. But we think it is a book for people who wish to see a great subject handled on a scale which befits it and with a perception of its real elements. It is a book which will have attractions for those who like to see a powerful mind applying itself without shrinking or holding back, without trick or reserve or show of any kind, as a wrestler closes body to body with his antagonist, to the strength of an adverse and powerful argument. A stern self-constraint excludes everything exclamatory, all glimpses and disclosures of what merely affects the writer, all advantages from an appeal, disguised and indirect perhaps, to the opinion of his own side. But though the work is not rhetorical, it is not the less eloquent; but it is eloquence arising from a keen insight at once into what is real and what is great, and from a singular power of luminous, noble, and expressive statement. There is no excitement about its close subtle trains of reasoning; and there is no affectation,—and therefore no affectation of impartiality. The writer has his conclusions, and he does not pretend to hold a balance between them and their opposites. But in the presence of such a subject he never loses sight of its greatness, its difficulty, its eventfulness; and these thoughts make him throughout his undertaking circumspect, considerate, and calm.

The point of view from which the subject of miracles is looked at in these Lectures is thus stated in the preface. It is plain that two great questions arise—first, Are miracles possible? next, If they are, can any in fact be proved? These two branches of the inquiry involve different classes of considerations. The first is purely philosophical, and stops the inquiry at once if it can be settled in the negative. The other calls in also the aid of history and criticism. Both questions have been followed out of late with great keenness and interest, but it is the first which at present assumes an importance which it never had before, with its tremendous negative answer, revolutionising not only the past, but the whole future of mankind; and it is to the first that Mr. Mozley's work is mainly addressed.

The difficulty which attaches to miracles in the period of thought through which we are now passing is one which is concerned not with their evidence, but with their intrinsic credibility. There has arisen in a certain class of minds an apparent perception of the impossibility of suspensions of physical law. This is one peculiarity of the time; another is a disposition to maintain the disbelief of miracles upon a religious basis, and in a connection with a declared belief in the Christian revelation.

The following Lectures, therefore, are addressed mainly to the fundamental question of the credibility of Miracles, their use and the evidences of them being only touched on subordinately and collaterally. It was thought that such an aim, though in itself a narrow and confined one, was most adapted to the particular need of the day.

As Mr. Mozley says, various points essential to the whole argument, such as testimony, and the criterion between true and false miracles, are touched upon; but what is characteristic of the work is the way in which it deals with the antecedent objection to the possibility and credibility of miracles. It is on this part of the subject that the writer strikes out a line for himself, and puts forth his strength. His argument may be described generally as a plea for reason against imagination and the broad impressions of custom. Experience, such experience as we have of the world and human life, has, in all ages, been really the mould of human thought, and with large exceptions, the main unconscious guide and controller of human belief; and in our own times it has been formally and scientifically recognised as such, and made the exclusive foundation of all possible philosophy. A philosophy of mere experience is not tolerant of miracles; its doctrines exclude them; but, what is of even greater force than its doctrines, the subtle and penetrating atmosphere of feeling and intellectual habits which accompanies it is essentially uncongenial and hostile to them. It is against the undue influence of such results of experience—an influence openly acting in distinct ideas and arguments, but of which the greater portion operates blindly, insensibly, and out of sight—that Mr. Mozley makes a stand on behalf of reason, to which it belongs in the last resort to judge of the lessons of experience. Reason, as it cannot create experience, so it cannot take its place and be its substitute; but what reason can do is to say within what limits experience is paramount as a teacher; and reason abdicates its functions if it declines to do so, for it was given us to work upon and turn to account the unmeaning and brute materials which experience gives us in the rough. The antecedent objection against miracles is, he says, one of experience, but not one of reason. And experience, flowing over its boundaries tyrannically and effacing its limits, is as dangerous to truth and knowledge as reason once was, when it owned no check in nature, and used no test but itself.

Mr. Mozley begins by stating clearly the necessity for coming to a decision on the question of miracles. It cannot remain one of the open questions, at least of religion. There is, as has been said, a disposition to pass by it, and to construct a religion without miracles. The thing is conceivable. We can take what are as a matter of fact the moral results of Christianity, and of that singular power with which it has presided over the improvement of mankind, and alloying and qualifying them with other elements, not on the face of the matter its products, yet in many cases indirectly connected with its working, form something which we may acknowledge as a rule of life, and which may satisfy our inextinguishable longings after the unseen and eternal. It is true that such a religion presupposes Christianity, to which it owes its best and noblest features, and that, as far as we can see, it is inconceivable if Christianity had not first been. Still, we may say that alchemy preceded chemistry, and was not the more true for being the step to what is true. But what we cannot say of such a religion is that it takes the place of Christianity, and is such a religion as Christianity has been and claims to be. There must ever be all the difference in the world between a religion which is or professes to be a revelation, and one which cannot be called such. For a revelation is a direct work and message of God; but that which is the result of a process and progress of finding out the truth by the experience of ages, or ot correcting mistakes, laying aside superstitions and gradually reducing the gross mass of belief to its essential truth, is simply on a level with all other human knowledge, and, as it is about the unseen, can never be verified. If there has been no revelation, there may be religious hopes and misgivings, religious ideas or dreams, religious anticipations and trust; but the truth is, there cannot be a religion in the world. Much less can there be any such thing as Christianity. It is only when we look at it vaguely in outline, without having before our mind what it is in fact and in detail, that we can allow ourselves to think so. There is no transmuting its refractory elements into something which is not itself; and it is nothing if it is not primarily a direct message from God. Limit as we may the manner of this communication, still there remains what makes it different from all other human possessions of truth, that it was a direct message. And that, to whatever extent, involves all that is involved in the idea of miracles. It is, as Mr. Mozley says, inconceivable without miracles.

If, then, a person of evident integrity and loftiness of character rose into notice in a particular country and community eighteen centuries ago, who made these communications about himself—that he had existed before his natural birth, from all eternity, and before the world was, in a state of glory with God; that he was the only-begotten Son of God; that the world itself had been made by him; that he had, however, come down from heaven and assumed the form and nature of man for a particular purpose—viz. to be the Lamb of God that taketh away the sins of the world; that he thus stood in a mysterious and supernatural relation to the whole of mankind; that through him alone mankind had access to God; that he was the head of an invisible kingdom, into which he should gather all the generations of righteous men who had lived in the world; that on his departure from hence he should return to heaven to prepare mansions there for them; and, lastly, that he should descend again at the end of the world to judge the whole human race, on which occasion all that were in their graves should hear his voice and come forth, they that had done good unto the resurrection of life, and they that had done evil unto the resurrection of damnation,—if this person made these assertions about himself, and all that was done was to make the assertions, what would be the inevitable conclusion of sober reason respecting that person? The necessary conclusion of sober reason respecting that person would be that he was disordered in his understanding. What other decision could we come to when a man, looking like one of ourselves, and only exemplifying in his life and circumstances the ordinary course of nature, said this about himself, but that when reason had lost its balance a dream of extraordinary and unearthly grandeur might be the result? By no rational being could a just and benevolent life be accepted as proof of such astonishing announcements. Miracles are the necessary complement then of the truth of such announcements, which without them are purposeless and abortive, the unfinished fragments of a design which is nothing unless it is the whole. They are necessary to the justification of such announcements, which, indeed, unless they are supernatural truths, are the wildest delusions. The matter and its guarantee are the two parts of a revelation, the absence of either of which neutralises and undoes it.

A revelation, in any sense in which it is more than merely a result of the natural progress of the human mind and the gradual clearing up of mistakes, cannot in the nature of things be without miracles, because it is not merely a discovery of ideas and rules of life, but of facts undiscoverable without it. It involves *constituent* miracles, to use De Quincey's phrase, as part of its substance, and could not claim a hearing without *evidential* or *polemic* ones. No other portion or form of proof, however it may approve itself to the ideas of particular periods or minds, can really make up for this. The alleged sinlessness of the Teacher, the internal evidence from adaptation to human nature, the historical argument of the development of Christendom, are, as Mr. Mozley points out, by themselves inadequate, without that further guarantee which is contained in miracles, to prove the Divine origin of a religion. The tendency has been of late to fall back on these attractive parts of the argument, which admit of such varied handling and expression, and come home so naturally to the feelings of an age so busy and so keen in pursuing the secrets of human character, and so fascinated with its unfolding wonders. But take any of them, the argument from results, for instance, perhaps the most powerful of them all. "We cannot," as Mr. Mozley says, "rest too much upon it, so long as we do not charge it with more of the burden of proof than it is in its own nature equal to—viz. the whole. But that it cannot bear." The hard, inevitable question remains at the end, for the most attenuated belief in Christianity as a religion from God—what is the ultimate link which connects it directly with God? The readiness with which we throw ourselves on more congenial topics of proof does not show that, even to our own minds, these proofs could suffice by themselves, miracles being really taken away. The whole power of a complex argument and the reasons why it tells do not always appear on its face. It does not depend merely on what it states, but also on unexpressed, unanalysed, perhaps unrealised grounds, the real force of which would at once start forth if they were taken away. We are told of the obscure rays of the spectrum, rays which have their proof and their effect, only not the same proof and effect as the visible ones which they accompany; and the background and latent suppositions of a great argument are as essential to it as its more prominent and elaborate constructions. And they show their importance sometimes in a remarkable and embarrassing way, when, after a long debate, their presence at the bottom of everything, unnoticed and perhaps unallowed for, is at length disclosed by some obvious and decisive question, which some person had been too careless to think of, and another too shy to ask. We may not care to obtrude miracles; but take them away, and see what becomes of the argument for Christianity.

It must be remembered that when this part of Christian evidence comes so forcibly home to us, and creates that inward assurance which it does, it does this in connection with the proof of miracles in the background, which though it may not for the time be brought into actual view, is still known to be there, and to be ready for use upon being wanted. The *indirect* proof from results has the greater force, and carries with it the deeper persuasion, because it is additional and auxiliary to the *direct* proof behind it, upon which it leans all the time, though we may not distinctly notice and estimate this advantage. Were the evidence of moral result to be taken rigidly alone as the one single guarantee for a Divine revelation, it would then be seen that we had calculated its single strength too highly. If there is a species of evidence which is directly appropriate to the thing believed, we cannot suppose, on the strength of the indirect evidence we possess, that we can do without the direct. But miracles are the direct credentials of a revelation; the visible supernatural is the appropriate witness to the invisible supernatural—that proof which goes straight to the point, and, a token being wanted of a Divine communication, is that token. We cannot, therefore, dispense with this evidence. The position that the revelation proves the miracles, and not the miracles the revelation, admits of a good qualified meaning; but, taken literally, it is a double offence against the rule that things are properly proved by the proper proof of them; for a supernatural fact *is* the proper proof of a supernatural doctrine, while a supernatural doctrine, on the other hand, is certainly *not* the proper proof of a supernatural fact.

So that, whatever comes of the inquiry, miracles and revelation must go together. There is no separating them. Christianity may claim in them the one decisive proof that could be given of its Divine origin and the truth of its creed; but, at any rate, it must ever be responsible for them.

But suppose a person to say, and to say with truth, that his own individual faith does not rest upon miracles, is he, therefore, released from the defence of miracles? Is the question of their truth or falsehood an irrelevant one to him? Is his faith secure if they are disproved? By no means; if miracles were, although only at the commencement, necessary to Christianity, and were actually wrought, and therefore form part of the Gospel record and are bound up with the Gospel scheme and doctrines, this part of the structure cannot be abandoned without the sacrifice of the other too. To shake the authority of one-half of this body of statement is to shake the authority of the whole. Whether or not the individual makes *use* of them for the support of his own faith, the miracles are there; and if they are there they must be there either as true miracles or as false ones. If he does not avail himself of their evidence, his belief is still affected by their refutation. Accepting, as he does, the supernatural truths of Christianity and its miracles upon the same report from the same witnesses, upon the authority of the same documents, he cannot help having at any rate this negative interest in them. For if those witnesses and documents deceive us with regard to the miracles, how can we trust them with regard to the doctrines? If they are wrong upon the evidences of a revelation, how can we depend upon their being right as to the nature of that revelation? If their account of visible facts is to be received with an explanation, is not their account of doctrines liable to a like explanation? Revelation, then, even if it does not need the truth of miracles for the benefit of their proof, still requires it in order not to be crushed under the weight of their falsehood. . . . Thus miracles and the supernatural contents of Christianity must stand or fall together. These two questions—the *nature* of the revelation, and the *evidence* of the revelation—cannot be disjoined. Christianity as a dispensation undiscoverable by human reason, and Christianity as a dispensation authenticated by miracles—these two are in necessary combination. If any do not include the supernatural character of Christianity in their definition of it, regarding the former only as one interpretation of it or one particular traditional form of it, which is separable from the essence—for Christianity as thus defined the support of miracles is not wanted, because the moral truths are their own evidence. But Christianity cannot be maintained as a revelation undiscoverable by human reason, a revelation of a supernatural scheme for man's salvation, without the evidence of miracles.

The question of miracles, then, of the supernatural disclosed in the world of nature, is the vital point for everything that calls itself Christianity. It may be forgotten or disguised; but it is vain to keep it back and put it out of sight. It must be answered; and if we settle it that miracles are incredible, it is idle to waste our time about accommodations with Christianity, or reconstitutions of it. Let us be thankful for what it has done for the world; but let us put it away, both name and thing. It is an attempt after what is in the nature of things impossible to man—a revealed religion, authenticated by God. The shape which this negative answer takes is, as Mr. Mozley points out, much more definite now than it ever was. Miracles were formerly assailed and disbelieved on mixed and often confused grounds; from alleged defect of evidence, from their strangeness, or because they would be laughed at. Foes and defenders looked at them from the outside and in the gross; and perhaps some of those who defended them most keenly had a very imperfect sense of what they really were. The difficulty of accepting them now arises not mainly from want of external evidence, but from having more keenly realised what it is to believe a miracle. As Mr. Mozley says—

How is it that sometimes when the same facts and truths have been before men all their lives, and produced but one impression, a moment comes when they look different from what they did? Some minds may abandon, while others retain, their fundamental position with respect to those facts and truths, but to both they look stranger; they excite a certain surprise which they did not once do. The reasons of this change then it is not always easy for the persons themselves to trace, but of the result they are conscious; and in some this result is a change of belief.

An inward process of this kind has been going on recently in many minds on the subject of miracles; and in some with the latter result. When it came to the question—which every one must sooner or later put to himself on this subject—Did these things really take place? Are they matters of fact?—they have appeared to themselves to be brought to a standstill, and to be obliged to own an inner refusal of their whole reason to admit them among the actual events of the past. This strong repugnance seemed to be the witness of its own truth, to be accompanied by a clear and vivid light, to be a law to the understanding, and to rule without appeal the question of fact. . . . But when the reality of the past is once apprehended and embraced, then the miraculous occurrences in it are realised too; being realised they excite surprise, and surprise, when it comes in, takes two directions—it either makes belief more real, or it destroys belief. There is an element of doubt in surprise; for this emotion arises *because* an event is strange, and an event is strange because it goes counter to and jars with presumption. Shall surprise, then, give life to belief or stimulus to doubt? The road of belief and unbelief in the history of some minds thus partly lies over common ground; the two go part of their journey together; they have a common perception in the insight into the real astonishing nature of the facts with which they deal. The majority of mankind, perhaps, owe their belief rather to the outward influence of custom and education than to any strong principle of faith within; and it is to be feared that many, if they came to perceive how wonderful what they believed was, would not find their belief so easy and so matter-of-course a thing as they appear to find it. Custom throws a film over the great facts of religion, and interposes a veil between the mind and truth, which, by preventing wonder, intercepts doubt too, and at the same time excludes from deep belief and protects from disbelief. But deeper faith and disbelief throw off in common the dependence on mere custom, draw aside the interposing veil, place themselves face to face with the contents of the past, and expose themselves alike to the ordeal of wonder.

It is evident that the effect which the visible order of nature has upon some minds is, that as soon as they realise what a miracle is, they are stopped by what appears to them a simple sense of its impossibility. So long as they only believe by habit and education, they accept a miracle without difficulty, because they do not realise it as an event which actually took place in the world; the alteration of the face of the world, and the whole growth of intervening history, throw the miracles of the Gospel into a remote perspective in which they are rather seen as a picture than real occurrences. But as soon as they see that, if these miracles are true, they once really happened, what they feel then is the apparent sense of their impossibility. It is not a question of evidence with them: when they realise, *e.g.*, that our Lord's resurrection, if true, was a visible fact or occurrence, they have the seeming certain perception that it is an impossible occurrence. "I cannot," a person says to himself in effect, "tear myself from the type of experience and join myself to another. I cannot quit order and law for what is eccentric. There is a repulsion between such facts and my belief as strong as that between physical substances. In the mere effort to conceive these amazing scenes as real ones, I fall back upon myself and upon that type of reality which the order of nature has impressed upon me."

The antagonism to the idea of miracles has grown

stronger and more definite with the enlarged and more widely-spread conception of invariable natural law, and also, as Mr. Mozley points out, with that increased power in our time of realising the past, which is not the peculiarity of individual writers, but is "part of the thought of the time." But though it has been quickened and sharpened by these influences, it rests ultimately on that sense which all men have in common of the customary and regular in their experience of the world. The world, which we all know, stands alone, cut off from any other; and a miracle is an intrusion, "an interpolation of one order of things into another, confounding two systems which are perfectly distinct." The broad, deep resistance to it which is awakened in the mind when we look abroad on the face of nature is expressed in Emerson's phrase—"A miracle is a monster. It is not one with the blowing clouds or the falling rain." Who can dispute it? Yet the rejoinder is obvious, and has often been given—that neither is man. Man, who looks at nature and thinks and feels about its unconscious unfeeling order; man, with his temptations, his glory, and his shame, his heights of goodness, and depths of infamy, is not one with those innocent and soulless forces so sternly immutable—"the blowing clouds and falling rain." The two awful phenomena which Kant said struck him dumb—the starry heavens, and right and wrong—are vainly to be reduced to the same order of things. Nothing can be stranger than the contrast between the rigid, inevitable sequences of nature, apparently so elastic only because not yet perfectly comprehended, and the consciousness of man in the midst of it. Nothing can be stranger than the juxtaposition of physical law and man's sense of responsibility and choice. Man is an "insertion," an "interpolation in the physical system"; he is "insulated as an anomaly in the midst of matter and material law." Mr. Mozley's words are striking:—

The first appearance, then, of man in nature was the appearance of a new being in nature; and this fact was relatively to the then order of things miraculous; no more physical account can be given of it than could be given of a resurrection to life now. What more entirely new and eccentric fact, indeed, can be imagined than a human soul first rising up amidst an animal and vegetable world? Mere consciousness—was not that of itself a new world within the old one? Mere knowledge—that nature herself became known to a being within herself, was not that the same? Certainly man was not all at once the skilled interpreter of nature, and yet there is some interpretation of nature to which man as such is equal in some degree. He derives an impression from the sight of nature which an animal does not derive; for though the material spectacle is imprinted on its retina, as it is on man's, it does not see what man sees. The sun rose, then, and the sun descended, the stars looked down upon the earth, the mountains climbed to heaven, the cliffs stood upon the shore, the same as now, countless ages before a single being existed who *saw* it. The counterpart of this whole scene was wanting—the understanding mind; that mirror in which the whole was to be reflected; and when this arose it was a new birth for creation itself, that it became *known*,—an image in the mind of a conscious being. But even consciousness and knowledge were a less strange and miraculous introduction into the world than conscience.

Thus wholly mysterious in his entrance into this scene, man is *now* an insulation in it; he came in by no physical law, and his freewill is in utter contrast to that law. What can be more incomprehensible, more heterogeneous, a more ghostly resident in nature, than the sense of right and wrong? What is it? Whence is it? The obligation of man to sacrifice himself for right is a truth which springs out of an abyss, the mere attempt to look down into which confuses the reason. Such is the juxtaposition of mysterious and physical contents in the same system. Man is alone, then, in nature: he alone of all the creatures communes with a Being out of nature; and he divides himself from all other physical life by prophesying, in the face of universal visible decay, his own immortality.

And till this anomaly has been removed—that is, till the last trace of what is moral in man has disappeared under the analysis of science, and what ought to be is resolved into a mere aspect of what is, this deep exception to the dominion of physical law remains as prominent and undeniable as physical law itself.

It is, indeed, avowed by those who reduce man in

in nature, that upon the admission of free-will, the objection to the miraculous is over, and that it is absurd to allow exception to law in man, and reject it in nature.

But the broad, popular sense of natural order, and the instinctive and common repugnance to a palpable violation of it, have been forged and refined into the philosophical objection to miracles. Two great thinkers of past generations, two of the keenest and clearest intellects which have appeared since the Reformation, laid the foundations of it long ago. Spinoza urged the uselessness of miracles, and Hume their incredibility, with a guarded subtlety and long-sighted refinement of statement which made them in advance of their age except with a few. But their reflections have fallen in with a more advanced stage of thought and a taste for increased precision and exactness, and they are beginning to bear their fruit. The great and telling objection to miracles is getting to be, not their want of evidence, but, prior to all question of evidence, the supposed impossibility of fitting them in with a scientific view of nature. Reason, looking at nature and experience, is said to raise an antecedent obstacle to them which no alleged proof of fact can get over. They cannot be, because they are so unlike to everything else in the world, even of the strangest kind, in this point—in avowedly breaking the order of nature. And reason cannot be admitted to take cognizance of their claims and to consider their character, their purpose, their results, their credentials, because the mere supposition of them violates the fundamental conception and condition of science, absolute and invariable law, as well as that common-sense persuasion which everybody has, whether philosopher or not, of the uniformity of the order of the world.

II

To make room for reason to come in and pronounce upon miracles on their own merits—to clear the ground for the consideration of their actual claims by disposing of the antecedent objection of impossibility, is Mr. Mozley's main object.

Whatever difficulty there is in believing in miracles in general arises from the circumstance that they are in contradiction to or unlike the order of nature. To estimate the force of this difficulty, then, we must first understand what kind of belief it is which we have in the order of nature; for the weight of the objection to the miraculous must depend on the nature of the belief to which the miraculous is opposed.

His examination of the alleged impossibility of miracles may be described as a very subtle turning the tables on Hume and the empirical philosophy. For when it is said that it is contrary to reason to believe in a suspension of the order of nature, he asks on what ground do we believe in the order of nature; and Hume himself supplies the answer. There is nothing of which we have a firmer persuasion. It is the basis of human life and knowledge. We assume at each step, without a doubt, that the future will be like the past. But why? Hume has carefully examined the question, and can find no answer, except the fact that we do assume it. "I apprehend," says Mr. Mozley, accepting Hume's view of the nature of probability, "that when we examine the different reasons which may be assigned for this connection, *i.e.* for the belief that the future will be like the past, they all come at last to be mere statements of the belief itself, and not reasons to account for it."

Let us imagine the occurrence of a particular physical phenomenon for the first time. Upon that single occurrence we should have but the very faintest expectation of another. If it did occur again once or twice, so far from counting on another recurrence, a cessation would come as the more natural event to us. But let it occur a hundred times, and we should feel no hesitation in inviting persons from a distance to see it; and if it occurred every day for years, its recurrence would then be a certainty to us, its cessation a marvel. But what has taken place in the interim to produce this total change in our belief? From the mere repetition do we know anything more about its cause? No. Then what have we got besides the past repetition itself? Nothing. Why, then, are we so certain of its *future* repetition? All we can say is that the known casts its shadow before; we project into unborn time the existing types, and the secret skill of nature intercepts the darkness of the future by ever suspending before our eyes, as it were in a mirror, a reflection of the past. We really look at a blank before us, but the mind, full of the scene behind, sees it again in front. . . .

What ground of reason, then, can we assign for our expectation that any part of the course of nature will the *next* moment be like what it has been up to *this* moment, *i.e.* for our belief in the uniformity of nature?   None. No demonstrative reason can be given, for the contrary to the recurrence of a fact of nature is no contradiction. No probable reason can be given, for all probable reasoning respecting the course of nature is founded *upon* this presumption of likeness, and therefore cannot be the foundation of it. No reason can be given for this belief. It is without a reason. It rests upon no rational ground and can be traced to no rational principle. Everything connected with human life depends upon this belief, every practical plan or purpose that we form implies it, every provision we make for the future, every safeguard and caution we employ against it, all calculation, all adjustment of means to ends, supposes this belief; it is this principle alone which renders our experience of the slightest use to us, and without it there would be, so far as we are concerned, no order of nature and no laws of nature; and yet this belief has no more producible reason for it than a speculation of fancy. A natural fact has been repeated; it will be repeated:—I am conscious of utter darkness when I try to see why one of these follows from the other: I not only see no reason, but I perceive that I see none, though I can no more help the expectation than I can stop the circulation of my blood. There is a premiss, and there is a conclusion, but there is a total want of connection between the two. The inference, then, from the one of these to the other rests upon no ground of the understanding; by no search or analysis, however subtle or minute, can we extract from any corner of the human mind and intelligence, however remote, the very faintest reason for it.

Hume, who had urged with great force that miracles were contrary to that probability which is created by experience, had also said that this probability had no producible ground in reason; that, universal, unfailing, indispensable as it was to the course of human life, it was but an instinct which defied analysis, a process of thought and inference for which he vainly sought the rational steps. There is no absurdity, though the greatest impossibility, in supposing this order to stop to-morrow; and, if the world ends at all, its end will be in an increasing degree improbable up to the very last moment. But, if this whole ground of belief is in its own nature avowedly instinctive and independent of reason, what right has it to raise up a bar of intellectual necessity, and to shut out reason from entertaining the question of miracles? They may have grounds which appeal to reason; and an unintelligent instinct forbids reason from fairly considering what they are. Reason cannot get beyond the actual fact of the present state of things for believing in the order of nature; it professes to find no necessity for it; the interruption of that order, therefore, whether probable or not, is not against reason. Philosophy itself, says

Mr. Mozley, cuts away the ground on which it had raised its preliminary objection to miracles.

And now the belief in the order of nature being thus, however powerful and useful, an unintelligent impulse of which we can give no rational account, in what way does this discovery affect the question of miracles? In this way, that this belief not having itself its foundation in reason, the ground is gone upon which it could be maintained that miracles as opposed to the order of nature were opposed to reason. There being no producible reason why a new event should be like the hitherto course of nature, no decision of reason is contradicted by its unlikeness. A miracle, in being opposed to our experience, is not only not opposed to necessary reasoning, but to any reasoning. Do I see by a certain perception the connection between these two—It *has* happened so, it *will* happen so; then may I reject a new reported fact which has *not* happened so as an impossibility. But if I do not see the connection between these two by a certain perception, or by any perception, I cannot. For a miracle to be rejected as such, there must, at any rate, be some proposition in the mind of man which is opposed to it; and that proposition can only spring from the quarter to which we have been referring—that of elementary experimental reasoning. But if this experimental reasoning is of that nature which philosophy describes it as being of, *i.e.* if it is not itself a process of reason, how can there from an irrational process of the mind arise a proposition at all,—to make which is the function of the rational faculty alone? There cannot; and it is evident that the miraculous does not stand in any opposition whatever to reason. . . .

Thus step by step has philosophy loosened the connection of the order of nature with the ground of reason, befriending, in exact proportion as it has done this, the principle of miracles. In the argument against miracles the first objection is that they are against *law;* and this is answered by saying that we know nothing in nature of law in the sense in which it prevents miracles. Law can only prevent miracles by *compelling* and making necessary the succession of nature, *i.e.* in the sense of causation; but science has itself proclaimed the truth that we see no causes in nature, that the whole chain of physical succession is to the eye of reason a rope of sand, consisting of antecedents and consequents, but without a rational link or trace of necessary connection between them. We only know of law in nature in the sense of recurrences in nature, classes of facts, *like* facts in nature —a chain of which, the junction not being reducible to reason, the interruption is not against reason. The claim of law settled, the next objection in the argument against miracles is that they are against *experience;* because we expect facts *like* to those of our experience, and miracles are *unlike* ones. The weight, then, of the objection of unlikeness to experience depends on the reason which can be produced for the expectation of likeness; and to this call philosophy has replied by the summary confession that we have *no* reason. Philosophy, then, could not have overthrown more thoroughly than it has done the order of nature as a necessary course of things, or cleared the ground more effectually for the principle of miracles.

Nor, he argues, does this instinct change its nature, or become a necessary law of reason, when it takes the form of an inference from induction. For the last step of the inductive process, the creation of its supposed universal, is, when compared with the real standard of universality acknowledged by reason, an incomplete and more or less precarious process; "it gets out of facts something more than what they actually contain"; and it can give no reason for itself but what the common faith derived from experience can give, the anticipation of uniform recurrence. "The inductive principle," he says, "is only the unreasoning impulse applied to a scientifically ascertained fact, instead of to a vulgarly ascertained fact. . . . Science has led up to the fact, but there it stops, and for converting the fact into a law a totally unscientific principle comes in, the same as that which generalises the commonest observations in nature."

The scientific part of induction being only the pursuit of a particular fact, miracles cannot in the nature of the case receive any blow from the scientific part of induction; because the existence of one fact does not interfere with the existence of another dissimilar fact. That which *does* resist the miraculous is the *un*scientific part of induction, or the instinctive generalisation upon this fact. . . . It does not belong to this principle to lay down speculative positions, and to say what can or cannot take place in the world. It does not belong to it to control religious belief, or to determine that certain acts of God for the revelation of His will to man, reported to have taken place, have not taken place. Such decisions are totally out of its sphere; it can assert the universal as a *law*, but the universal as a law and the universal as a proposition are wholly distinct. The one asserts the universal as a fact, the other as a presumption; the one as an absolute certainty, the other as a practical certainty, when there is no reason to expect the contrary. The one contains and includes the particular, the other does not; from the one we argue mathematically to the falsehood of any opposite particular; from the other we do not. . . . For example, one signal miracle, pre-eminent for its grandeur, crowned the evidence of the supernatural character and office of our Lord—our Lord's ascension—His going up with His body of flesh and bones into the sky in the presence of His disciples. "He lifted up His hands, and blessed them. And while He blessed them, He was parted from them, and carried up into heaven. And they looked stedfastly toward heaven as He went up, and a cloud received Him out of their sight."

Here is an amazing scene, which strikes even the devout believer, coming across it in the sacred page suddenly or by chance, amid the routine of life, with a fresh surprise. Did, then, this event really take place? Or is the evidence of it forestalled by the inductive principle compelling us to remove the scene *as such* out of the category of matters of fact? The answer is, that the inductive principle is in its own nature only an *expectation;* and that the expectation, that what is unlike our experience will not happen, is quite consistent with its occurrence in fact. This principle does not pretend to decide the question of fact, which is wholly out of its province and beyond its function. It can only decide the fact by the medium of a universal; the universal proposition that no man has ascended to heaven. But this is a statement which exceeds its power; it is as radically incompetent to pronounce it as the taste or smell is to decide on matters of sight; its function is practical, not logical. No antecedent statement, then, which touches my belief in this scene, is allowed by the laws of thought. Converted indeed into a universal proposition, the inductive principle is omnipotent, and totally annihilates every particular which does not come within its range. The universal statement that no man has ascended into heaven absolutely falsifies the fact that One Man has. But, thus transmuted, the inductive principle issues out of this metamorphose, a fiction not a truth; a weapon of air, which even in the hands of a giant can inflict no blow because it is itself a shadow. The object of assault receives the unsubstantial thrust without a shock, only exposing the want of solidity in the implement of war. The battle against the supernatural has been going on long, and strong men have conducted it, and are conducting it—but what they want is a weapon. The logic of unbelief wants a universal. But no real universal is forthcoming, and it only wastes its strength in wielding a fictitious one.

It is not in reason, which refuses to pronounce upon the possible merely from experience of the actual, that the antecedent objection to miracles is rooted. Yet that the objection is a powerful one the consciousness of every reflecting mind testifies.

What, then, is the secret of its force? In a lecture of singular power Mr. Mozley gives his answer. What tells beforehand against miracles is not reason, but imagination. Imagination is often thought to favour especially the supernatural and miraculous. It does do so, no doubt. But the truth is, that imagination tells both ways—as much against the miraculous as for it. The imagination, that faculty by which we give life and body and reality to our intellectual conceptions, takes its character from the intellectual conceptions with which it is habitually associated. It accepts the miraculous or shrinks from it and throws it off, according to the leaning of the mind of which it is the more vivid and, so to speak, passionate expression. And as it may easily exaggerate on one side, so it may just as easily do the same on the other. Every one is familiar with that imaginative exaggeration which fills the world with miracles. But there is another form of imagination, not so distinctly recognised, which is oppressed by the presence of unchanging succession and visible uniformity, which cannot shake off the yoke of custom or allow anything different to seem to it real. The sensitiveness and impressibility of the imagination are affected, and unhealthily affected, not merely by strangeness, but by sameness; to one as to the other it may "passively submit and surrender itself, give way to the mere form of attraction, and, instead of grasping something else, be itself grasped and mastered by some dominant idea." And it is then, in one case as much as in the other, "not a power, but a failing and weakness of nature."

The passive imagination, then, in the present case exaggerates a practical expectation of the uniformity of nature, implanted in us for practical ends, into a scientific or universal proposition; and it does this by surrendering itself to the impression produced by the constant spectacle of the regularity of visible nature. By such a course a person allows the weight and pressure of this idea to grow upon him till it reaches the point of actually restricting his sense of possibility to the mould of physical order. . . . The order of nature thus stamps upon some minds the idea of its immutability simply by its repetition. The imagination we usually indeed associate with the acceptance of the supernatural rather than with the denial of it; but the passive imagination is in truth neutral; it only increases the force and tightens the hold of any impression upon us, to whatever class the impression may belong, and surrenders itself to a superstitious or a physical idea, as it may be. Materialism itself is the result of imagination, which is so impressed by matter that it cannot realise the existence of spirit.

The great opponent, then, of miracles, considered as possible occurrences, is not reason, but something which on other great subjects is continually found on the opposite side to reason, resisting and counteracting it; that powerful overbearing sense of the actual and the real, which when it is opposed by reason is apt to make reason seem like the creator of mere ideal theories; which gives to arguments implying a different condition of things from one which is familiar to present experience the disadvantage of appearing like artificial and unsubstantial refinements of thought, such as, to the uncultivated mind, appear not merely metaphysical discussions, but what are known to be the most certain reasonings of physical and mathematical science. It is that measure of the probable, impressed upon us by the spectacle, to which we are accustomed all our lives long, of things as we find them, and which repels the possibility of a break or variation; that sense of probability which the keenest of philosophers declares to be incapable of rational analysis, and pronounces allied to irrational portions of our constitution, like custom, and the effect of time, and which is just as much an enemy to invention, to improvement, to a different state of things in the future, as it is to the belief and realising of a different state of things in the past. The antecedent objection to the miraculous is not reason, but an argument which limits and narrows the domain of reason; which excludes dry, abstract, passionless reason—with its appeals to considerations remote from common experience, its demands for severe reflection, its balancing and long chains of thought—from pronouncing on what seems to belong to the flesh and blood realities of life as we know it. Against this tyrannical influence, which may be in a vulgar and popular as in a scientific form, which may be the dull result of habit or the more specious effect of a sensitive and receptive imagination, but which in all cases is at bottom the same, Mr. Mozley claims to appeal to reason:—

To conclude, then, let us suppose an intelligent Christian of the present day asked, not what evidence he has of miracles, but how he can antecedently to all evidence think such amazing occurrences *possible*, he would reply, "You refer me to a certain sense of impossibility which you suppose me to possess, applying not to mathematics but to facts. Now, on this head, I am conscious of a certain natural resistance in my mind to events unlike the order of nature. But I resist many things which I know to be certain: infinity of space, infinity of time, eternity past, eternity future, the very idea of a God and another world. If I take mere resistance, therefore, for denial, I am confined in every quarter of my mind; I cannot carry out the very laws of reason, I am placed under conditions which are obviously false. I conclude, therefore, that I may resist and believe at the same time. If Providence has implanted in me a certain expectation of uniformity or likeness in nature, there is implied in that very expectation resistance to an *un*like event, which resistance does not cease even when upon evidence I *believe* the event, but goes on as a mechanical impression, though the reason counterbalances it. Resistance, therefore, is not disbelief, unless by an act of my own reason I *give* it an absolute veto, which I do *not* do. My reason is clear upon the point, that there is no disagreement between itself and a miracle as such."
. . . Nor is it dealing artificially with ourselves to exert a force upon our minds against the false certainty of the resisting imagination—such a force as is necessary to enable reason to stand its ground, and bend back again

that spring of impression against the miraculous which has illegally tightened itself into a law to the understanding. Reason does not always prevail spontaneously and without effort even in questions of belief; so far from it, that the question of faith against reason may often be more properly termed the question of reason against imagination. It does not seldom require faith to believe reason, isolated as she may be amid vast irrational influences, the weight of custom, the power of association, the strength of passion, the *vis inertiae* of sense, the mere force of the uniformity of nature as a spectacle—those influences which make up that power of the world which Scripture always speaks of as the antagonist of faith.

The antecedent questions about miracles, before coming to the question of the actual evidence of any, are questions about which reason—reason disengaged and disembarrassed from the arbitrary veto of experience—has a right to give its verdict. Miracles presuppose the existence of God, and it is from reason alone that we get the idea of God; and the antecedent question then is, whether they are really compatible with the idea of God which reason gives us. Mr. Mozley remarks that the question of miracles is really "shut up in the enclosure of one assumption, that of the existence of God"; and that if we believe in a personal Deity with all power over nature, that belief brings along with it the possibility of His interrupting natural order for His own purposes. He also bids us observe that the idea of God which reason gives us is exposed to resistance of the same kind, and from precisely the same forces, in our mental constitution, as the idea of miracles. When reason has finished its overwhelming proof, still there is a step to be taken before the mind embraces the equally overwhelming conclusion—a step which calls for a distinct effort, which obliges the mind, satisfied as it may be, to beat back the counteracting pressure of what is visible and customary. After reason—not opposed to it or independent of it, but growing out of it, yet a distinct and further movement—comes faith. This is the case, not specially in religion, but in all subjects, where the conclusions of reason cannot be subjected to immediate verification. How often, as he observes, do we see persons "who, when they are in possession of the best arguments, and what is more, understand those arguments, are still shaken by almost any opposition, because they want the faculty to *trust* an argument when they have got one."

Not, however, that the existence of a God is so clearly seen by reason as to dispense with faith; not from any want of cogency in the reasons, but from the amazing nature of the conclusion—that it is so unparalleled, transcendent, and inconceivable a truth to believe. It requires trust to commit oneself to the conclusion of any reasoning, however strong, when such as this is the conclusion: to put enough dependence and reliance upon any premisses, to accept upon the strength of them so immense a result. The issue of the argument is so astonishing that if we do not tremble for its safety, it must be on account of a practical principle in our minds which enables us to *confide* and trust in reasons, when they are really strong and good ones. . . . Faith, when for convenience' sake we do distinguish it from reason, is not distinguished from reason by the want of premisses, but by the nature of the conclusions. Are our conclusions of the customary type? Then custom imparts the full sense of security. Are they not of the customary, but of a strange and unknown type? Then the mechanical sense of security is wanting, and a certain trust is required for reposing in them, which we call faith. But that which draws these conclusions is in either case reason. We infer, we go upon reasons, we use premisses in either case. The premisses of faith are not so palpable as those of ordinary reason, but they are as real and solid premisses all the same. Our faith in the existence of a God and a future state is founded upon reasons as much so as the belief in the commonest kind of facts. The reasons are in themselves as strong, but, because the conclusions are marvellous and are not seconded and backed by known parallels or by experience, we do not so passively acquiesce in them; there is an exertion of confidence in depending upon them and assuring ourselves of their force. The inward energy of the reason has to be evoked, when she can no longer lean upon the outward prop of custom, but is thrown back upon herself and the intrinsic force of her premisses. Which reason, not leaning upon custom, is faith; she obtains the latter name when she depends entirely upon her own insight into certain grounds, premisses, and evidences, and follows it though it leads to transcendent, unparalleled, and supernatural conclusions. . . .

Indeed, does not our heart bear witness to the fact

that to believe in a God is an exercise of faith? That the universe was produced by the will of a personal Being, that its infinite forces are all the power of that one Being, its infinite relations the perceptions of one Mind—would not this, if any truth could, demand the application of the maxim, *Credo quia impossibile*? Look at it only as a conception, and does the wildest fiction of the imagination equal it? No premisses, no arguments therefore, can so accommodate this truth to us as not to leave the belief in it an act of mental ascent and trust, of faith as distinguished from sight. *Divest* reason of its trust, and the universe stops at the impersonal stage—there is no God; and yet, if the first step in religion is the greatest, how is it that the freest and boldest speculator rarely declines it? How is it that the most mysterious of all truths is a universally accepted one? What is it which guards this truth? What is it which makes men shrink from denying it? Why is atheism a crime? Is it that authority still reigns upon one question, and that the voice of all ages is too potent to be withstood?

But the progress of civilisation and thought has impressed this amazing idea on the general mind. It is no matter-of-course conception. The difficulties attending it were long insuperable to the deepest thought as well as to popular belief; and the triumph of the modern and Christian idea of God is the result not merely of the eager forwardness of faith, but of the patient and inquiring waiting of reason. And the question, whether we shall pronounce the miraculous to be impossible as such, is really the question whether we shall once more let this belief go.

The conception of a limited Deity then, *i.e.* a Being really circumscribed in power, and not verbally only by a confinement to necessary truth, is at variance with our fundamental idea of a God; to depart from which is to retrograde from modern thought to ancient, and to go from Christianity back again to Paganism. The God of ancient religion was either not a personal Being or not an omnipotent Being; the God of modern religion is both. For, indeed, civilisation is not opposed to faith. The idea of the Supreme Being in the mind of European society now is more primitive, more childlike, more imaginative than the idea of the ancient Brahman or Alexandrian philosopher; it is an idea which both of these would have derided as the notion of a child—a *negotiosus Deus,* who interposes in human affairs and answers prayers. So far from the philosophical conception of the Deity having advanced with civilisation, and the poetical receded, the philosophical has receded and the poetical advanced. The God of whom it is said, "Are not five sparrows sold for two farthings, and not one of them is forgotten before God; but even the very hairs of your head are numbered," is the object of modern worship. Nor, again, has civilisation shown any signs of rejecting doctrine. Certain ages are, indeed, called the ages of faith; but the bulk of society in *this* age believes that it lives under a supernatural dispensation, and accepts truths which are not less supernatural, though they have more proof, than some doctrines of the Middle Ages; and, if so, *this* is an age of faith. It is true that most people do not live up to their faith now; neither did they in the Middle Ages.

Has not modern philosophy, again, shown both more strength and acuteness, and also more faith, than the ancient? I speak of the main current. Those ancient thinkers who reduced the Supreme Being to a negation, with all their subtlety, wanted strength, and settled questions by an easier test than that of modern philosophy. The merit of a modern metaphysician is, like that of a good chemist or naturalist, accurate observation in noting the facts of mind. Is there a contradiction in the idea of creation? Is there a contradiction in the idea of a personal Infinite Being? He examines his own mind, and if he does not see one, he passes the idea. But the ancient speculators decided, without examination of the true facts of mind, by a kind of philosophical fancy; and, according to this loose criterion, the creation of matter and a personal Infinite Being were impossibilities, for they mistook the inconceivable for the impossible. And thus a stringent test has admitted what a loose but capricious test discarded, and the true notion of God has issued safe out of the crucible of modern metaphysics. Reason has shown its strength, but then it has turned that strength back upon itself; it has become its own critic; and in becoming its own critic it has become its own check.

If the belief, then, in a personal Deity lies at the bottom of all religious and virtuous practice, and if the removal of it would be a descent for human nature, the withdrawal of its inspiration and support, and a fall in its whole standard; the failure of the very breath of moral life in the individual and in society; the decay and degeneration of the very stock of mankind;—does a theory which would withdraw miraculous action from the Deity interfere with that belief? If it would, it is but prudent to count the cost of that interference. Would a Deity deprived of miraculous action possess action at all? And would a God who cannot act be a God? If this would be the issue, such an issue is the very last which religious men can desire. The question here has been all throughout, not whether upon any ground, but whether upon a religious ground and by religious believers, the miraculous as such could be rejected. But to that there is but one answer—that it is impossible in reason to separate religion from the supernatural, and upon a religious basis to overthrow miracles. . . .

And so we arrive again by another route at the old turning question; for the question whether man is or is not the *vertex* of nature, is the question whether there is or is not a God. Does free agency stop at the human stage, or is there a sphere of free-will above the human, in which, as in the human, not physical law but spirit moves matter? And does that free-will penetrate the universal frame invisibly to us, an omnipresent agent? If so, every miracle in Scripture is as natural an event in the universe as any chemical experiment in the physical world; if not, the seat of the great Presiding Will is empty, and nature has no Personal Head; man is her highest point; he finishes her ascent; though by this very supremacy he falls, for under fate he is not free himself; all nature either ascends to God, or descends to law. Is there above the level of material causes a region of Providence? If there is, nature there is moved by the Supreme Free Agent ; and of such a realm a miracle is the natural production.

Two rationales of miracles thus present themselves to our choice ; one more accommodating to the physical imagination and easy to fall in with, on a level with custom, common conceptions, and ordinary history, and requiring no ascent of the mind to embrace, viz. the solution of miracles as the growth of fancy and legend ; the other requiring an ascent of the reason to embrace it, viz. the rationale of the supremacy of a Personal Will in nature. The one is the explanation to which we fall when we dare not trust our reason, but mistake its inconceivable truths for sublime but unsubstantial visions ; the other is that to which we rise when we dare trust our reason, and the evidences which it lays before us of the existence of a Personal Supreme Being.

The belief in a personal God thus bringing with it the possibility of miracles, what reason then has to judge is whether it can accept miracles as such, or any set of miracles, as worthy of a reasonable conception of the Divine Nature, and whether it can be fairly said that such miracles have answered a purpose which approves itself to our reason. Testimony will always speak at a disadvantage till we are assured on these points. Into the subject of testimony Mr. Mozley enters only in a general way, though his remarks on the relation of testimony to facts of so exceptional a nature as miracles, and also on the distinct peculiarities of Christian evidence as contrasted with the evidence of all other classes of alleged miracles, are marked by a characteristic combination of acuteness, precision, and broad practical sobriety and moderation. He rebukes with quiet and temperate and yet resolute plainness of statement the misplaced ingenuity which, on different sides, to serve very different causes, has tried to confuse and perplex the claims of the great Christian miracles by comparisons which it is really mere wantonness to make with later ones; for, be they what they may, it is certain that the Gospel miracles, in nature, in evidence, and in purpose and result, are absolutely unique in the world, and have nothing like them. And though the book mainly confines itself to its proper subject, the antecedent question of credibility, some of the most striking remarks in it relate to the way in which the purpose of miracles is visible in those of Christianity, and has been served by them. A miracle is an instrument— an instrument without which revelation is impossible; and Mr. Mozley meets Spinoza's objection to the unmeaning isolation of a miracle by insisting on the distinction, which Spinoza failed to see, between a miracle simply as a wonder for its own sake, and as a means, deriving its use and its value simply from the end which it was to serve. He observes that all the stupendous "marvels of nature do not speak to us in that way in which one miracle does, because they do not tell us that we are not like themselves"; and he remarks on the "perverse determination of Spinoza to look at miracles in that aspect which does not belong to them, and not to look at them in that aspect which does."

He compares miracles with nature, and then says how wise is the order of nature, how meaningless the violation of it; how expressive of the Almighty Mind the one, what a concealment of it the other! But no one pretends to say that a miracle competes with nature, in physical purpose and effectiveness. That is not its object. But a miracle, though it does not profess to compete with nature upon its rival's own ground, has a ghostly force and import which nature has not. If real, it is a token, more pointed and direct than physical order can be, of another world, and of Moral Being and Will in that world.

Thus, regarding miracles as means to fulfil a purpose, Mr. Mozley shows what has come of them. His lecture on "Miracles regarded in their Practical Result" is excelled by some of the others as examples of subtle and searching thought and well-balanced and compact argument; but it is a fine example of the way in which a familiar view can have fresh colour and force thrown into it by the way in which it is treated. He shows that it is impossible in fact to separate from the miracles in which it professed to begin, the greatest and deepest moral change which the world has ever known. This change was made not by miracles but by certain doctrines. The Epistle to the Romans surveyed the moral failure of the world; St. Paul looked on the chasm between knowledge and action, the "unbridged gulf, this incredible inability of man to do what was right, with profound wonder"; but in the face of this hopeless spectacle he dared to prophesy the moral elevation which we have witnessed, and the power to which he looked to bring it about was the Christian doctrines. St. Paul "takes what may be called the high view of human nature—*i.e.* what human nature is capable of when the proper motive and impulse is applied to it." He sees in Christian doctrine that strong force which is to break down "the *vis inertiae* of man, to set human nature going, to touch the spring of man's heart"; and he compares with St. Paul's doctrines and hopefulness the doctrinal barrenness, the despair of Mohammedanism:—

If one had to express in a short compass the character of its remarkable founder as a teacher, it would be that that great man had no faith in human nature. There were two things which he thought man could do and would do for the glory of God—transact religious forms, and fight; and upon those two points he was severe; but within the sphere of common practical life, where man's great trial lies, his code exhibits the disdainful laxity of a legislator who accommodates his rule to the recipient, and shows his estimate of the recipient by the accommodation which he adopts. Did we search history for a contrast, we could hardly discover a deeper one than that between St. Paul's overflowing standard of the capabilities of human nature and the oracular cynicism of the great false Prophet. The writer of the Koran does, indeed, if any discerner of hearts ever did, take the measure of mankind; and his measure is the same that Satire has taken, only expressed with the majestic brevity of one who had once lived in the realm of Silence. "Man is weak," says Mahomet.

And upon that maxim he legislates. . . . The keenness of Mahomet's insight into human nature, a wide knowledge of its temptations, persuasives, influences under which it acts, a vast immense capacity of forbearance for it, half grave half genial, half sympathy half scorn, issue in a somewhat Horatian model, the character of the man of experience who despairs of any change in man, and lays down the maxim that we must take him as we find him. It was indeed his supremacy in both faculties, the largeness of the passive nature and the splendour of action, that constituted the secret of his success. The breadth and flexibility of mind that could negotiate with every motive of interest, passion, and pride in man is surprising; there is boundless sagacity; what is wanting is hope, a belief in the capabilities of human nature. There is no upward flight in the teacher's idea of man. Instead of which, the notion of the power of earth, and the impossibility of resisting it, depresses his whole aim, and the shadow of the tomb falls upon the work of the great false Prophet.

The idea of God is akin to the idea of man. "He knows us," says Mahomet. God's *knowledge*, the vast *experience*, so to speak, of the Divine Being, His infinite acquaintance with man's frailties and temptations, is appealed to as the ground of confidence. "He is the Wise, the Knowing One," "He is the Knowing, the Wise," "He is easy to be reconciled." Thus is raised a notion of the Supreme Being, which is rather an extension of the character of the large-minded and sagacious man of the world than an extension of man's virtue and holiness. He forgives because He knows too much to be rigid, because sin universal ceases to be sin, and must be given way to. Take a man who has had large opportunity of studying mankind, and has come into contact with every form of human weakness and corruption; such a man is indulgent as a simple consequence of his knowledge, because nothing surprises him. So the God of Mahomet forgives by reason of His vast knowledge.

In contrast with the fruit of this he observes that "the prophecy in the Epistle to the Romans has been fulfilled, and that doctrine has been historically at the bottom of a great change of moral practice in mankind." The key has been found to set man's moral nature in action, to check and reverse that course of universal failure manifest before; and this key is Christian doctrine. "A stimulus has been given to human nature which has extracted an amount of action from it which no Greek or Roman could have believed possible." It is inconceivable that but for such doctrine such results as have been seen in Christendon would have followed; and were it now taken away we cannot see anything else that would have the faintest expectation of taking its place. "Could we commit mankind to a moral Deism without trembling for the result?" Can the enthusiasm for the divinity of human nature stand the test of clear, unsparing observation? Would it not issue in such an estimate of human nature as Mahomet took? "A deification of humanity upon its own grounds, an exaltation which is all height and no depth, wants power because it wants truth. It is not founded upon the facts of human nature, and therefore issues in vain and vapid aspiration, and injures the solidity of man's character." As he says, "The Gospel doctrine of the Incarnation and its effects alone unites the sagacious view of human nature with the enthusiastic." And now what is the historical root and basis from which this one great moral revolution in the world's history, so successful, so fruitful, so inexhaustible, has started?

But if, as the source and inspiration of practice, doctrine has been the foundation of a new state of the world, and of that change which distinguishes the world under Christianity from the world before it, miracles, as the proof of that doctrine, stand before us in a very remarkable and peculiar light. Far from being mere idle feats of power to gratify the love of the marvellous; far even from being mere particular and occasional rescues from the operation of general laws,—they come before us as means for accomplishing the largest and most important practical object that has ever been accomplished in the history of mankind. They lie at the bottom of the difference of the modern from the ancient world; so far, *i.e.*, as that difference is moral. We see as a fact a change in the moral condition of mankind, which marks ancient and modern society as two different states of mankind. What has produced this change, and elicited this new power of action? Doctrine. And what was the proof of that doctrine, or essential to the proof of it? Miracles. The greatness of the result thus throws light upon the propriety of the means, and shows the fitting object which was presented for the introduction of such means—the fitting occasion which had arisen for the use of them; for, indeed, no more weighty, grand, or solemn occasion can be conceived than the foundation of such a new order of things in the world. Extraordinary action of Divine power for such an end has the benefit of a justifying object of incalculable weight; which though not of itself, indeed, proof of the fact, comes with striking force upon the mind in connection with the proper proof. It is reasonable, it is inevitable, that we should be impressed by such a result; for it shows that the miraculous system has been a practical one; that it has been a step in the ladder of man's ascent, the means of introducing those powerful truths which have set his moral nature in action.

Of this work, remarkable in so many ways, we will add but one thing more. It is marked throughout with the most serious and earnest conviction, but it is without a single word, from first to last, of asperity or insinuation against opponents; and this, not from any deficiency of feeling as to the importance of the issue, but from a deliberate and resolutely maintained self-control, and from an overruling ever-present sense of the duty, on themes like these, of a more than judicial calmness.

IX

ECCE HOMO[1]

This is a dangerous book to review. The critic of it, if he is prudent, will feel that it is more than most books a touchstone of his own capacity, and that in giving his judgment upon it he cannot help giving his own measure and betraying what he is himself worth. All the unconscious guiding which a name, even if hitherto unknown, gives to opinion is wanting. The first aspect of the book is perplexing; closer examination does not clear up all the questions which present themselves; and many people, after they have read it through, will not feel quite certain what it means. Much of what is on the surface and much of what is inherent in the nature of the work will jar painfully on many minds; while others who begin to read it under one set of impressions may by the time they have got to the end complain of having been taken in. There can be no doubt on which side the book is; but it may be open to debate from which side it

[1] *Ecce Homo: A Survey of the Life and Work of Jesus Christ.* *Guardian*, 7th February 1866.

has come. The unknown champion who comes into the lists with barred vizor and no cognisance on his shield leaves it not long uncertain for which of the contending parties he appears; but his weapons and his manner of fighting are not the ordinary ones of the side which he takes; and there is a force in his arm, and a sweep in his stroke, which is not that of common men. The book is one which it is easy to take exception to, and perhaps still easier to praise at random; but the subject is put before us in so unusual a way, and one so removed from the ordinary grooves of thought, that in trying to form an adequate estimate of the work as a whole, a man feels as he does when he is in the presence of something utterly unfamiliar and unique, when common rules and inferences fail him, and in pronouncing upon which he must make something of a venture.

In making our own venture we will begin with what seems to us incontestable. In the first place, but that it has been questioned, we should say that there could be no question of the surpassing ability which the book displays. It is far beyond the power of the average clever and practised writer of our days. It is the work of a man in whom thought, sympathy, and imagination are equally powerful and wealthy, and who exercises a perfect and easy command over his own conceptions, and over the apt and vivid language which is their expression. Few men have entered so deeply into the ideas and feelings of the time, or have looked at the world, its history and its conditions, with so large and piercing an insight. But it is idle to dwell on what must strike, at first sight, any one who but opens the book. We go on to observe, what is equally beyond dispute, the deep tone of religious seriousness which pervades the work. The writer's way of speaking is very different from that of the ascetic or the devotee; but no ascetic or devotee could be more profoundly penetrated with the great contrast between holiness and evil, and show more clearly in his whole manner of thinking the ineffaceable impression of the powers of the world to come. Whatever else the book may be, this much is plain on the face of it—it is the work of a mind of extreme originality, depth, refinement, and power; and it is also the work of a very religious man: Thomas à Kempis had not a more solemn sense of things unseen and of what is meant by the Imitation of Christ.

What the writer wishes his book to be understood to be we must gather from his Preface:—

Those who feel dissatisfied with the current conceptions of Christ, if they cannot rest content without a definite opinion, may find it necessary to do what to persons not so dissatisfied it seems audacious and perilous to do. They may be obliged to reconsider the whole subject from the beginning, and placing themselves in imagination at the time when he whom we call Christ bore no such name, but was simply, as St. Luke describes him, a young man of promise, popular with those who knew him, and appearing to enjoy the Divine favour, to trace his biography from point to point, and accept those conclusions about him, not which church doctors or even apostles have sealed with their authority, but which the facts themselves, critically weighed, appear to warrant.

This is what the present writer undertook to do for the satisfaction of his own mind, and because, after reading a good many books on Christ, he felt still constrained to confess that there was no historical character whose motives, objects, and feelings remained so incomprehensible to him. The inquiry which proved serviceable to himself may chance to be useful to others.

What is now published is a fragment. No theological questions whatever are here discussed. Christ. as the creator of modern theology and religion, will make the subject of another volume, which, however, the author does not hope to publish for some time to come. In the meanwhile he has endeavoured to furnish an answer to the question, What was Christ's object in founding the Society which is called by his name, and how is it adapted to attain that object?

Thus the book comes before us as a serious facing of difficulties. And that the writer lays stress on its being so viewed appears further from a letter which he wrote to the *Spectator*, repeating emphatically that the book is not one "written after the investigation was completed, but the *investigation* itself." The letter may be taken to complete the statement of the Preface :—

I endeavoured in my Preface to describe the state of mind in which I undertook my book. I said that the character and objects of Christ were at that time altogether incomprehensible to me, and that I wished to try whether an independent investigation would relieve my perplexity. Perhaps I did not distinctly enough state that *Ecce Homo* is not a book written after the investigation was completed, but the *investigation* itself.

The Life of Christ is partly easy to understand and partly difficult. This being so, what would a man do who wished to study it methodically? Naturally he would take the easy part first. He would collect, arrange, and carefully consider all the facts which are simple, and until he has done this, he would carefully avoid all those parts of his subject which are obscure, and which cannot be explained without making bold hypotheses. By this course he would limit the problem, and in the meanwhile arrive at a probable opinion concerning the veracity of the documents, and concerning the characteristics, both intellectual and moral, of the person whose high pretensions he wished to investigate.

This is what I have done. I have postponed altogether the hardest questions connected with Christ, as questions which cannot properly be discussed until a considerable quantity of evidence has been gathered about his character and views. If this evidence, when collected, had appeared to be altogether conflicting and inconsistent, I should have been saved the trouble of proceeding any further; I should have said that Christ is a myth. If it had been consistent, and had disclosed to me a person of mean and ambitious aims, I should have said, Christ is a deceiver. Again, if it had exhibited a person of weak understanding and strong impulsive sensibility, I should have said Christ is a bewildered enthusiast.

In all these cases you perceive my method would have saved me a good deal of trouble. As it is, I certainly feel bound to go on, though, as I say in my Preface, my progress will necessarily be slow. But I am much engaged and have little time for theological study. But pray do not suppose that postponing questions is only another name for evading them. I think I have gained much by this postponement. I have now a very definite notion of Christ's character and that of his followers. I shall be able to judge how far he was likely to deceive himself or them. It is possible I may have put others, who can command more time than I, in a condition to take up the subject where for the present I leave it.

You say my picture suffers by my method. But *Ecce Homo* is not a picture: it is the very opposite of a picture; it is an analysis. It may be, you will answer, that the title suggests a picture. This may perhaps be true, and if so, it is no doubt a fault, but a fault in the title, not in the book. For titles are put to books, not books to titles.

Thus it appears that the writer found it his duty to investigate those awful questions which every thinking man feels to be full of the "incomprehensible" and unfathomable, but which many thinking men, for various reasons both good and bad, shrink from attempting to investigate, accepting on practical and very sufficient grounds the religious conclusions which are recommended and sanctioned by the agreement of Christendom. And finding it his duty to investigate them at all, he saw that he was bound to investigate in earnest. But under what circumstances this happened, from what particular pressure of need, and after what previous belief or state of opinion, we are not told. Whether from being originally on the doubting side—on the irreligious side we cannot suppose he ever could have been—he has risen through his investigation into belief; or whether, originally on the believing side, he found the aspect so formidable, to himself or to the world, of the difficulties and perplexities which beset belief, that he turned to bay upon the foes that dogged him—must be left to conjecture. It is impossible to question that he has been deeply impressed with the difficulties of believing; it is impossible to question that doubt has been overborne and trampled under foot. But here we have the record, it would not be accurate to say of the struggle, but of that resolute and unflinching contemplation of the realities of the case which decided it. Such plunging into such a question must seem, as he says, to those who do not need it, "audacious and perilous"; for if you plunge into a question in earnest, and do not under a thin disguise take a side, you must, whatever your bias and expectation, take your chance of the alternative answers which may come out. It is a simple fact that there are many people who feel "dissatisfied with the current conceptions" of our Lord—whether reasonably and justly dissatisfied is another question; but whatever we think of it they remain dissatisfied. In such emergencies it is conceivable that a man who believes, yet keenly realises and feels what disturbs or destroys the belief of others, should dare to put himself in their place; should enter the hospital and suffer the disease which makes such ravages; should descend into the shades and face the spectres. No one can deny the risk of dwelling on such thoughts as he must dwell on; but if he feels warmly with his kind, he may think it even a duty to face the risk. To any one accustomed to live on his belief it cannot but be a hard necessity, full of pain and difficulty, first to think and then to speak of what he believes, as if it *might not* be, or *could be* otherwise; but the changes of time bring up ever new hard necessities; and one thing is plain, that if ever such an investigation is undertaken, it ought to be a real one, in good earnest and not in play. If a man investigates at all, both for his own sake and for the sake of the effect of his investigation on others, he must accept the fair conditions of investigation. We may not ourselves be able to conceive the possibility of taking, even provisionally, a neutral position; but looking at what is going on all round us, we ought to be able to enlarge our thoughts sufficiently to take in the idea that a believing mind may feel it a duty to surrender itself boldly to the intellectual chances and issues of the inquiry, and to "let its thoughts take their course in the confidence that they will come home at last." It may be we ourselves who "have not faith enough to be patient of doubt"; there may be others who feel that if what they believe is real, they need not be afraid of the severest revisal and testing of the convictions on which they rest; who feel that, in the circumstances of the time, it is not left to their choice whether these convictions shall be sifted unsparingly and to the uttermost; and who think it a venture not unworthy of a Christian, to descend even to the depths to go through the thoughts of doubters, if so be that he may find the spell that shall calm them. We do not say that this book is the production of such a state of mind; we only think that it may be. One thing is clear, wherever the writer's present lot is cast, he has that in him which not only enables him, but forces him, to sympathise with what he sees in the opposite camp. If he is what is called a Liberal, his whole heart is yet pouring itself forth towards the great truths of Christianity. If he is what is called orthodox, his whole intellect is alive to the right and duty of freedom of thought. He will therefore attract and repel on both sides. And he appears to feel that the position of double sympathy gives him a special advantage, to attract to each side what is true in its opposite, and to correct in each what is false or inadequate.

What, then, is this investigation, and what course does it follow? At the first aspect, we might take it for one of those numerous attempts on the Liberal side, partly impatient, partly careless of Christianity, to put a fresh look on the Christian history, and to see it with new eyes. The writer's language is at starting neutral; he speaks of our Lord in the language indeed of the New Testament, but not in the usual language of later Christian writers. All through, the colour and tone is absolutely modern; and what would naturally be expressed in familiar theological terms is for the most part studiously put in other words. Persons acquainted with the writings of the late Mr. Robertson might be often reminded of his favourite modes of teaching; of his maxim that truth is made up of two opposites which seem contradictories; of the distinction which he was so fond of insisting upon between principles and rules; above all, of his doctrine that the true way to rise to the faith in our Lord's Divine Nature was by first realising His Human Life. But the resemblance is partial, if not superficial, and gives way on closer examination before broad and characteristic features of an entirely different significance. That one which at first arrests attention, and distinguishes this writer's line of thought from the common Liberal way of dealing with the subject, is that from the first page of the book to its last line the work of Christ is viewed, not simply as the foundation of a religious system, the introduction of certain great principles, the elevation of religious ideas, the delivery of Divine truths, the exhibition of a life and example, but as the call and creation of a definite, concrete, organised society of men. The subject of investigation is not merely the character and history of the Person, but the Person as connected with His work. Christ is regarded not simply in Himself or in His teaching, as the Founder of a philosophy, a morality, a theology in the abstract, but as the Author of a Divine Society, the Body which is called by His Name, the Christian Church Universal, a real and visible company of men, which, however we may understand it, exists at this moment as it has existed since His time, marked by His badges, governed by His laws, and working out His purpose. The writer finds the two joined in fact, and he finds them also joined in the recorded history of Christ's plan. The book might almost be described as the beginning of a new *De Civitate Dei*, written with the further experience of fourteen centuries and from the point of view of our own generation. This is one remarkable peculiarity of this investigation; another is the prominence given to the severe side of the Person and character of whom he writes, and what is even more observable, the way in which both the severity and the gentleness are apprehended and harmonised.

We are familiar with the attempts to resolve the Christianity of the New Testament into philanthropy; and, on the other hand, writers like Mr. Carlyle will not let us forget that the world is as dark and evil as the Bible draws it. This writer feels both in one. No one can show more sympathy with enlarged and varied ideas of human happiness, no one has connected them more fearlessly with Christian principles, or claimed from those principles more unlimited developments, even for the physical well-being of men. No one has extended wider the limits of Christian generosity, forbearance, and tolerance.

But, on the other hand, what is striking is, that all this is compatible, and is made to appear so, with the most profound and terrible sense of evil, with indignation and scorn which is scathing where it kindles and strikes, with a capacity and energy of deliberate religious hatred against what is impure and false and ungodly, which mark one who has dared to realise and to sympathise with the wrath of Jesus Christ.

The world has been called in these later days, and from opposite directions, to revise its judgments about Jesus Christ. Christians, on the one hand, have been called to do it by writers of whom M. Ernest Renan is the most remarkable and the most unflinching. But the sceptical and the unbelieving have likewise been obliged to change their ground and their tone, and no one with any self-respect or care for his credit even as a thinker and a man would like to repeat the superficial and shallow flippancy and irreligion of the last century. Two things have been specially insisted on. We have been told that if we are to see the truth of things as it is, we must disengage our minds from the deeply rooted associations and conceptions of a later theology, and try to form our impressions first-hand and unprompted from the earliest documents which we can reach. It has been further urged on us, in a more believing spirit, that we should follow the order by which in fact truth was unfolded, and rise from the full appreciation of our Lord's human nature to the acknowledgment of His Divine nature. It seems to us that the writer of this book has felt the force of both these appeals, and that his book is his answer to them. Here is the way in which he responds to both—to the latter indirectly, but with a significance which no one can mistake; to the former directly and avowedly. He undertakes, isolating himself from current beliefs, and restricting himself to the documents from which, if from any source at all, the original facts about Christ are to be learned, to examine what the genuine impression is which an attempt to realise the statements about him leaves on the mind. This has been done by others, with results supposed to be unfavourable to Christianity. He has been plainly moved by these results, though not a hint is given of the existence of Renan or Strauss. But the effect on his own mind has been to drive him back on a closer survey of the history in its first fountains, and to bring him from it filled more than ever with wonder at its astonishing phenomena, to protest against the poverty and shallowness of the most ambitious and confident of these attempts. They leave the historical Character which they pourtray still unsounded, its motives, objects, and feelings absolutely incomprehensible. He accepts the method to reverse the product. "Look at Christ historically," people say; "see Him as He really was." The answer here is, "Well, I will look at Him with whatever aid a trained historical imagination can look at Him. I accept your challenge; I admit your difficulties. I will dare to do what you do. I will try and look at the very facts themselves, with singleness and 'innocence of the eye,' trying to see nothing more than I really see, and trying to see all that my eye falls on. I will try to realise indeed what is recorded of Him. And *this* is what I see. This is the irresistible impression from the plainest and most elementary part of the history, if we are to accept any history at all. A miracle could not be more unlike the order of our experience than the Character set before us is unique and unapproachable in all known history. Further, all that makes the superiority of the modern world to the ancient, and is most permanent and pregnant with improvement in it, may be traced to the appearance of that Character, and to the work which He planned and did. You ask for a true picture of Him, drawn with freedom, drawn with courage; here, if you dare look at it, is what those who wrote of Him showed Him to be. Renan has tried to draw this picture. Take the Gospels as they stand; treat them simply as biographies; look, and see, and think of what they tell, and then ask yourself about Renan's picture, and what it looks like when placed side by side with the truth."

This, as we have ventured to express it in our own words, seems to be the writer's position. It is at any rate the effect of his book, to our minds. The inquiry, it must always be remembered, is a preliminary one, dealing, as he says, with the easiest and obvious elements of the problem; and much that seems inadequate and unsatisfactory may be developed hereafter. He starts from what, to those who already have the full belief, must appear a low level. He takes, as it will be seen, the documents as they stand. He takes little more than the first three Gospels, and these as a whole, without asking minute questions about them. The mythical theory he dismisses as false to nature, in dealing with such a Character and such results. He talks in his preface of "critically weighing" the facts; but the expression is misleading. It is true that we may talk of criticism of character; but the words naturally suggest that close cross-questioning of documents and details which has produced such remarkable results in modern investigations; and of this there is none. It is a work in no sense of criticism; it is a work of what he calls the "trained historical imagination"; a work of broad and deep knowledge of human nature and the world it works in and creates about it; a work of steady and large insight into character, and practical judgment on moral likelihoods. He answers Strauss as he answers Renan, by producing the interpretation of a character, so living, so in accordance with all before and after, that it overpowers and sweeps away objections; a picture, an analysis or outline, if he pleases, which justifies itself and is its own evidence, by its originality and internal consistency. Criticism in detail does not affect him. He assumes nothing of the Gospels, except that they are records; neither their inspiration in any theological sense, nor their authorship, nor their immunity from mistake, nor the absolute purity of their texts. But taking them as a whole he discerns in them a Character which, if you accept them at all and on any terms, you cannot mistake. Even if the copy is ever so imperfect, ever so unskilful, ever so blurred and defaced, there is no missing the features any more than a man need miss the principle of a pattern because it is rudely or confusedly traced. He looks at these "biographies" as a geologist might do at a disturbed series of strata; and he feeds his eye upon them till he gets such a view of the coherent whole as will stand independent of the right or wrong disposition of the particular fragments. To the mind which discerns the whole, the regulating principle, the general curves and proportions of the strata may be just as visible after the disturbance as before it. The Gospels bring before us the visible and distinct outlines of a life which, after all efforts to alter the idea of it, remains still the same; they present certain clusters of leading ideas and facts so embedded in their substance that no criticism of detail can possibly get rid of them, without absolutely obliterating the whole record. It is this leading idea, or cluster of ideas, to be gained by intent gazing, which the writer disengages from all questions of criticism in the narrow sense of the word, and sets before us as explaining the history of Christianity, and as proving themselves by that explanation. That the world has been moved we know. "Give me," he seems to say, "the Character which is set forth in the Gospels, and I can show how He moved it":—

It is in the object of the present treatise to exhibit

Christ's career in outline. No other career ever had so much unity; no other biography is so simple or can so well afford to dispense with details. Men in general take up scheme after scheme, as circumstances suggest one or another, and therefore most biographies are compelled to pass from one subject to another, and to enter into a multitude of minute questions, to divide the life carefully into periods by chronological landmarks accurately determined, to trace the gradual development of character and ripening or change of opinions. But Christ formed one plan and executed it; no important change took place in his mode of thinking, speaking, or acting; at least the evidence before us does not enable us to trace any such change. It is possible, indeed, for students of his life to find details which they may occupy themselves with discussing; they may map out the chronology of it, and devise methods of harmonising the different accounts; but such details are of little importance compared with the one grand question, what was Christ's plan, and throw scarcely any light upon that question. What was Christ's plan is the main question which will be investigated in the present treatise, and that vision of universal monarchy which we have just been considering affords an appropriate introduction to it. . . .

We conclude then, that Christ in describing himself as a king, and at the same time as king of the Kingdom of God—in other words as a king representing the Majesty of the Invisible King of a theocracy—claimed the character first of Founder, next of Legislator; thirdly, in a certain high and peculiar sense, of Judge, of a new divine society.

In defining as above the position which Christ assumed, we have not entered into controvertible matter. We have not rested upon single passages, nor drawn upon the fourth Gospel. To deny that Christ did undertake to found and to legislate for a new theocratic society, and that he did claim the office of Judge of mankind, is indeed possible, but only to those who altogether deny the credibility of the extant biographies of Christ. If those biographies be admitted to be generally trustworthy, then Christ undertook to be what we have described; if not, then of course this, but also every other account of him falls to the ground.

We have said that he starts from a low level; and he restricts himself so entirely at the opening to facts which do not involve dispute, that his views of them are necessarily incomplete, and, so to say, provisional and deliberate understatements. He begins no higher than the beginning of the public ministry, the Baptism, and the Temptation; and his account of these leaves much to say, though it suggests much of what is left unsaid. But he soon gets to the proper subject of his book—the absolute uniqueness of Him whose equally unique work has been the Christian Church. And this uniqueness he finds in the combination of "unbounded personal pretensions," and the possession, claimed and believed, of boundless power, with an absolutely unearthly use of His pretensions and His power, and with a goodness which has proved to be, and still is, the permanent and ever-flowing source of moral elevation and improvement in the world. He early comes across the question of miracles, and, as he says, it is impossible to separate the claim to them and the belief in them from the story. We find Christ, he says, "describing himself as a king, and at the same time as king of the Kingdom of God"; calling forth and founding a new and divine society, and claiming to be, both now and hereafter, the Judge without appeal of all mankind; "he considered, in short, heaven and hell to be in his hands." And we find, on the other hand, that as such He has been received. To such an astonishing chain of phenomena miracles naturally belong:—

When we contemplate this scheme as a whole, and glance at the execution and results of it, three things strike us with astonishment. First, its prodigious originality, if the expression may be used. What other man has had the courage or elevation of mind to say, "I will build up a state by the mere force of my will, without help from the kings of the world, without taking advantage of any of the secondary causes which unite men together —unity of interest or speech, or blood-relationship. I will make laws for my state which shall never be repealed, and I will defy all the powers of destruction that are at work in the world to destroy what I build"?

Secondly, we are astonished at the calm confidence with which the scheme was carried out. The reason why statesmen can seldom work on this vast scale is that it commonly requires a whole lifetime to gain that ascendency over their fellow-men which such schemes presuppose. Some of the leading organisers of the world have said, "I will work my way to supreme power, and then I will execute great plans." But Christ overleaped the first stage altogether. He did not work his way to royalty, but simply said to all men, "I am your king." He did not struggle forward to a position in which he could found a new state, but simply founded it.

Thirdly, we are astonished at the prodigious success of the scheme. It is not more certain that Christ presented himself to men as the founder, legislator, and judge of a divine society than it is certain that men have accepted him in these characters, that the divine society has been founded, that it has lasted nearly two thousand years, that it has extended over a large and the most highly-civilised portion of the earth's surface, and that it continues full of vigour at the present day.

Between the astonishing design and its astonishing success there intervenes an astonishing instrumentality— that of miracles. It will be thought by some that in asserting miracles to have been actually wrought by Christ we go beyond what the evidence, perhaps beyond what any possible evidence, is able to sustain. Waiving, then, for the present, the question whether miracles were actually wrought, we may state a fact which is fully capable of being established by ordinary evidence, and which is actually established by evidence as ample as any historical fact whatever — the fact, namely, that Christ *professed* to work miracles. We may go further, and assert with confidence that Christ was believed by his followers really to work miracles, and that it was mainly on this account that they conceded to him the pre-eminent dignity and authority which he claimed. The accounts which we have of these miracles may be exaggerated; it is possible that in some special cases stories have been related which have no foundation whatever; but on the whole, miracles play so important a part in Christ's scheme, that any theory which would represent them as due entirely to the imagination of his followers or of a later age destroys the credibility of the documents not partially but wholly, and leaves Christ a personage as mythical as Hercules. Now, the present treatise aims to show that the Christ of the Gospels is not mythical, by showing that the character those biographies portray is in all its large features strikingly consistent, and at the same time so peculiar as to be altogether beyond the reach of invention both by individual genius and still more by what is called the "consciousness of an age." Now, if the character depicted in the Gospels is in the main real and historical, they must be generally trustworthy, and if so, the responsibility of miracles is fixed on Christ. In this case the reality of the miracles themselves depends in a great degree on the opinion we form of Christ's veracity, and this opinion must arise gradually from the careful examination of his whole life. For our present purpose, which is to investigate the plan which Christ formed and the way in which he executed it, it matters nothing whether the miracles were real or imaginary; in either case, being believed to be real, they had the same effect. Provisionally, therefore, we may speak of them as real.

Without the belief in miracles, as he says, it is impossible to conceive the history of the Church :—

If we suppose that Christ really performed no miracles, and that those which are attributed to him were the product of self-deception mixed in some proportion or other with imposture, then no doubt the faith of St. Paul and St. John was an empty chimera, a mere misconception; but it is none the less true that those apparent miracles were essential to Christ's success, and that had he not pretended to perform them the Christian Church would never have been founded, and the name of Jesus of Nazareth would be known at this day only to the curious in Jewish antiquities.

But he goes on to point out what was the use which Christ made of miracles, and how it was that they did not, as they might have done, even impede His purpose of founding His kingdom on men's consciences and not on their terrors. In one of the most remarkable passages perhaps ever written on the Gospel miracles as they are seen when simply looked at as they are described, the writer says :—

He imposed upon himself a strict restraint in the use of his supernatural powers. He adopted the principle that he was not sent to destroy men's lives but to save them, and rigidly abstained in practice from inflicting any kind of damage or harm. In this course he persevered so steadily that it became generally understood. Every one knew that this *king*, whose royal pretensions were so prominent, had an absolutely unlimited patience, and that he would endure the keenest criticism, the bitterest and most malignant personal attacks. Men's mouths were open to discuss his claims and character with perfect freedom; so far from regarding him with that excessive fear which might have prevented them from receiving his doctrine intelligently, they learnt gradually to treat him, even while they acknowledged his extraordinary power, with a reckless animosity which they would have been afraid to show towards an ordinary enemy. With curious inconsistency they openly charged him with being leagued with the devil; in other words, they acknowledged that he was capable of boundless mischief, and yet they were so little afraid of him that they were ready to provoke him to use his whole power against themselves. The truth was that they believed him to be disarmed by his own deliberate resolution, and they judged rightly. He punished their malice only by verbal reproofs, and they gradually gathered courage to attack the life of one whose miraculous powers they did not question.

Meantime, while this magnanimous self-restraint saved him from false friends and mercenary or servile flatterers, and saved the kingdom which he founded from the corruption of self-interest and worldliness, it gave him a power over the good such as nothing else could have given. For the noblest and most amiable thing that can be seen is power mixed with gentleness, the reposing, self-restraining attitude of strength. These are the "fine strains of honour," these are "the graces of the gods"—

> To tear with thunder the wide cheeks o' the air,
> And yet to charge the sulphur with a bolt
> That shall but rive an oak.

And while he did no mischief under any provocation, his power flowed in acts of beneficence on every side. Men could approach near to him, could eat and drink with him, could listen to his talk and ask him questions, and they found him not accessible only, but warm-hearted, and not occupied so much with his own plans that he could not attend to a case of distress or mental perplexity. They found him full of sympathy and appreciation, dropping words of praise, ejaculations of admiration, tears. He surrounded himself with those who had tasted of his bounty, sick people whom he had cured, lepers whose death-in-life, demoniacs whose hell-in-life, he had terminated with a single powerful word. Among these came loving hearts who thanked him for friends and relatives rescued for them out of the jaws of premature death, and others whom he had saved, by a power which did not seem different, from vice and degradation.

This temperance in the use of supernatural power is the masterpiece of Christ. It is a moral miracle super-induced upon a physical one. This repose in greatness makes him surely the most sublime image ever offered to the human imagination. And it is precisely this trait which gave him his immense and immediate ascendency over men. If the question be put—Why was Christ so successful?—Why did men gather round him at his call, form themselves into a new society according to his wish, and accept him with unbounded devotion as their legislator and judge? some will answer, Because of the miracles which attested his divine character; others, Because of the intrinsic beauty and divinity of the great law of love which he propounded. But miracles, as we have seen, have not by themselves this persuasive power. That a man possesses a strange power which I cannot understand is no reason why I should receive his words as divine oracles of truth. The powerful man is not of necessity also wise; his power may terrify and yet not convince. On the other hand, the law of love, however divine, was but a precept. Undoubtedly it deserved that men should accept it for its intrinsic worth, but men are not commonly so eager to receive the words of wise men nor so unbounded in their gratitude to them. It was neither for his miracles nor for the beauty of his doctrine that Christ was worshipped. Nor was it for his winning personal character, nor for the persecutions he endured, nor for his martyrdom. It was for the inimitable unity which all these things made when taken together. In other words, it was for this that he whose power and greatness as shown in his miracles were overwhelming denied himself the use of his power, treated it as a slight thing, walked among men as though he were one of them, relieved them in distress, taught them to love each other, bore with undisturbed patience a perpetual hailstorm of calumny; and when his enemies grew fiercer, continued still to endure their attacks in silence, until, petrified and bewildered with astonishment, men saw him arrested and put to death with torture, refusing steadfastly to use in his own behalf the power he conceived he held for the benefit of others. It was the combination of greatness and self-sacrifice which won their hearts, the mighty powers held under a mighty control, the unspeakable condescension, the *Cross* of *Christ.*

And he goes on to describe the effect upon the world; and what it was that "drew all men unto Him":—

To sum up the results of this chapter. We began

by remarking that an astonishing plan met with an astonishing success, and we raised the question to what instrumentality that success was due. Christ announced himself as the Founder and Legislator of a new Society, and as the Supreme Judge of men. Now by what means did he procure that these immense pretensions should be allowed? He might have done it by sheer power, he might have adopted persuasion, and pointed out the merits of the scheme and of the legislation he proposed to introduce. But he adopted a third plan, which had the effect not merely of securing obedience, but of exciting enthusiasm and devotion. He laid men under an immense *obligation.* He convinced them that he was a person of altogether transcendent greatness, one who needed nothing at their hands, one whom it was impossible to benefit by conferring riches, or fame, or dominion upon him, and that, being so great, he had devoted himself of mere benevolence to their good. He showed them that for their sakes he lived a hard and laborious life, and exposed himself to the utmost malice of powerful men. They saw him hungry, though they believed him able to turn the stones into bread; they saw his royal pretensions spurned, though they believed that he could in a moment take into his hand all the kingdoms of the world and the glory of them; they saw his life in danger; they saw him at last expire in agonies, though they believed that, had he so willed it, no danger could harm him, and that had he thrown himself from the topmost pinnacle of the temple he would have been softly received in the arms of ministering angels. Witnessing his sufferings, and convinced by the miracles they saw him work that they were voluntarily endured, men's hearts were touched, and pity for weakness blending strangely with wondering admiration of unlimited power, an agitation of gratitude, sympathy, and astonishment, such as nothing else could ever excite, sprang up in them; and when, turning from his deeds to his words, they found this very self-denial which had guided his own life prescribed as the principle which should guide theirs, gratitude broke forth in joyful obedience, self-denial produced self-denial, and the Law and Lawgiver together were enshrined in their inmost hearts for inseparable veneration.

It is plain that whatever there is novel in such a line of argument must depend upon the way in which it is handled; and it is the extraordinary and sustained power with which this is done which gives its character to the book. The writer's method consists in realising with a depth of feeling and thought which it would not be easy to match, what our Lord was in His human ministry, as that ministry is set before us by those who witnessed it; and next, in showing in detail the connection of that ministry, which wrought so much by teaching, but still more by the Divine example, "not sparing words but resting most on deeds," with all that is highest, purest, and best in the morality of Christendom, and with what is most fruitful and most hopeful in the differences between the old world and our own. We cannot think we are wrong when we say that no one could speak of our Lord as this writer speaks, with the enthusiasm, the overwhelming sense of His inexpressible authority, of

His unapproachable perfection, with the profound faith which lays everything at His feet, and not also believe all that the Divine Society which Christ founded has believed about Him. And though for the present his subject is history, and human morality as it appears to have been revolutionised and finally fixed by that history, and not the theology which subsequent in date is yet the foundation of both, it is difficult to imagine any reader going along with him and not breaking out at length into the burst, " My Lord and my God." If it is not so, then the phenomenon is strange indeed; for a belief below the highest and truest has produced an appreciation, a reverence, an adoration which the highest belief has only produced in the choicest examples of those who have had it, and by the side of which the ordinary exhibitions of the divine history are pale and feeble. To few, indeed, as it seems to us, has it been given to feel, and to make others feel, what in all the marvellous complexity of high and low, and in all the Divine singleness of His goodness and power, the Son of Man appeared in the days of His flesh. It is not more vivid or more wonderful than what the Gospels with so much detail tell us of that awful ministry in real flesh and blood, with a human soul and with all the reality of man's nature; but most of us, after all, read the Gospels with sealed and unwondering eyes. But, dwelling on the Manhood, so as almost to overpower us with the contrast between the distinct and living truth and the dead and dull familiarity of our thoughts of routine and custom, he does so in such a way that it is impossible to doubt, though the word Incarnation never occurs in the volume, that all the while he has before his thoughts the "taking of the manhood into God." What is the Gospel picture?

And let us pause once more to consider that which remains throughout a subject of ever-recurring astonishment, the unbounded personal pretensions which Christ advances. It is common in human history to meet with those who claim some superiority over their fellows. Men assert a pre-eminence over their fellow-citizens or fellow-countrymen and become rulers of those who at first were their equals, but they dream of nothing greater than some partial control over the actions of others for the short space of a lifetime. Few indeed are those to whom it is given to influence future ages. Yet some men have appeared who have been "as levers to uplift the earth and roll it in another course." Homer by creating literature, Socrates by creating science, Caesar by carrying civilisation inland from the shores of the Mediterranean, Newton by starting science upon a career of steady progress, may be said to have attained this eminence. But these men gave a single impact like that which is conceived to have first set the planets in motion; Christ claims to be a perpetual attractive power like the sun which determines their orbit. They contributed to men some discovery and passed away; Christ's discovery is himself. To humanity struggling with its passions and its destiny he says, Cling to me, cling ever closer to me. If we believe St. John, he represented himself as the Light of the world, as the Shepherd of the souls of men, as the Way to immortality, as the Vine or Life-tree of humanity. And if we refuse to believe that he used those words, we cannot deny, without rejecting all the evidence before us, that he used words which have substantially the same meaning. We cannot deny that he commanded men to leave everything and attach themselves to him; that he declared himself king, master, and judge of men; that he promised to give rest to all the weary and heavy-laden; that he instructed his followers to hope for life from feeding on his body and blood.

But it is doubly surprising to observe that these enormous pretensions were advanced by one whose special peculiarity, not only among his contemporaries but among the remarkable men that have appeared before and since, was an almost feminine tenderness and humility. This characteristic was remarked, as we have seen, by the Baptist, and Christ himself was fully conscious of it. Yet so clear to him was his own dignity and infinite importance to the human race as an objective fact with which his own opinion of himself had nothing to do, that in the same breath in which he asserts it in the most unmeasured language, he alludes, apparently with entire unconsciousness, to his *humility*. "Take my yoke upon you, and learn of me; *for I am meek and lowly of heart.*" And again, when speaking to his followers of the arrogance of the Pharisees, he says, "They love to be called Rabbi; but be not you called Rabbi: *for one is your master, even Christ.*"

Who is the humble man? It is he who resists with special watchfulness and success the temptations which the conditions of his life may offer to exaggerate his own importance. . . . If he judged himself correctly, and if the Baptist described him well when he compared him to a lamb, and, we may add, if his biographers have delineated his character faithfully, Christ was one naturally contented with obscurity, wanting the restless desire for distinction and eminence which is common in great men, hating to put forward personal claims, disliking competition and "disputes who should be greatest," finding something bombastic in the titles of royalty, fond of what is simple and homely, of children, of poor people, occupying himself so much with the concerns of others, with the relief of sickness and want, that the temptation to exaggerate the importance of his own thoughts and plans was not likely to master him; lastly, entertaining for the human race a feeling so singularly fraternal that he was likely to reject as a sort of treason the impulse to set himself in any manner above them. Christ, it appears, was this humble man. When we have fully pondered the fact we may be in a condition to estimate the force of the evidence which, submitted to his mind, could induce him, in direct opposition to all his tastes and instincts, to lay claim, persistently, with the calmness of entire conviction, in opposition to the whole religious world, in spite of the offence which his own followers conceived, to a dominion more transcendent, more universal, more complete, than the most delirious votary of glory ever aspired to in his dreams.

And what is it that our Lord has done for man by being so truly man?

This then it is which is wanted to raise the feeling of humanity into an enthusiasm; when the precept of love has been given, an image must be set before the eyes of those who are called upon to obey it, an ideal or type of man which may be noble and amiable enough to raise the whole race and make the meanest member of it sacred with reflected glory.

Did not Christ do this? Did the command to love go forth to those who had never seen a human being they could revere? Could his followers turn upon him and say, How can we love a creature so degraded, full of vile wants and contemptible passions, whose little life is most harmlessly spent when it is an empty round of eating and sleeping; a creature destined for the grave and for oblivion when his allotted term of fretfulness and folly has expired? Of this race Christ himself was a member, and to this day is it not the best answer to all blasphemers of the species, the best consolation when our sense of its degradation is keenest, that a human brain was behind his forehead, and a human heart beating in his breast, and that within the whole creation of God nothing more elevated or more attractive has yet been found than he? And if it be answered that there was in his nature something exceptional and peculiar, that humanity must not be measured by the stature of Christ, let us remember that it was precisely thus that he wished it to be measured, delighting to call himself the Son of Man, delighting to call the meanest of mankind his brothers. If some human beings are abject and contemptible, if it be incredible to us that they can have any high dignity or destiny, do we regard them from so great a height as Christ? Are we likely to be more pained by their faults and deficiencies than he was? Is our standard higher than his? And yet he associated by preference with the meanest of the race; no contempt for them did he ever express, no suspicion that they might be less dear than the best and wisest to the common Father, no doubt that they were naturally capable of rising to a moral elevation like his own. There is nothing of which a man may be prouder than of this; it is the most hopeful and redeeming fact in history; it is precisely what was wanting to raise the love of man as man to enthusiasm. An eternal glory has been shed upon the human race by the love Christ bore to it. And it was because the Edict of Universal Love went forth to men whose hearts were in no cynical mood, but possessed with a spirit of devotion to a man, that words which at any other time, however grandly they might sound, would have been but words, penetrated so deeply, and along with the law of love the power of love was given. Therefore also the first Christians were enabled to dispense with philosophical phrases, and instead of saying that they loved the ideal of man in man, could simply say and feel that they loved Christ in every man.

We have here the very kernel of the Christian moral scheme. We have distinctly before us the end Christ proposed to himself, and the means he considered adequate to the attainment of it. . . .

But how to give to the meagre and narrow hearts of men such enlargement? How to make them capable of a universal sympathy? Christ believed it possible to bind men to their kind, but on one condition—that they were first bound fast to himself. He stood forth as the representative of men, he identified himself with the cause and with the interests of all human beings; he was destined, as he began before long obscurely to intimate, to lay down his life for them. Few of us sympathise originally and directly with this devotion; few of us can perceive in human nature itself any merit sufficient to evoke it. But it is not so hard to love and venerate him who felt it. So vast a passion of love, a devotion so comprehensive, elevated, deliberate, and profound, has not elsewhere been in any degree approached save by some of his imitators. And as love provokes love, many have found it possible to conceive for Christ an attachment the closeness of which no words can describe, a veneration so possessing and absorbing the man within them, that they have said, "I live no more, but Christ lives in me."

And what, in fact, has been the result, after the utmost and freest abatement for the objections of those who criticise the philosophical theories or the practical effects of Christianity?

But that Christ's method, when rightly applied, is really of mighty force may be shown by an argument which the severest censor of Christians will hardly refuse to admit. Compare the ancient with the modern world: "Look on this picture and on that." The broad distinction in the characters of men forces itself into prominence. Among all the men of the ancient heathen world there were scarcely one or two to whom we might venture to apply the epithet "holy." In other words, there were not more than one or two, if any, who, besides being virtuous in their actions, were possessed with an unaffected enthusiasm of goodness, and besides abstaining from vice, regarded even a vicious thought with horror. Probably no one will deny that in Christian countries this higher-toned goodness, which we call holiness, has existed. Few will maintain that it has been exceedingly rare. Perhaps the truth is that there has scarcely been a town in any Christian country since the time of Christ, where a century has passed without exhibiting a character of such elevation that his mere presence has shamed the bad and made the good better, and has been felt at times like the presence of God Himself. And if this be so, has Christ failed? or can Christianity die?

The principle of feeling and action which Christ implanted in that Divine Society which He founded, or in other words, His morality, had two peculiarities; it sprang, and it must spring still, from what this writer calls all through an "enthusiasm"; and this enthusiasm was kindled and maintained by the influence of a Person. There can be no goodness without impulses to goodness, any more than these impulses are enough without being directed by truth and reason; but the impulses must come before the guidance, and "Christ's Theocracy" is described "as a great attempt to set all the virtues of the world on this basis, and to give it a visible centre and fountain." He thus describes how personal influence is the great instrument of moral quickening and elevation :—

How do men become for the most part " pure, generous, and humane"? By personal, not by logical influences. They have been reared by parents who had these qualities, they have lived in a society which had a high tone, they have been accustomed to see just acts done, to hear gentle words spoken, and the justness and the gentleness have passed into their hearts, and slowly moulded their habits and made their moral discernment clear; they remember commands and prohibitions which it is a pleasure to obey for the sake of those who gave them; often they think of those who may be dead and say, "How would this action appear to him? Would he approve that word or disapprove it?" To such no baseness appears a small baseness because its consequences may be small, nor does the yoke of law seem burdensome although it is ever on their necks, nor do they dream of covering a sin by an atoning act of virtue. Often in solitude they blush when some impure fancy sails across the clear heaven of their minds, because they are never alone, because the absent Examples, the Authorities they still revere, rule not their actions only but their inmost hearts; because their conscience is indeed awake and alive, representing all the nobleness with which they stand in sympathy, and reporting their most hidden indecorum before a public opinion of the absent and the dead.

Of these two influences—that of Reason and that of Living Example—which would a wise reformer reinforce? Christ chose the last. He gathered all men into a common relation to himself, and demanded that each should set him on the pedestal of his heart, giving a lower place to all other objects of worship, to father and mother, to husband or wife. In him should the loyalty of all hearts centre; he should be their pattern, their Authority and Judge. Of him and his service should no man be ashamed, but to those who acknowledged it morality should be an easy yoke, and the law of right as spontaneous as the law of life; sufferings should be easy to bear, and the loss of worldly friends repaired by a new home in the bosom of the Christian kingdom; finally, in death itself their sleep should be sweet upon whose tombstone it could be written "Obdormivit in Christo."

In his treatment of this part of the subject, the work of Christ as the true Creator, through the Christian Church, of living morality, what is peculiar and impressive is the way in which sympathy with Christianity in its antique and original form, in its most austere, unearthly, exacting aspects, is combined with sympathy with the practical realities of modern life, with its boldness, its freedom, its love of improvement, its love of truth. It is no common grasp which can embrace both so easily and so firmly. He is one of those writers whose strong hold on their ideas is shown by the facility with which they can afford to make large admissions, which are at first sight startling. Nowhere are more tremendous passages written than in this book about the corruptions of that Christianity which yet the writer holds to be the one hope and safeguard of mankind. He is not afraid to pursue his investigation independently of any inquiry into the peculiar claims to authority of the documents on which it rests. He at once goes to their substance and their facts, and the Person and Life and Character which they witness to. He is not afraid to put Faith on exactly the same footing as

Life, neither higher nor lower, as the title to membership in the Church; a doctrine which, if it makes imperfect and rudimentary faith as little a disqualification as imperfect and inconsistent life, obviously does not exclude the further belief that deliberate heresy is on the same level with deliberate profligacy. But the clear sense of what is substantial, the power of piercing through accidents and conditions to the real kernel of the matter, the scornful disregard of all entanglement of apparent contradictions and inconsistencies, enable him to bring out the lesson which he finds before him with overpowering force. He sees before him immense mercy, immense condescension, immense indulgence; but there are also immense requirements—requirements not to be fulfilled by rule or exhausted by the lapse of time, and which the higher they raise men the more they exact—an immense seriousness and strictness, an immense care for substance and truth, to the disregard, if necessary, of the letter and the form. The "Dispensation of the Spirit" has seldom had an interpreter more in earnest and more determined to see meaning in his words. We have room but for two illustrations. He is combating the notion that the work of Christianity and the Church nowadays is with the good, and that it is waste of hope and strength to try to reclaim the bad and the lost:—

Once more, however, the world may answer, Christ may be consistent in this, but is he wise? It may be true that he does demand an enthusiasm, and that such an enthusiasm may be capable of awakening the moral sense in hearts in which it seemed dead. But if, notwithstanding this demand, only a very few members of the Christian Church are capable of the enthusiasm, what use in imposing on the whole body a task which the vast majority are not qualified to perform? Would it not be well to recognise the fact which we cannot alter, and to abstain from demanding from frail human nature what human nature cannot render? Would it not be well for the Church to impose upon its ordinary members only ordinary duties? When the Bernard or the Whitefield appears let her by all means find occupation for him. Let her in such cases boldly invade the enemy's country. But in ordinary times would it not be well for her to confine herself to more modest and practicable undertakings? There is much for her to do even though she should honestly confess herself unable to reclaim the lost. She may reclaim the young, administer reproof to slight lapses, maintain a high standard of virtue, soften manners, diffuse enlightenment. Would it not be well for her to adapt her ends to her means?

No, it would not be well; it would be fatal to do so; and Christ meant what he said, and said what was true, when he pronounced the Enthusiasm of Humanity to be everything, and the absence of it to be the absence of everything. The world understands its own routine well enough; what it does not understand is the mode of changing that routine. It has no appreciation of the nature or measure of the power of enthusiasm, and on this matter it learns nothing from experience, but after every fresh proof of that power, relapses from its brief astonishment into its old ignorance, and commits precisely the same miscalculation on the next occasion. The power of enthusiasm is, indeed, far from being unlimited; in some cases it is very small. . . .

But one power enthusiasm has almost without limit— the power of propagating itself; and it was for this that Christ depended on it. He contemplated a Church in which the Enthusiasm of Humanity should not be felt by two or three only, but widely. In whatever heart it might be kindled, he calculated that it would pass rapidly into other hearts, and that as it can make its heat felt outside the Church, so it would preserve the Church itself from lukewarmness. For a lukewarm Church he would not condescend to legislate, nor did he regard it as at all inevitable that the Church should become lukewarm. He laid it as a duty upon the Church to reclaim the lost, because he did not think it utopian to suppose that the Church might be not in its best members only, but through its whole body, inspired by that ardour of humanity that can charm away the bad passions of the wildest heart, and open to the savage and the outlaw lurking in moral wildernesses an entrancing view of the holy and tranquil order that broods over the streets and palaces of the city of God. . . .

Christianity is an enthusiasm or it is nothing; and if there sometimes appear in the history of the Church instances of a tone which is pure and high without being enthusiastic, of a mood of Christian feeling which is calmly favourable to virtue without being victorious against vice, it will probably be found that all that is respectable in such a mood is but the slowly-subsiding movement of an earlier enthusiasm, and all that is produced by the lukewarmness of the time itself is hypocrisy and corrupt conventionalism.

Christianity, then, would sacrifice its divinity if it abandoned its missionary character and became a mere educational institution. Surely this Article of Conversion is the true *articulus stantis aut cadentis ecclesiae*. When the power of reclaiming the lost dies out of the Church, it ceases to be the Church. It may remain a useful institution, though it is most likely to become an immoral and mischievous one. Where the power remains, there, whatever is wanting, it may still be said that "the tabernacle of God is with men."

One more passage about those who in all Churches and sects think that all that Christ meant by His call was to give them a means to do what the French call *faire son salut*:—

It appears throughout the Sermon on the Mount that there was a class of persons whom Christ regarded with peculiar aversion—the persons who call themselves one thing and are another. He describes them by a word which originally meant an "actor." Probably it may in Christ's time have already become current in the sense which we give to the word "hypocrite." But no doubt whenever it was used the original sense of the word was distinctly remembered. And in this Sermon, whenever Christ denounces any vice, it is with the words "Be not you like the actors." In common with all great reformers, Christ felt that honesty in word and deed was the fundamental virtue; dishonesty, including affectation, self-consciousness, love of stage effect, the one incurable vice. Our thoughts, words, and deeds are to be of a piece.

For example, if we would pray to God, let us go into some inner room where none but God shall see us; to pray at the corner of the streets, where the passing crowd may admire our devotion, is to *act* a prayer. If we would keep down the rebellious flesh by fasting, this concerns ourselves only; it is acting to parade before the world our self-mortification. And if we would put down sin let us put it down in ourselves first; it is only the actor who begins by frowning at it in others. But there are subtler forms of hypocrisy, which Christ does not denounce, probably because they have sprung since out of the corruption of a subtler creed. The hypocrite of that age wanted simply money or credit with the people. His ends were those of the vulgar, though his means were different. Christ endeavoured to cure both alike of their vulgarity by telling them of other riches and another happiness laid up in heaven. Some, of course, would neither understand nor regard his words, others would understand and receive them. But a third class would receive them without understanding them, and instead of being cured of their avarice and sensuality, would simply transfer them to new objects of desire. Shrewd enough to discern Christ's greatness, instinctively believing what he said to be true, they would set out with a triumphant eagerness in pursuit of the heavenly riches, and laugh at the short-sighted and weak-minded speculator who contented himself with the easy but insignificant profits of a worldly life. They would practise assiduously the rules by which Christ said heaven was to be won. They would patiently turn the left cheek, indefatigibly walk the two miles, they would bless with effusion those who cursed them, and pray fluently for those who used them spitefully. To love their enemies, to love any one, they would certainly find impossible, but the outward signs of love might easily be learnt. And thus there would arise a new class of actors, not like those whom Christ denounced, exhibiting before an earthly audience and receiving their pay from human managers, but hoping to be paid for their performance out of the incorruptible treasures, and to impose by their dramatic talent upon their Father in heaven.

We have said that one peculiarity of this work is the connection which is kept in view from the first between the Founder and His work; between Christ and the Christian Church. He finds it impossible to speak of Him without that still existing witness of His having come, which is only less wonderful and unique than Himself. This is where, for the present, he leaves the subject :—

For the New Jerusalem, as we witness it, is no more exempt from corruption than was the Old. . . . First the rottenness of dying superstitions, their barbaric manners, their intellectualism preferring system and debate to brotherhood, strangling Christianity with theories and framing out of it a charlatan's philosophy which madly tries to stop the progress of science—all these corruptions have in the successive ages of its long life infected the Church, and many new and monstrous perversions of individual character have disgraced it. The creed which makes human nature richer and larger makes men at the same time capable of profounder sins; admitted into a holier sanctuary, they are exposed to the temptation of a greater sacrilege; awakened to the sense of new obligations, they sometimes lose their simple respect for the old ones; saints that have resisted the subtlest temptations sometimes begin again, as it were, by yielding without a struggle to the coarsest; hypocrisy has become tenfold more ingenious and better supplied with disguises; in short, human nature has inevitably developed downwards as well as upwards, and if the Christian ages be compared with those of heathenism, they are found worse as well as better, and it is possible to make it a question whether mankind has gained on the whole. . . .

But the triumph of the Christian Church is that it is *there*—that the most daring of all speculative dreams, instead of being found impracticable, has been carried into effect, and when carried into effect, instead of being confined to a few select spirits, has spread itself over a vast space of the earth's surface, and when thus diffused, instead of giving place after an age or two to something more adapted to a later time, has endured for two thousand years, and at the end of two thousand years, instead of lingering as a mere wreck spared by the tolerance of the lovers of the past, still displays vigour and a capacity of adjusting itself to new conditions, and lastly, in all the transformations it undergoes, remains visibly the same thing and inspired by its Founder's universal and unquenchable spirit.

It is in this and not in any freedom from abuses that the divine power of Christianity appears. Again, it is in this, and not in any completeness or all-sufficiency. . . .

But the achievement of Christ in founding by his

single will and power a structure so durable and so universal, is like no other achievement which history records. The masterpieces of the men of action are coarse and common in comparison with it, and the masterpieces of speculation flimsy and insubstantial. When we speak of it the commonplaces of admiration fail us altogether. Shall we speak of the originality of the design, of the skill displayed in the execution? All such terms are inadequate. Originality and contriving skill operated indeed, but, as it were, implicitly. The creative effort which produced that against which, it is said, the gates of hell shall not prevail, cannot be analysed. No architects' designs were furnished for the New Jerusalem, no committee drew up rules for the Universal Commonwealth. If in the works of Nature we can trace the indications of calculation, of a struggle with difficulties, of precaution, of ingenuity, then in Christ's work it may be that the same indications occur. But these inferior and secondary powers were not consciously exercised; they were implicitly present in the manifold yet single creative act. The inconceivable work was done in calmness; before the eyes of men it was noiselessly accomplished, attracting little attention. Who can describe that which unites men? Who has entered into the formation of speech which is the symbol of their union? Who can describe exhaustively the origin of civil society? He who can do these things can explain the origin of the Christian Church. For others it must be enough to say, "the Holy Ghost fell on those that believed." No man saw the building of the New Jerusalem, the workmen crowded together, the unfinished walls and unpaved streets; no man heard the chink of trowel and pickaxe; it descended *out of heaven from God.*

And here we leave this remarkable book. It seems to us one of those which permanently influence opinion, not so much by argument as such, as by opening larger views of the familiar and the long-debated, by deepening the ordinary channels of feeling, and by bringing men back to seriousness and rekindling their admiration, their awe, their love, about what they know best. We have not dwelt on minute criticisms about points to which exception might be taken. We have not noticed even positions on which, without further explanation, we should more or less widely disagree. The general scope of it, and the seriousness as well as the grandeur and power with which the main idea is worked out, seem to make mere secondary objections intolerable. It is a fragment, with the disadvantages of a fragment. What is put before us is far from complete, and it needs to be completed. In part at least an answer has been given to the question *what* Christ was; but the question remains, not less important, and of which the answer is only here foreshadowed, *who* He was. But so far as it goes, what it does is this: in the face of all attempts to turn Christianity into a sentiment or a philosophy, it asserts, in a most remarkable manner, a historical religion and a historical Church; but it also seeks, in a manner equally remarkable, to raise and elevate the thoughts of all, on all sides, about Christ, as He showed Himself in the world, and about what Christianity was meant to be; to touch new springs of feeling; to carry back the Church to its "hidden fountains," and pierce through the veils which hide from us the reality of the wonders in which it began.

The book is indeed a protest against the stiffness of all cast-iron systems, and a warning against trusting in what is worn out. But it shows how the modern world, so complex, so refined, so wonderful, is, in all that it accounts good, but a reflection of what is described in the Gospels, and its civilisation, but an application of the laws of Christ, changing, it may be, indefinitely in outward form, but depending on their spirit as its ever-living spring. If we have misunderstood this book, and its cautious understatements are not understatements at all, but represent the limits beyond which the writer does not go, we can only say again it is one of the strangest among books. If we have not misunderstood him, we have before us a writer who has a right to claim deference from those who think deepest and know most, when he pleads before them that not Philosophy can save and reclaim the world, but Faith in a Divine Person who is worthy of it, allegiance to a Divine Society which He founded, and union of hearts in the object for which He created it.

X

THE AUTHOR OF "ROBERT ELSMERE" ON A NEW REFORMATION[1]

MRS. WARD, in the *Nineteenth Century*, develops with warmth and force the theme and serious purpose of *Robert Elsmere;* and she does so, using the same literary method which she used, certainly with effect, in the story itself. Every age has its congenial fashion of discussing the great questions which affect, or seem to affect, the fate of mankind. According to the time and its circumstances, it is a *Summa Theologiae*, or a *Divina Commedia*, or a *Novum Organum*, or a Calvin's *Institutes*, or a Locke *On the Understanding*, or an *Encyclopedia*, or a *Candide*, which sets people thinking more than usual and comparing their thoughts. Long ago in the history of human questioning, Plato and Cicero discovered the advantages over dry argument of character and easy debate, and so much of story as clothed abstractions and hard notions with human life and affections. It is a

[1] *Guardian*, 6th March 1889.

weighty precedent. And as the prophetess of a "New Reformation" Mrs. Ward has reverted to what is substantially the same method. She is within her right. We do not blame her for putting her argument into the shape of a novel, and bringing out the points of her case in the trials and passionate utterances of imaginary persons, or in a conversation about their mental history. But she must take the good with the bad. Such a method has its obvious advantages, in freedom, and convenience, and range of illustration. It has its disadvantages. The dealer in imagination may easily become the unconscious slave of imagination; and, living in a self-constructed world, may come to forget that there is any other; and the temptation to unfairness becomes enormous when all who speak, on one side or the other, only speak as you make or let them speak.

It is to imagination that *Robert Elsmere* makes its main appeal, undoubtedly a powerful and pathetic one. It bids us ask ourselves what, with the phenomena before us, we can conceive possible and real. It implies, of course, much learning, with claims of victory in the spheres of history and science, with names great in criticism, of whom few readers probably can estimate the value, though all may be affected by the formidable array. But it is not in these things, as with a book like *Supernatural Religion*, that the gist of the argument lies. The alleged results of criticism are taken for granted; whether rightly or wrongly the great majority of readers certainly cannot tell. But then the effect of the book, or the view which it represents, begins. Imagine a man, pure-minded, earnest, sensitive, self-devoted, plunged into the tremendous questions of our time. Bit by bit he finds what he thought to be the truth of truths breaking away. In the darkness and silence with which nature covers all beyond the world of experience he thought he had found light and certainty from on high. He thought that he had assurances and pledges which could not fail him, that God was in the world, governed it, loved it, showed Himself in it. He thought he had a great and authentic story to fall back upon, and a Sacred Book, which was its guaranteed witness, and by which God still spoke to his soul. He thought that, whatever he did not know, he knew this, and this was a hope to live and die in; with all that he saw round him, of pain and sin and misery, here was truth on which he could rest secure, in his fight with evil. Like the rest of us, he knew that terrible, far-reaching, heart-searching questions were abroad; that all that to him was sacred and unapproachable in its sanctity was not so to all—was not so, perhaps, to men whom he felt to be stronger and more knowing than himself—was not so, perhaps, to some who seemed to him to stand, in character and purpose, at a moral height above him. Still he thought himself in full possession of the truth which God had given him, till at length, in one way or another, the tide of questioning reached him. Then begins the long agony. He hears that what he never doubted is said to be incredible, and is absolutely given up. He finds himself surrounded by hostile powers of thought, by an atmosphere which insensibly but irresistibly governs opinion, by doubt and denial in the air, by keen and relentless intellect, before which he can only be silent; he sees and hears all round the disintegrating process going on in the creeds and institutions and intellectual statements of Christianity. He is assured, and sees some reason to believe it, that the intellect of the day is against him and his faith; and further, that unreality taints everything, belief and reasoning, and profession and conduct. Step by step he is forced from one position and another; the process was a similar and a familiar one when the great Roman secession was going on fifty years ago. But now, in Robert Elsmere, comes the upshot. He is not landed, as some logical minds have been, which have gone through the same process, in mere unbelief or indifference. He is too good for that. Something of his old Christianity is too deeply engrained in him. He cannot go back from the moral standard to which it accustomed him. He will serve God in a Christian spirit and after the example of Christ, though not in what can claim to be called a Christian way. He is the beginner of one more of the numberless attempts to find a new mode of religion, purer than any of the old ones could be— of what Mrs. Ward calls in her new paper "A New Reformation."

In this paper, which is more distinctly a dialogue on the Platonic model, she isolates the main argument on which the story was based, but without any distinct reference to any of the criticisms on her book. *Robert Elsmere* rests on the achievements of historic criticism, chiefly German criticism. From the traditional, old-fashioned Christian way of regarding and using the old records which we call the Bible, the ground, we are told, is hopelessly and for ever cut away by German historical criticism. And the difference between the old and the modern way of regarding and using them is expressed by the difference between *bad translation* and *good;* the old way of reading, quoting, and estimating ancient documents of all kinds was purblind, lifeless, narrow, mechanical, whereas the modern comparative and critical method not only is more sure in important questions of authenticity, but puts true life and character and human feeling and motives into the personages who wrote these documents, and of whom they speak. These books were entirely misunderstood, even if people knew the meaning of their words; now, at last, we can enter into their real spirit and meaning. And where such a change of method and point of view, as regards these documents, is wholesale and sweeping, it involves a wholesale and sweeping change in all that is founded on them. Revised ideas about the Bible mean a revised and reconstructed Christianity—" A New Reformation."

Mrs. Ward lays more stress than everybody will agree to on what she likens to the difference between *good translation* and *bad*, in dealing with the materials of history. Doubtless, in our time, the historical imagination, like the historical conscience, has been awakened. In history, as in other things, the effort after the real and the living has been very marked; it has sometimes resulted, as we know, in that parading of the real which we call the realistic. The mode of telling a story or stating a case varies, even characteristically, from age to age, from Macaulay to Hume, from Hume to Rapin, from Rapin to Holinshed or Hall; but after all, the story in its main features remains, after allowing for the differences in the mode of presenting it. German criticism, to which we are expected to defer, has its mode. It combines two elements—a diligent, searching, lawyer-like habit of cross-examination, laborious, complete and generally honest, which, when it is not spiteful or insolent, deserves all the praise it receives; but with it a sense of the probable, in dealing with the materials collected, and a straining after attempts to construct theories and to give a vivid reality to facts and relations, which are not always so admirable; which lead, in fact, sometimes to the height of paradox, or show mere incapacity to deal with the truth and depth of life, or make use of a poor and mean standard—*mesquin* would be the French word—in the interpretation of actions and aims. It has impressed on us the lesson—not to be forgotten when we read Mrs. Ward's lists of learned names—that weight and not number is the test of good evidence. German learning is decidedly imposing. But after all there are Germans and Germans;

and with all that there has been of great in German work there has been also a large proportion of what is bad—conceited, arrogant, shallow, childish. German criticism has been the hunting-ground of an insatiable love of sport—may we not say, without irreverence, the scene of the discovery of a good many mares' nests? When the question is asked, why all this mass of criticism has made so little impression on English thought, the answer is, because of its extravagant love of theorising, because of its divergences and variations, because of its negative results. Those who have been so eager to destroy have not been so successful in construction. Clever theories come to nothing; streams which began with much noise at last lose themselves in the sand. Undoubtedly, it presents a very important, and, in many ways, interesting class of intellectual phenomena, among the many groups of such inquiries, moral, philosophical, scientific, political, social, of which the world is full, and of which no sober thinker expects to see the end. If this vaunted criticism is still left to scholars, it is because it is still in the stage in which only scholars are competent to examine and judge it; it is not fit to be a factor in the practical thought and life of the mass of mankind. Answers, and not merely questions, are what we want, who have to live, and work, and die. Criticism has pulled about the Bible without restraint or scruple. We are all of us steeped in its daring assumptions and shrewd objections. Have its leaders yet given us an account which it is reasonable to receive, clear, intelligible, self-consistent and consistent with all the facts, of what this mysterious book is?

Meanwhile, in the face of theories and conjectures and negative arguments, there is something in the world which is fact, and hard fact. The Christian Church is the most potent fact in the most important ages of the world's progress. It is an institution like the world itself, which has grown up by its own strength and according to its own principle of life, full of good and evil, having as the law of its fate to be knocked about in the stern development of events, exposed, like human society, to all kinds of vicissitudes and alternations, giving occasion to many a scandal, and shaking the faith and loyalty of many a son, showing in ample measure the wear and tear of its existence, battered, injured, sometimes degenerate, sometimes improved, in one way or another, since those dim and long distant days when its course began; but showing in all these ways what a real thing it is, never in the extremity of storms and ruin, never in the deepest degradation of its unfaithfulness, losing hold of its own central unchanging faith, and never in its worst days of decay and corruption losing hold of the power of self-correction and hope of recovery. *Solvitur ambulando* is an argument to which Mrs. Ward appeals, in reply to doubts about the solidity of the "New Reformation." It could be urged more modestly if the march of the "New Reformation" had lasted for even half of one of the Christian centuries. The Church is in the world, as the family is in the world, as the State is in the world, as morality is in the world, a fact of the same order and greatness. Like these it has to make its account with the "all-dissolving" assaults of human thought. Like these it has to prove itself by living, and it does do so. In all its infinite influences and ministries, in infinite degrees and variations, it is the public source of light and good and hope. If there are select and aristocratic souls who can do without it, or owe it nothing, the multitude of us cannot. And the Christian Church is founded on a definite historic fact, that Jesus Christ who was crucified rose from the dead; and, coming from such an author, it comes to us, bringing with it the Bible. The fault of a book like *Robert Elsmere* is that it is written with a deliberate ignoring that these two points are not merely important, but absolutely fundamental, in the problems with which it deals. With these not faced and settled it is like looking out at a prospect through a window of which all the glass is ribbed and twisted, distorting everything. It may be that even yet we imperfectly understand our wondrous Bible. It may be that we have yet much to learn about it. It may be that there is much that is very difficult about it. Let us reverently and fearlessly learn all we can about it. Let us take care not to misuse it, as it has been terribly misused. But coming to us from the company and with the sanction of Christ risen, it never can be merely like other books. A so-called Christianity, ignoring or playing with Christ's resurrection, and using the Bible as a sort of Homer, may satisfy a class of clever and cultivated persons. It may be to them the parent of high and noble thoughts, and readily lend itself to the service of mankind. But it is well in so serious a matter not to confuse things. This new religion may borrow from Christianity as it may borrow from Plato, or from Buddhism, or Confucianism, or even Islam. But it is not Christianity. *Robert Elsmere* may be true to life, as representing one of those tragedies which happen in critical moments of history. But a Christianity which tells us to think of Christ doing good, but to forget and put out of sight Christ risen from the dead, is not true to life. It is as delusive to the conscience and the soul as it is illogical to reason.

XI

RENAN'S "VIE DE JÉSUS"[1]

UNBELIEF is called upon nowadays, as well as belief, to give its account of the origin of that undeniable and most important fact which we call the Christian religion. And if it is true that in some respects the circumstances under which the controversy is carried on are, as it has been alleged, more than heretofore favourable to unbelief, it is also true that in some other respects the case of unbelief has difficulties which it had not once. It has to accept and admit, if it wishes to gain a favourable hearing from the present generation, the unique and surpassing moral grandeur, depth, and attractiveness of Christianity. The polemic method which set Christianity in broad contrast with what was supposed to be best and highest in human nature, and therefore found no difficulty in tracing to a bad source what was itself represented to be bad, is not a method suited to the ideas and feelings of our time; and the

[1] *Histoire des Origines du Christianisme.* Livre I.—*Vie de Jésus.* Par Ernest Renan. *Guardian*, 9th September 1863.

sneers and sarcasms of the last century, provoked by abuses and inconsistencies which have since received their ample and memorable punishment, cease to produce any effect on readers of the present day, except to call forth a passing feeling of repugnance at what is shallow and profane, mixed, it may be, sometimes, with an equally passing admiration for what is witty and brilliant. Even in M. Renan's view, Voltaire has done his work, and is out of date. Those who now attack Christianity have to attack it under the disadvantage of the preliminary admission that its essential and distinguishing elements are, on the whole, in harmony and not in discordance with the best conceptions of human duty and life, and that its course and progress have been, at any rate, concurrent with all that is best and most hopeful in human history. First allowing that as a fact it contains in it things than which we cannot imagine anything better, and without which we should never have reached to where we are, they then have to dispute its divine claims. No man could write persuasively on religion now, *against* it any more than *for* it, who did not show that he was fully penetrated not only with its august and beneficent aspect, but with the essential and everlasting truths which, in however imperfect shapes, or whencesoever derived, are embodied in it and are ministered by it to society.

That Christianity is, as a matter of fact, a successful and a living religion, in a degree absolutely without parallel in any other religion, is the point from which its assailants have now to start. They have also to take account of the circumstance, to the recognition of which the whole course of modern thought and inquiry has brought us, that it has been successful, not by virtue merely of any outward and accidental favouring circumstances, but of its intrinsic power and of principles which are inseparable from its substance. This being the condition of the question, those who deny its claim to a direct Divine origin have to frame their theory of it so as to account, on principles supposed to be common to it and other religions, not merely for its rise and its conquests, but for those broad and startling differences which separate it, in character and in effects, from all other known religions. They have to show how that which is instinct with never-dying truth sprang out of what was false and mistaken, if not corrupt; how that which alone has revealed God to man's conscience had no other origin than what in other instances has led men through enthusiasm and imposture to a barren or a mischievous superstition.

Such an attempt is the work before us—a work destined, probably, both from its ability and power and from its faults, to be for modern France what the work of Strauss was for Germany, the standard expression of an unbelief which shrinks with genuine distaste from the coarse and negative irreligion of older infidelity, and which is too refined, too profound and sympathetic in its views of human nature, to be insensible to those numberless points in which as a fact Christianity has given expression to the best and highest thoughts that man can have. Strauss, to account for what we see, imagined an idea, or a set of ideas, gradually worked out into the shape of a history, of which scarcely anything can be taken as real matter of fact, except the bare existence of the person who was clothed in the process of time with the attributes created by the idealising legend. Such a view is too vague and indistinct to satisfy French minds. A theory of this sort, to find general acceptance in France, must start with concrete history, and not be history held in solution in the cloudy shapes of myths which vanish as soon as touched. M. Renan's process is in the main the reverse of Strauss's. He undertakes to extract the real history recorded in the Gospels; and not only so, but to make it even more palpable and interesting, if not more wonderful, than it seems at first sight in the original records, by removing the crust of mistake and exaggeration which has concealed the true character of what the narrative records; by rewriting it according to those canons of what is probable and intelligible in human life and capacity which are recognised in the public whom he addresses.

Two of these canons govern the construction of the book. One of them is the assumption that in no part of the history of man is the supernatural to be admitted. This, of course, is not peculiar to M. Renan, though he lays it down with such emphasis in all his works, and is so anxious to bring it into distinct notice on every occasion, that it is manifestly one which he is desirous to impress on all who read him, as one of the ultimate and unquestionable foundations of all historical inquiry. The other canon is one of moral likelihood, and it is, that it is credible and agreeable to what we gather from experience, that the highest moral elevation ever attained by man should have admitted along with it, and for its ends, conscious imposture. On the first of these assumptions, all that is miraculous in the Gospel narratives is, not argued about, or, except perhaps in one instance—the raising of Lazarus—attempted to be accounted for or explained, but simply left out and ignored. On the second, the fact from which there is no escape—that He whom M. Renan venerates with a sincerity which no one can doubt as the purest and greatest of moral reformers, did claim power from God to work miracles—is harmonised with the assumption that the claim could not possibly have been a true one.

M. Renan professes to give an historical account of the way in which the deepest, purest, most enduring religious principles known among men were, not merely found out and announced, but propagated and impressed upon the foremost and most improved portions of mankind, by the power of a single character. It is impossible, without speaking of Jesus of Nazareth as Christians are used to do, to speak of His character and of the results of His appearance in loftier terms than this professed unbeliever in His Divine claims. But when the account is drawn out in detail, of a cause alleged to be sufficient to produce such effects, the apparent inadequacy of it is most startling. When we think of what Christianity is and has done, and that, in M. Renan's view, Christ, the Christ whom he imagines and describes, is all in all to Christianity, and then look to what he conceives to have been the original spring and creative impulse of its achievements, the first feeling is that no shifts that belief has sometimes been driven to, to keep within the range of the probable, are greater than those accepted by unbelief, in its most enlightened and reflecting representations. To suppose such an one as M. Renan paints, changing the whole course of history, overturning and converting the world, and founding the religion which M. Renan thinks the lasting religion of mankind, involves a force upon our imagination and reason to which it is not easy to find a parallel.

His view is that a Galilean peasant, in advance of his neighbours and countrymen only in the purity, force, and singleness of purpose with which he realised the highest moral truths of Jewish religious wisdom, first charming a few simple provincials by the freshness and native beauty of his lessons, was then led on, partly by holy zeal against falsehood and wickedness, partly by enthusiastic delusions as to his own mission and office, to attack the institutions of Judaism, and perished in the conflict—and that this was the cause why Christianity and Christendom came to be and exist. This is the explanation which a great critical historian, fully acquainted with the history of other religions, presents, as a satisfactory one, of a phenomenon so astonishing and unique as that of a religion which has suited itself with undiminished vitality to the changes, moral, social, and political, which have marked the eighteen centuries of European history. There have been other enthusiasts for goodness and truth, more or less like the character which M. Renan draws in his book, but they have never yet founded a universal religion, or one which had the privilege of perpetual youth and unceasing self-renovation. There have been other great and imposing religions, commanding the allegiance for century after century of millions of men; but who will dare assert that any of these religions, that of Sakya-Mouni, of Mahomet, or that of the Vedas, could possibly be the religion, or satisfy the religious ideas and needs, of the civilised West?

When M. Renan comes to detail he is as strangely insensible to what seem at first sight the simplest demands of probability. As it were by a sort of reaction to the minute realising of particulars which has been in vogue among some Roman Catholic writers, M. Renan realises too—realises with no less force and vividness, and, according to his point of view, with no less affectionate and tender interest. He popularises the Gospels; but not for a religious set of readers—nor, we must add, for readers of thought and sense, whether interested for or against Christianity, but for a public who study life in the subtle and highly wrought novels of modern times. He appeals from what is probable to those representations of human nature which aspire to pass beyond the conventional and commonplace, and especially he dwells on neglected and unnoticed examples of what is sweet and soft and winning. But it is hard to recognise the picture he has drawn in the materials out of which he has composed it. The world is tolerably familiar with them. If there is a characteristic, consciously or unconsciously acknowledged in the Gospel records, it is that of the gravity, the plain downright seriousness, the laborious earnestness, impressed from first to last on the story. When we turn from these to his pages it is difficult to exaggerate the astounding impression which his epithets and descriptions have on the mind. We are told that there is a broad distinction between the early Galilean days of hope in our Lord's ministry, and the later days of disappointment and conflict; and that if we look, we shall find in Galilee the "*fin et joyeux moraliste,*" full of a "*conversation pleine de gaieté et de charme,*" of "*douce gaieté et aimables plaisanteries,*" with a "*prédication suave et douce, toute pleine de la nature et du parfum des champs,*" creating out of his originality of mind his "*innocents aphorismes,*" and the "*genre délicieux*" of parabolic teaching; "*le charmant docteur qui pardonnait à tous pourvu qu'on l'aimât.*" He lived in what was then an earthly paradise, in "*la joyeuse Galilée,*" in the midst of the "*nature ravissante*" which gave to everything about the Sea of Galilee "*un tour idyllique et charmant.*" So the history of Christianity at its birth is a "*délicieuse pastorale,*" an "*idylle,*" a "*milieu enivrant*" of joy and hope. The master was surrounded by a "*bande de joyeux enfants,*" a "*troupe gaie et vagabonde,*" whose existence in the open air was a "perpetual enchantment." The disciples were "*ces petits comités de bonnes gens,*" very simple, very credulous, and like their country full of a "*sentiment gai et tendre de la vie,*" and of an "*imagination riante.*" Everything is spoken of as "delicious"—"*délicieuse pastorale,*" "*délicieuse beauté,*" "*délicieuses sentences,*" "*délicieuse théologie d'amour.*" Among the "tender and delicate souls of the North"—it is not quite thus that Josephus describes the Galileans—was set up an "*aimable communisme.*" Is it possible to imagine a more extravagant distortion than the following, both in its general effect and in the audacious generalisation of a very special incident, itself inaccurately conceived of?—

Il parcourait ainsi la Galilée au milieu *d'une fête perpétuelle.* Il se servait d'une mule, monture en Orient si bonne et si sûre, et dont le grand œil noir, ombragé de longs cils, a beaucoup de douceur. Ses disciples déployaient quelquefois autour de lui une pompe rustique, dont leurs vêtements, tenant lieu de tapis, faisaient les frais. Ils les mettaient sur la mule qui le portait, ou les étendaient à terre sur son passage.

History has seen strange hypotheses; but of all extravagant notions, that one that the world has been conquered by what was originally an idyllic gipsying party is the most grotesque. That these "*petits comités de bonnes gens,*" though influenced by a great example and wakened out of their "delicious pastoral" by a heroic death, should have been able to make an impression on Judaean faith, Greek intellect, and Roman civilisation, and to give an impulse to mankind which has lasted to this day, is surely one of the most incredible hypotheses ever accepted, under the desperate necessity of avoiding an unwelcome alternative.

M. Renan is willing to adopt everything in the Gospel history except what is miraculous. If he is difficult to satisfy as to the physical possibility or the proof of miracles, at least he is not hard to satisfy on points of moral likelihood; and he draws on his ample power of supposing the combination of moral opposites in order to get rid of the obstinate and refractory supernatural miracle. To some extent, indeed, he avails himself of that inexhaustible resource of unlimited guessing, by means of which he reverses the whole history, and makes it take a shape which it is hard to recognise in its original records. The feeding of the five thousand, the miracle described by all the four Evangelists, is thus curtly disposed of:— "Il se retira au désert. Beaucoup de monde l'y suivit. *Grâce à une extrême frugalité* la troupe sainte y vécut; *on crut naturellement* voir en cela un miracle."

This is all he has to say. But miracles are too closely interwoven with the whole texture of the Gospel history to be, as a whole, thus disposed of. He has, of course, to admit that miracles are so mixed up with it that mere exaggeration is not a sufficient account of them. But he bids us remember that the time was one of great credulity, of slackness and incapacity in dealing with matters of evidence, a time when it might be said that there was an innocent disregard of exact and literal truth where men's souls and affections were deeply interested. But, even supposing that this accounted for a belief in certain miracles growing up—which it does not, for the time was not one of mere childlike and uninquiring belief, but was as perfectly familiar as we are with the notion of false claims to miraculous power which could not stand examination—still this does not meet the great difficulty of all, to which he is at last brought. It is undeniable that our Lord professed to work miracles. They were not merely attributed to Him by those who came after Him. If we accept in any degree the Gospel account, He not only wrought miracles, but claimed to do so; and M. Renan admits it—that is, he admits that the highest, purest, most Divine person ever seen on earth (for all this he declares in the most unqualified terms) stooped to the arts of Simon Magus or Apollonius of Tyana. He was a "thaumaturge"—"tard et à contre-cœur"—"avec une sorte de mauvaise humeur'—"en cachette"— "malgré lui"—"sentant le vanité de l'opinion";

but still a "thaumaturge." Moreover, He was so almost of necessity; for M. Renan holds that without the support of an alleged supernatural character and power, His work must have perished. Everything, to succeed and be realised, must, we are told, be fortified with something of alloy. We are reminded of the "loi fatale qui condamne l'idée à déchoir dès qu'elle cherche à convertir les hommes." "Concevoir de bien, en effet, ne suffit pas; il faut le faire réussir parmi les hommes. Pour cela, des voies moins pures sont nécessaires." If the Great Teacher had kept to the simplicity of His early lessons, He would have been greater, but "the truth would not have been promulgated." "He had to choose between these two alternatives, either renouncing his mission or becoming a 'thaumaturge.'" The miracles "were a violence done to him by his age, a concession which was wrung from him by a passing necessity." And if we feel startled at such a view, we are reminded that we must not measure the sincerity of Orientals by our own rigid and critical idea of veracity; and that "such is the weakness of the human mind, that the best causes are not usually won but by bad reasons," and that the greatest of discoverers and founders have only triumphed over their difficulties "by daily taking account of men's weakness and by not always giving the true reasons of the truth."

L'histoire est impossible si l'on n'admet hautement qu'il y a pour la sincerité plusieurs mesures. Toutes les grandes choses se font par le peuple, or on ne conduit pas le peuple qu'en se prêtant à ses idées. Le philosophe, qui sachant cela, s'isole et se retranche dans sa noblesse, est hautement louable. Mais celui qui prend l'humanité avec ses illusions et cherche à agir sur elle et avec elle, ne saurait être blamé. César savait fort bien qu'il n'était pas fils de Vénus ; la France ne serait pas ce qu'elle est si l'on n'avait cru mille ans à la sainte ampoule de Reims. Il nous est facile à nous autres, impuissants que nous sommes, d'appeler cela mensonge, et fiers de notre timide honnêteté, de traiter avec dédain les héros qui ont accepté dans d'autres conditions la lutte de la vie. Quand nous aurons fait avec nos scrupules ce qu'ils firent avec leurs mensonges, nous aurons le droit d'être pour eux sévères.

Now let M. Renan or any one else realise what is involved, on his supposition, not merely, as he says, of "illusion or madness," but of wilful deceit and falsehood, in the history of Lazarus, even according to his lame and hesitating attempt to soften it down and extenuate it; and then put side by side with it the terms in which M. Renan has summed up the moral greatness of Him of whom he writes:—

La foi, l'enthousiasme, la constance de la première génération chrétienne ne s'expliquent qu'en supposant à l'origine de tout le mouvement un homme de proportions colossales . . . . Cette sublime personne, qui chaque jour préside encore au destin du monde, il est permis de l'appeler divine, non en ce sens que Jésus ait absorbé tout le divin, mais en ce sens que Jésus est l'individu qui a fait faire à son espèce le plus grand pas vers le divin. . . . Au milieu de cette uniforme vulgarité, des colonnes s'élèvent vers le ciel et attestent une plus noble destinée. Jésus est la plus haute de ces colonnes qui montrent à l'homme d'où il vient et où il doit tendre. En lui s'est condensé tout ce qu'il y a de bon et d'élevé dans notre nature. . . Quels que puissent être les phénomènes inattendus de l'avenir, Jésus ne sera pas surpassé . . . Tous les siècles proclameront qu'entre les fils des hommes il n'en est pas né de plus grand que Jésus.

And of such an one we are told that it is a natural and reasonable view to take, not merely that He claimed a direct communication with God, which disordered reason could alone excuse Him for claiming, but that He based His whole mission on a pretension to such supernatural powers as a man could not pretend to without being conscious that they were delusions. The conscience of that age as to veracity or imposture was quite clear on such a point. Jew and Greek and Roman would have condemned as a deceiver one who, not having the power, took on him to say that by the finger of God he could raise the dead. And yet to a conscience immeasurably above his age, it seems, according to M. Renan, that this might be done. It is absurd to say that we must not judge such a proceeding by the ideas of our more exact and truth-loving age, when it would have been abundantly condemned by the ideas recognised in the religion and civilisation of the first century.

M. Renan repeatedly declares that his great aim is to save religion by relieving it of the supernatural.

He does not argue; but instead of the old familiar view of the Great History, he presents an opposite theory of his own, framed to suit that combination of the revolutionary and the sentimental which just now happens to be in favour in the unbelieving schools. And this is the result: a representation which boldly invests its ideal with the highest perfections of moral goodness, strength, and beauty, and yet does not shrink from associating with it also—and that, too, as the necessary and inevitable condition of success—a deliberate and systematic willingness to delude and insensibility to untruth. This is the religion and this is the reason which appeals to Christ in order to condemn Christianity.

XII

RENAN'S "LES APÔTRES"[1]

In his recent volume, *Les Apôtres*, M. Renan has undertaken two tasks of very unequal difficulty. He accounts for the origin of the Christian belief and religion, and he writes the history of its first propagation. These are very different things, and to do one of them is by no means to do the other. M. Renan's historical sketch of the first steps of the Christian movement is, whatever we may think of its completeness and soundness, a survey of characters and facts, based on our ordinary experience of the ways in which men act and are influenced. Of course it opens questions and provokes dissent at every turn; but, after all, the history of a religion once introduced into the world is the history of the men who give it shape and preach it, who accept or oppose it. The spread and development of all religions have certain broad features in common, which admit of philosophical treatment simply as phenomena, and receive

[1] *Histoire des Origines du Christianisme.* Livre II.—*Les Apôtres.* Par Ernest Renan. *Saturday Review,* 14th July 1866.

light from being compared with parallel examples of the same kind; and whether a man's historical estimate is right, and his picture accurate and true, depends on his knowledge of the facts, and his power to understand them and to make them understood. No one can dispute M. Renan's qualifications for being the historian of a religious movement. The study of religion as a phenomenon of human nature and activity has paramount attractions for him. His interest in it has furnished him with ample and varied materials for comparison and generalisation. He is a scholar and a man of learning, quick and wide in his sympathies, and he commands attention by the singular charm of his graceful and lucid style. When, therefore, he undertakes to relate how, as a matter of fact, the Christian Church grew up amid the circumstances of its first appearance, he has simply to tell the story of the progress of a religious cause; and this is a comparatively light task for him. But he also lays before us what he appears to consider an adequate account of the origin of the Christian belief. The Christian belief, it must be remembered, means, not merely the belief that there was such a person as he has described in his former volume, but the belief that one who was crucified rose again from the dead, and lives for evermore above. It is in this belief that the Christian religion had its beginning; there is no connecting Christ and Christianity, except through the Resurrection. The origin, therefore, of the belief in the Resurrection, in the shape in which we have it, lies across M. Renan's path to account for; and neither the picture which he has drawn in his former volume, nor the history which he follows out in this, dispense him from the necessity of facing this essential and paramount element in the problem which he has to solve. He attempts to deal with this, the knot of the great question. But his attempt seems to us to disclose a more extraordinary insensibility to the real demands of the case, and to what we cannot help calling the pitiable inadequacy of his own explanation, than we could have conceived possible in so keen and practised a mind.

The Resurrection, we repeat, bars the way in M. Renan's scheme for making an intelligible transition, from the life and character which he has sought to reproduce from the Gospels, to the first beginnings and preaching of Christianity. The Teacher, he says, is unique in wisdom, in goodness, in the height of his own moral stature and the Divine elevation of his aims. The religion is, with all abatements and imperfections, the only one known which could be the religion of humanity. After his portraiture of the Teacher, follows, naturally enough, as the result of that Teacher's influence and life, a religion of corresponding elevation and promise. The passage from a teaching such as M. Renan supposes to a religion such as he allows Christianity to be may be reasonably understood as a natural consequence of well-known causes, but for one thing—the interposition between the two of an alleged event which simply throws out all reasonings drawn from ordinary human experience. From the teaching and life of Socrates follow, naturally enough, schools of philosophy, and an impulse which has affected scientific thought ever since. From the preaching and life of Mahomet follows, equally naturally, the religion of Islam. In each case the result is seen to be directly and distinctly linked on to the influences which gave it birth, and nothing more than these influences is wanted, or makes any claim, to account for it. So M. Renan holds that all that is needed to account for Christianity is such a personality and such a career as he has described in his last volume. But the facts will not bend to this. Christianity hangs on to Christ not merely as to a Person who lived and taught and died, but as to a Person who rose again from death. That is of the very essence of its alleged derivation from Christ. It knows Christ only as Christ risen; the only reason of its own existence that it recognises is the Resurrection. The only claim the Apostles set forth for preaching to the world is that their Master who was crucified was alive once more. Every one knows that this was the burden of all their words, the corner-stone of all their work. We may believe them or not. We may take Christianity or leave it. But we cannot derive Christianity from Christ, without meeting, as the bond which connects the two, the Resurrection. But for the Resurrection, M. Renan's scheme might be intelligible. A Teacher unequalled for singleness of aim and nobleness of purpose lives and dies, and leaves the memory and the leaven of His teaching to disciples, who by them, even though in an ill-understood shape, and with incomparably inferior qualities themselves, purify and elevate the religious ideas and feelings of mankind. If that were all, if there were nothing but the common halo of the miraculous which is apt to gather about great names, the interpretation might be said to be coherent. But a theory of Christianity cannot neglect the most prominent fact connected with its beginning. It is impossible to leave it out of the account, in judging both of the Founder and of those whom his influence moulded and inspired.

M. Renan has to account for the prominence given to the Resurrection in the earliest Christian teaching, without having recourse to the supposition of conscious imposture and a deliberate conspiracy to deceive; for such a supposition would not harmonise either with the portrait he has drawn of the Master, or with his judgment of the seriousness and moral elevation of the men who, immeasurably inferior as they were to Him, imbibed His spirit, and represented and transmitted to us His principles. And this is something much more than can be accounted for by the general disposition of the age to assume the supernatural and the miraculous. The way in which the Resurrection is circumstantially and unceasingly asserted, and made on every occasion and from the first the foundation of everything, is something very different from the vague legends which float about of kings or saints whom death has spared, or from a readiness to see the direct agency of heaven in health or disease. It is too precise, too matter-of-fact, too prosaic in the way in which it is told, to be resolved into ill-understood dreams and imaginations. The various recitals show little care to satisfy our curiosity, or to avoid the appearance of inconsistency in detail; but nothing can be more removed from vagueness and hesitation than their definite positive statements. It is with them that the writer on Christianity has to deal.

M. Renan's method is—whilst of course not believing them, yet not supposing conscious fraud—to treat these records as the description of natural, unsought visions on the part of people who meant no harm, but who believed what they wished to believe. They are the story of a great mistake, but a mistake proceeding simply, in the most natural way in the world, from excess of "idealism" and attachment. Unaffected by the circumstance that there never were narratives less ideal, and more straightforwardly real—that they seem purposely framed to be a contrast to professed accounts of visions, and to exclude the possibility of their being confounded with such accounts; and that the alleged numbers who saw, the alleged frequency and repetition and variation of the instances, and the alleged time over which the appearances extended, and after which they absolutely ceased, make the hypothesis of involuntary and undesigned allusions of regret and passion infinitely different from what it might be in the case of one or two persons, or for a transitory period of excitement and crisis—unaffected by such considerations, M. Renan proceeds to tell, in his own way, the story of what he supposes to have occurred, without, of course, admitting the smallest real foundation for what was so positively asserted, but with very little reproach or discredit to the ardent and undoubting assertors. He begins with a statement which is meant to save the character of the Teacher. "Jesus, though he spoke unceasingly of resurrection, of new life, had never said quite clearly that he should rise again in the flesh." He says this with the texts before him, for he quotes them and classifies them in a note. But this is his point of departure, laid down without qualification. Yet if there is anything which the existing records do say distinctly, it is that Jesus Christ said over and over again that He should rise again, and that He fixed the time within which He should rise. M. Renan is not bound to believe them. But he must take them as he finds them; and on this capital point either we know nothing at all, and have no evidence to go upon, or the evidence is simply inverted by M. Renan's assertion. There may, of course, be reasons for believing one part of a man's evidence and disbelieving another; but there is nothing in this case but incompatibility with a theory to make this part of the evidence either more or less worthy of credit than any other part. What is certain is that it is in the last degree weak and uncritical to lay down, as the foundation and first pre-requisite of an historical view, a position which the records on which the view professes to be based emphatically and unambiguously contradict. Whatever we may think of it, the evidence undoubtedly is, if evidence there is at all, that Jesus Christ did say, though He could not get His disciples at the time to understand and believe Him, that He should rise again on the third day. What M. Renan had to do, if he thought the contrary, was not to assume, but to prove, that in these repeated instances in which they report His announcements, the Evangelists mistook or misquoted the words of their Master.

He accepts, however, their statement that no one at first hoped that the words would be made good; and he proceeds to account for the extraordinary belief which, in spite of this original incredulity, grew up, and changed the course of things and the face of the world. We admire and respect many things in M. Renan; but it seems to us that his treatment of this matter is simply the *ne plus ultra* of the degradation of the greatest of issues by the application to it of sentiment unworthy of a silly novel. In the first place, he lays down on general grounds that, though the disciples had confessedly given up all hope, it yet *was natural* that they should expect to see their master alive again. "Mais l'enthousiasme et l'amour ne connaissent pas les situations sans issue." Do they not? Are death and separation such light things to triumph over that imagination finds it easy to cheat them? "Ils se jouent de l'impossible et, plutôt que d'abdiquer l'espérance, ils font violence à toute réalité." Is this an account of the world of fact or the world of romance? The disciples did not hope; but, says M. Renan, vague words about the future had dropped from their master, and these were enough to build upon, and to suggest that they would soon see him back. In vain it is said that in fact they did not expect it. "Une telle croyance était d'ailleurs si naturelle, que la foi des disciples aurait suffi pour la créer de toutes pièces." Was it indeed—in spite of Enoch and Elias, cases of an entirely different kind—so natural to think that the ruined leader of a crushed cause, whose hopeless followers had seen the last of him amid the lowest miseries of torment and scorn, should burst the grave?

Il devait arriver [he proceeds] pour Jésus ce qui arrive pour tous les hommes qui ont captivé l'attention de leurs semblables. Le monde, habitué à leur attribuer des vertus surhumaines, ne peut admettre qu'ils aient subi la loi injuste, révoltante, inique, du trépas commun. . . . La mort est chose si absurde quand elle frappe l'homme de génie ou l'homme d'un grand cœur, que le peuple ne croit pas à la possibilité d'une telle erreur de la nature. Les héros ne meurent pas.

The history of the world presents a large range of instances to test the singular assertion that death is so "absurd" that "the people" cannot believe that great and good men literally die. But would it be easy to match the strangeness of a philosopher and a man of genius gravely writing this down as a reason— not why, at the interval of centuries, a delusion should grow up—but why, on the very morrow of a crucifixion and burial, the disciples should have believed that all the dreadful work they had seen a day or two before was in very fact and reality reversed? We confess we do not know what human experience is if it countenances such a supposition as this.

From this antecedent probability he proceeds to the facts. "The Sabbath day which followed the burial was occupied with these thoughts. . . . Never was the rest of the Sabbath so fruitful." They all, the women especially, thought of him all day long in his bed of spices, watched over by angels; and the assurance grew that the wicked men who had killed him would not have their triumph, that he would not be left to decay, that he would be wafted on high to that Kingdom of the Father of which he had spoken. "Nous le verrons encore; nous entendrons sa voix charmante; c'est en vain qu'ils l'auront tué." And as, with the Jews, a future life implied a resurrection of the body, the shape which their hope took was settled. "Reconnaître que la mort pouvait être victorieuse de Jésus, de celui qui venait de supprimer son empire, c'était le comble de l'absurdité." It is, we suppose, irrelevant to remark that we find not the faintest trace of this sense of absurdity. The disciples, he says, had no choice between hopelessness and "an heroic affirmation"; and he makes the bold surmise that "un homme pénétrant aurait pu annoncer *dès le samedi* que Jésus revivrait." This may be history, or philosophy, or criticism; what it is *not* is the inference naturally arising from the only records we have of the time spoken of. But the force of historical imagination dispenses with the necessity of extrinsic support. "La petite société chrétienne, ce jour-là, opéra le véritable miracle : elle ressuscita Jésus en son cœur par l'amour intense qu'elle lui porta. Elle décida que Jésus ne mourrait pas." The Christian Church has done many remarkable things; but it never did anything so strange, or which so showed its power, as when it took that resolution.

How was the decision, involuntary and unconscious, and guiltless of intentional deception, if we can conceive of such an attitude of mind, carried out? M. Renan might leave the matter in obscurity. But he sees his way, in spite of incoherent traditions and the contradictions which they present, to a "sufficient degree of probability." The belief in the Resurrection originated in an hallucination of the disordered fancy of Mary Magdalen, whose mind was thrown off its balance by her affection and sorrow; and, once suggested, the idea rapidly spread, and produced, through the Christian society, a series of corresponding visions, firmly believed to be real. But Mary Magdalen was the founder of it all :—

> Elle eut, en ce moment solennel, une part d'action tout à fait hors ligne. C'est elle qu'il faut suivre pas à pas;

car elle porta, ce jour-là, pendant une heure, tout le travail de la conscience chrétienne ; son témoignage décida la foi de l'avenir. . . . La vision légère s'écarte et lui dit : " Ne me touche pas ! " Peu à peu l'ombre disparaît. Mais le miracle de l'amour est accompli. Ce que Céphas n'a pu faire, Marie l'a faite ; elle a su tirer la vie, la parole douce et pénétrante, du tombeau vide. Il ne s'agit plus de conséquences à déduire ni de conjectures à former. Marie a vu et entendu. La résurrection a son premier témoin immédiat.

He proceeds to criticise the accounts which ascribe the first vision to others; but in reality Mary Magdalen, he says, has done most, after the great Teacher, for the foundation of Christianity. " Queen and patroness of idealists," she was able to "impose upon all the sacred vision of her impassioned soul." All rests upon her first burst of enthusiasm, which gave the signal and kindled the faith of others. "Sa grande affirmation de femme, 'il est ressuscité,' a été la base de la foi de l'humanité " :—

Paul ne parle pas de la vision de Marie et reporte tout l'honneur de la première apparition sur Pierre. Mais cette expression est très-inexacte. Pierre ne vit que le caveau vide, le suaire et le linceul. Marie seule aima assez pour dépasser la nature et faire revivre le fantôme du maître exquis. Dans ces sortes de crises merveilleuses, voir après les autres n'est rien ; tout le mérite est de voir pour la première fois ; car les autres modèlent ensuite leur vision sur le type reçu. C'est le propre des belles organisations de concevoir l'image promptement, avec justesse et par une sorte de sens intime du dessin. La gloire de la résurrection appartient donc à Marie de Magdala. Après Jésus, c'est Marie qui a le plus fait pour la fondation du Christianisme. L'ombre créée par les sens délicats de Madeleine plane encore sur le monde. . . . Loin d'ici, raison impuissante ! Ne va pas appliquer une froide analyse à ce chef-d'œuvre de l'idéalisme et de l'amour. Si la sagesse renonce à consoler cette pauvre race humaine, trahie par le sort, laisse la folie tenter l'aventure. Où est le sage qui a donné au monde autant de joie, que la possédée Marie de Magdala ?

He proceeds to describe, on the same supposition, the other events of the day, which he accepts as having in a certain very important sense happened, though, of course, only in the sense which excludes their reality. No doubt, for a series of hallucinations, anything will do in the way of explanation. The scene of the evening was really believed to have taken place as described, though it was the mere product of chance noises and breaths of air on minds intently expectant ; and we are bidden to remember "that in these decisive hours a current of wind, a creaking window, an accidental rustle, settle the belief of nations for centuries." But at any rate it was a decisive hour :—

Tels furent les incidents de ce jour qui a fixé le sort de l'humanité. L'opinion que Jésus était ressuscité s'y fonda d'une manière irrévocable. La secte, qu'on avait cru éteindre en tuant le maître, fut dès lors assurée d'un immense avenir.

We are willing to admit that Christian writers have often spoken unreally and unsatisfactorily enough in their comments on this subject. But what Christian comment, hard, rigid, and narrow in its view of possibilities, ever equalled this in its baselessness and supreme absence of all that makes a view look like the truth? It puts the most extravagant strain on documents which, truly or falsely, but at any rate in the most consistent and uniform manner, assert something different. What they assert in every conceivable form, and with distinct detail, are facts; it is not criticism, but mere arbitrary license, to say that all these stand for visions. The issue of truth or falsehood is intelligible; the middle supposition of confusion and mistake in that which is the basis of everything, and is definitely and in such varied ways repeated, is trifling and incredible. We may disbelieve, if we please, St Paul's enumeration of the appearances after the Resurrection; but to resolve it into a series of visions is to take refuge in the most unlikely of guesses. And, when we take into view the whole of the case—not merely the life and teaching out of which everything grew, but the aim and character of the movement which ensued, and the consequences of it, long tested and still continuing, to the history and development of mankind—we find it hard to measure the estimate of probability which is satisfied with the supposition that the incidents of one day of folly and delusion irrevocably decided the belief of ages, and the life and destiny of millions. Without the belief in the Resurrection there would have been no Christianity; if anything may be laid down as certain, this may. We should probably never have even heard of the great Teacher; He would not have been believed in, He would not have been preached to the world; the impulse to conversion would have been wanting; and all that was without parallel good and true and fruitful in His life would have perished, and have been lost in Judaea. And the belief in the Resurrection M. Renan thinks due to an hour of over-excited fancy in a woman agonized by sorrow and affection. When we are presented with an hypothesis on the basis of intrinsic probability, we cannot but remember that the power of delusion and self-deception, though undoubtedly shown in very remarkable instances, must yet be in a certain proportion to what it originates and produces, and that it is controlled by the numerous antagonistic influences of the world. Crazy women have founded superstitions; but we cannot help thinking that it would be more difficult than M. Renan supposes for crazy women to found a world-wide religion for ages, branching forth into infinite forms, and tested by its application to all varieties of civilisation, and to national and personal character. M. Renan points to La Salette. But the assumption would be a bold one that the La Salette people could have invented a religion for Christendom which would stand the wear of eighteen centuries, and satisfy such different minds. Pious frauds, as he says, may have built cathedrals. But you must take Christianity for what it has proved itself to be in its hard and unexampled trial. To start an order, a sect, an institution, even a local tradition or local set of miracles, on foundations already laid, is one thing; it is not the same to be the spring of the most serious and the deepest of moral movements for the improvement of the world, the most unpretending and the most careless of all outward form and show, the most severely searching and universal and lasting in its effects on mankind. To trace that back to the Teacher without the intervention of the belief in the Resurrection is manifestly impossible. We know what He is said to have taught; we know what has come of that teaching in the world at large; but if the link which connects the two be not a real one, it is vain to explain it by the dreams of affection. It was not a matter of a moment or an hour, but of days and weeks continually; not the assertion of one imaginative mourner or two, but of a numerous and variously constituted body of people. The story, if it was not true, was not delusion, but imposture. We certainly cannot be said to know much of what happens in the genesis of religions. But that between such a teacher and such teaching there should intervene such a gigantic falsehood, whether imposture or delusion, is unquestionably one of the hardest violations of probability conceivable, as well as one of the most desperate conclusions as regards the capacity of mankind for truth. Few thoughts can be less endurable than that the wisest and best of our race, men of the soberest and most serious tempers, and most candid and judicial minds, should have been the victims and dupes of the mad affection of a crazy Magdalen, of "ces touchantes démoniaques, ces pécheresses converties, ces vraies fondatrices du Christianisme." M. Renan shrinks from solving such a question by the hypothesis of conscious fraud. To solve it by sentiment is hardly more respectful either to the world or to truth.

We have left ourselves no room to speak of the best part of M. Renan's new volume, his historical comment on the first period of Christianity. We do not pretend to go along with him in his general principles of judgment, or in many of his most important historical conclusions. But here he is, what he is not in the early chapters, on ground where his critical faculty comes fairly into play. He is, we think, continually paradoxical and reckless in his statements; and his book is more thickly strewn than almost any we know with half-truths, broad axioms which require much paring down to be of any use, but which are made by him to do duty for want of something stronger. But, from so keen and so deeply interested a writer, it is our own fault if we do not learn a good deal. And we may study in its full development that curious combination, of which M. Renan is the most conspicuous example, of profound veneration for Christianity and sympathy with its most characteristic aspects, with the scientific impulse to destroy in the public mind the belief in its truth.

XIII

M. RENAN'S HIBBERT LECTURES[1]

I

THE object of M. Renan's lectures at St. George's Hall is, as we understand him, not merely to present a historical sketch of the influence of Rome on the early Church, but to reconcile the historical imagination with the results of his own and kindred speculations on the origin of Christianity. He has, with a good faith which we do not question, investigated the subject and formed his conclusions upon it. He on the present occasion assumes these investigations, and that he, at any rate, is satisfied with their result. He hardly pretends to carry the mixed popular audience whom he addresses into any real inquiry into the grounds on which he has satisfied himself that the received account of Christianity is not the true one. But he is aware that all minds are more or less consciously impressed with the broad difficulty that, after all attempts to trace the origin of

[1] *Guardian*, 14th April 1880.

Christianity to agencies and influences of well-understood human character, the disproportion between causes and effects still continues to appear excessive. The great Christian tradition with its definite beliefs about the conditions of man's existence, which has shaped the fortunes and determined the future of mankind on earth, is in possession of the world as much as the great tradition of right and wrong, or of the family, or of the State. How did it get there? It is most astonishing that it should have done so, what is the account of it? Of course people may inquire into this question as they may inquire into the basis of morality, or the origin of the family or the State. But here, as on those subjects, reason, and that imagination which is one of the forces of reason, by making the mind duly sensible of the magnitude of ideas and alternatives, are exacting. M. Renan's task is to make the purely human origin of Christianity, its origin in the circumstances, the beliefs, the ideas, and the moral and political conditions of the first centuries, seem to us *natural*—as natural in the history of the world as other great and surprising events and changes — as natural as the growth and the fall of the Roman Empire, or as the Reformation, or the French Revolution. He is well qualified to sound the depths of his undertaking and to meet its heavy exigencies. With a fuller knowledge of books, and a closer familiarity than most men with the thoughts and the events of the early ages, with a serious value for the idea of religion as such, and certainly with no feeble powers of recalling the past and investing it with colour and life, he has to show how these things can be—how a religion with such attributes as he freely ascribes to the Gospel, so grand, so pure, so lasting, can have sprung up not merely *in* but *from* a most corrupt and immoral time, and can have its root in the most portentous and impossible of falsehoods. It must be said to be a bold undertaking.

M. Renan has always aimed at doing justice to what he assailed; Christians, who realise what they believe, will say that he patronises their religion, and naturally they resent such patronage. Such candour adds doubtless to the literary effect of his method; but it is only due to him to acknowledge the fairness of his admissions. He starts with the declaration that there never was a nobler moment in human history than the beginnings of the Christian Church. It was the "most heroic episode in the annals of mankind." "Never did man draw forth from his bosom more devotion, more love of the ideal, than in the 150 years which elapsed between the sweet Galilean vision and the death of Marcus Aurelius." It was not only that the saints were admirable and beautiful in their lives; they had the secret of the future, and laid down the lines on which the goodness and hope of the coming world were to move. "Never was the religious conscience more eminently creative, never did it lay down with more authority the law of future ages."

Now, if this is not mere rhetoric, what does it come to? It means not merely that there was here a phenomenon, not only extraordinary but unique, in the development of human character, but that here was created or evolved what was to guide and form the religious ideas of mankind; here were the springs of what has reached through all the ages of expanding humanity to our own days, of what is best and truest and deepest and holiest. M. Renan, at any rate, does not think this an illusion of Christian prepossessions, a fancy picture of a mythic age of gold, of an unhistorical period of pure and primitive antiquity. Put this view of things by the side of any of the records or the literature of the time remaining to us; if not St. Paul's Epistles nor Tacitus nor Lucian, then Virgil and Horace and Cicero, or Seneca or Epictetus or Marcus Aurelius. Is it possible by any effort of imagination to body forth the links which can solidly connect the ideas which live and work and grow on one side, with the ideas which are represented by the facts and principles of the other side? Or is it any more possible to connect what we know of Christian ideas and convictions by a bond of natural and intelligible, if not necessary derivation, with what we know of Jewish ideas and Jewish habits of thought at the time in question? Yet that is the thing to be done, to be done rigorously, to be done clearly and distinctly, by those who are satisfied to find the impulses and faith which gave birth to Christianity amid the seething confusions of the time which saw its beginning; absolutely identical with those wild movements in origin and nature, and only by a strange, fortunate accident immeasurably superior to them.

This question M. Renan has not answered; as far as we can see he has not perceived that it is the first question for him to answer, in giving a philosophical account of the history of Christianity. Instead, he tells us, and he is going still further to tell us, how Rome and its wonderful influences acted on Christianity, and helped to assure its victories. But, first of all, what is that Christianity, and whence did it come, which Rome so helped? It came, he says, from Judaism; "it was Judaism under its Christian form which Rome propagated without wishing it, yet with such mighty energy that from a certain epoch Romanism and Christianity became synonymous words"; it was Jewish monotheism, the religion the Roman hated and despised, swallowing up by its contrast all that was local, legendary, and past belief, and presenting one religious law to the countless nationalities of the Empire, which like itself was one, and like itself above all nationalities.

This may all be true, and is partially true; but how did that hated and partial Judaism break through its trammels, and become a religion for all men, and a religion to which all men gathered? The Roman organisation was an admirable vehicle for Christianity; but the vehicle does not make that which it carries, or account for it. M. Renan's picture of the Empire abounds with all those picturesque details which he knows so well where to find, and knows so well, too, how to place in an interesting light. There were then, of course, conditions of the time more favourable to the Christian Church than would have been the conditions of other times. There was a certain increased liberty of thought, though there were also some pretty strong obstacles to it. M. Renan has Imperial proclivities, and reminds us truly enough that despotisms are sometimes more tolerant than democracies, and that political liberty is not the same as spiritual and mental freedom, and does not always favour it. It may be partially true, as he says, that "Virgil and Tibullus show that Roman harshness and cruelty were softening down"; that "equality and the rights of men were preached by the Stoics"; that "woman was more her own mistress, and slaves were better treated than in the days of Cato"; that "very humane and just laws were enacted under the very worst emperors; that Tiberius and Nero were able financiers"; that "after the terrible butcheries of the old centuries, mankind was crying with the voice of Virgil for peace and pity." A good many qualifications and abatements start up in our minds on reading these statements, and a good many formidable doubts suggest themselves, if we can at all believe what has come down to us of the history of these times. It is hard to accept quite literally the bold assertion that "love for the poor, sympathy with all men, almsgiving, were becoming virtues."

But allow this as the fair and hopeful side of the Empire. Yet all this is a long way from accounting for the effects on the world of Christianity, even in the dim, vaporous form in which M. Renan imagines it, much more in the actual concrete reality in which, if we know anything, it appeared. "Christianity," he says, "responded to the cry for peace and pity of all weary and tender souls." No doubt it did; but what was it that responded, and what was its consolation, and whence was its power drawn? What was there in the known thoughts or hopes or motives of men at the time to furnish such a response? "Christianity," he says, "could only have been born and spread at a time when men had no longer a country"; "it was that explosion of social and religious ideas which became inevitable after Augustus had put an end to political struggles," after his policy had killed "patriotism." It is true enough that the first Christians, believing themselves subjects of an Eternal King and in view of an eternal world, felt themselves strangers and pilgrims in this; yet did the rest of the Roman world under the Caesars feel that they had no country, and was the idea of patriotism extinct in the age of Agricola? But surely the real question worth asking is, What was it amid the increasing civilisation and prosperous peace of Rome under the first Emperors which made these Christians relinquish the idea of a country? From whence did Christianity draw its power to set its followers in inflexible opposition to the intensest worship of the State that the world has ever known?

To tell us the conditions under which all this occurred is not to tell us the cause of it. We follow with interest the sketches which M. Renan gives of these conditions, though it must be said that his generalisations are often extravagantly loose and misleading. We do indeed want to know more of those wonderful but hidden days which intervene between the great Advent, with its subsequent Apostolic age, and the days when the Church appears fully constituted and recognised. German research and French intelligence and constructiveness have done something to help us, but not much. But at the end of all such inquiries appears the question of questions, What was the beginning and root of it all? Christians have a reasonable answer to the question. There is none, there is not really the suggestion of one, in M. Renan's account of the connection of Christianity with the Roman world.

II[1]

M. RENAN has pursued the line of thought indicated in his first lecture, and in his succeeding lectures has developed the idea that Christianity, as we know it, was born in Imperial Rome, and that in its visible form and active influence on the world it was the manifest

[1] *Guardian*, 21st April 1880.

product of Roman instincts and habits; it was the spirit of the Empire passing into a new body and accepting in exchange for political power, as it slowly decayed and vanished, a spiritual supremacy as unrivalled and as astonishing. The "Legend of the Roman Church—Peter and Paul," "Rome the Centre in which Church Authority grew up," and "Rome the Capital of Catholicism," are the titles of the three lectures in which this thesis is explained and illustrated. A lecture on Marcus Aurelius, at the Royal Institution, though not one of the series, is obviously connected with it, and concludes M. Renan's work in England.

Except the brilliant bits of writing which, judging from the full abstracts given in translation in the *Times*, appear to have been interspersed, and except the undoubting self-confidence and *aplomb* with which a historical survey, reversing the common ideas of mankind, was delivered, there was little new to be learned from M. Renan's treatment of his subject. Perhaps it may be described as the Roman Catholic theory of the rise of the Church, put in an infidel point of view. It is Roman Catholic in concentrating all interest, all the sources of influence and power in the Christian religion and Christian Church, from the first moment at Rome. But for Rome the Christian Church would not have existed. The Church is inconceivable without Rome, and Rome as the seat and centre of its spiritual activity. Everything else is forgotten.

There were Christian Churches all over the Empire, in Syria, in Egypt, in Africa, in Asia Minor, in Gaul, in Greece. A great body of Christian literature, embodying the ideas and character of Christians all over the Empire, was growing up, and this was not Roman and had nothing to do with Rome; it was Greek as much as Latin, and local, not metropolitan, in its characteristics. Christianity was spreading here, there, and everywhere, slowly and imperceptibly as the tide comes in, or as cells multiply in the growing tissues of organised matter; it was spreading under its many distinct guides and teachers, and taking possession of the cities and provinces of the Empire. All this great movement, the real foundation of all that was to be, is overlooked and forgotten in the attention which is fixed on Rome and confined to it. As in the Roman Catholic view, M. Renan brings St. Paul and St. Peter together to Rome, to found that great Imperial Church in which the manifold and varied history of Christendom is merged and swallowed up. Only, of course, M. Renan brings them there as "fanatics" instead of Apostles and martyrs. We know something about St. Peter and St. Paul. We know them at any rate from their writings. In M. Renan's representation they stand opposed to one another as leaders of factions, to whose fierce hatreds and jealousies there is nothing comparable. "All the differences," he is reported to say, "which divide orthodox folks, heretics, schismatics, in our own day, are as nothing compared with the dissension between Peter and Paul." It is, as every one knows, no new story; but there it is in M. Renan in all its crudity, as if it were the most manifest and accredited of truths. M. Renan first brings St. Paul to Rome. "It was," he says, "a great event in the world's history, almost as pregnant with consequences as his conversion." How it was so M. Renan does not explain; but he brings St. Peter to Rome also, "following at the heels of St. Paul," to counteract and neutralise his influence. And who is this St Peter? He represents the Jewish element; and what that element was at Rome M. Renan takes great pains to put before us. He draws an elaborate picture of the Jews and Jewish quarter of Rome—a "longshore population" of beggars and pedlars, with a Ghetto resembling the Alsatia of *The Fortunes of Nigel*, seething with dirt and fanaticism. These were St. Peter's congeners at Rome, whose ideas and claims, "timid trimmer" though he was, he came to Rome to support against the Hellenism and Protestantism of St. Paul. And at Rome they, both of them, probably, perished in Nero's persecution, and that is the history of the success of Christianity. "Only fanatics can found anything. Judaism lives on because of the intense frenzy of its prophets and annalists, Christianity by means of its martyrs."

But a certain Clement arose after their deaths, to arrange a reconciliation between the fiercely antagonistic factions of St. Peter and St. Paul. How he harmonised them M. Renan leaves us to imagine; but he did reconcile them; he gathered in his own person the authority of the Roman Church; he lectured the Corinthian Church on its turbulence and insubordination; he anticipated, M. Renan remarked, almost in words, the famous saying of the French Archbishop of Rouen, "My clergy are my regiment, and they are drilled to obey like a regiment." On this showing, Clement might almost be described as the real founder of Christianity, of which neither St. Peter nor St. Paul, with their violent oppositions, can claim to be the complete representative; at any rate he was the first Pope, complete in all his attributes. And in accordance with this beginning M. Renan sees in the Roman Church, first, the centre in which Church authority grew up, and next, the capital of Catholicism. In Rome the congregation gave up its rights to its elders, and these rights the elders surrendered to the single ruler or Bishop. The creation of the Episcopate was eminently the work of Rome; and this Bishop of Rome caught the full spirit of the Caesar, on whose decay he became great; and troubling himself little about the deep questions which exercised the minds and wrung the hearts of thinkers and mystics, he made himself the foundation of order, authority, and subordination to all parts of the Imperial world.

Such is M. Renan's explanation of the great march and triumph of the Christian Church. The Roman Empire, which we had supposed was the natural enemy of the Church, was really the founder of all that made the Church strong, and bequeathed to the Church its prerogatives and its spirit, and partly its machinery. We should hardly gather from this picture that there was, besides, a widespread Catholic Church, with its numerous centres of life and thought and teaching, and with very slight connection, in the early times, with the Church of the capital. And, in the next place, we should gather from it that there was little more in the Church than a powerful and strongly built system of centralised organisation and control; we should hardly suspect the existence of the real questions which interested or disturbed it ; we should hardly suspect the existence of a living and all-engrossing theology, or the growth and energy in it of moral forces, or that the minds of Christians about the world were much more busy with the discipline of life, the teaching and meaning of the inspired words of Scripture, and the ever-recurring conflict with perverseness and error, than with their dependent connection on the Imperial Primacy of Rome, and the lessons they were to learn from it.

Disguised as it may be, M. Renan's lectures represent not history, but scepticism as to all possibility of history. Pictures of a Jewish Ghetto, with its ragged mendicants smelling of garlic, in places where Christians have been wont to think of the Saints ; ingenious explanations as to the way in which the "club" of the Christian Church surrendered its rights to a *bureau* of its officers ; exhortations to liberty and tolerance ; side-glances at the contrasts of national gifts and destinies and futures in the first century and in the nineteenth ; felicitous parallels and cunning epigrams, subtle combinations of the pathetic, the egotistical, and the cynical, all presented with calm self-reliance and in the most finished and distinguished of styles, may veil for the moment from the audience which such things amuse, and even interest, the hollowness which lies beneath. But the only meaning of the lectures is to point out more forcibly than ever that besides the obvious riddles of man's life there is one stranger and more appalling still—that a religion which M. Renan can never speak of without admiration and enthusiasm is based on a self-contradiction and deluding falsehood, more dreadful in its moral inconsistencies than the grave.

We cannot help feeling that M. Renan himself is a true representative of that highly cultivated society of the Empire which would have crushed Christianity, and which Christianity vanquished. He still owes something, and owns it, to what he has abandoned— "I am often tempted to say, as Job said, in our Latin version, *Etiam si occiderit me, in ipso sperabo.* But the next moment all is gone—all is but a symbol and a dream." There is no possibility of solving the religious problem. He relapses into profound disbelief of the worth and success of moral efforts after truth. His last word is an exhortation to tolerance for "fanatics," as the best mode of extinguishing them. "If, instead of leading *Polyeucte* to punishment, the magistrate, with a smile and shake of the hand, had sent him home again, *Polyeucte* would not have been caught offending again; perhaps, in his old age, he would even have laughed at his escapade, and would have become a sensible man." It is as obvious and natural in our days to dispose of such difficulties in this way with a smile and a sneer as it was in the first century with a shout—"*Christiani ad leones.*" But Corneille was as good a judge of the human heart as M. Renan. He had gauged the powers of faith and conviction; he certainly would have expected to find his *Polyeucte* more obstinate.

XIV

RENAN'S "SOUVENIRS D'ENFANCE"[1]

THE sketches which M. Renan gives us of his early life are what we should have looked for from the writer of the *Vie de Jésus*. The story of the disintegration of a faith is supposed commonly to have something tragic about it. We expect it to be a story of heart-breaking disenchantments, of painful struggles, of fierce recoils against ancient beliefs and the teachers who bolstered them up; of indignation at having been so long deceived; of lamentation over years wasted in the service of falsehood. The confessions of St. Augustine, the biography of Blanco White, the letters of Lamennais, at least agree in the witness which they bear to the bitter pangs and anxieties amid which, in their case, the eventful change came about. Even Cardinal Newman's *Apologia*, self-restrained and severely controlled as it is, shows no doubtful traces of the conflicts and sorrows out of which he believed himself to

[1] *Souvenirs d'Enfance et de Jeunesse.* Par Ernest Renan. *Guardian*, 18th July 1883.

have emerged to a calmer and surer light. But M. Renan's story is an idyl, not a tragedy. It is sunny, placid, contented. He calls his life the "*charmante promenade*" which the "cause of all good," whatever that may be, has granted him through the realities of existence. There are in it no storms of passion, no cruelties of circumstances, no deplorable mistakes, no complaints, no recriminations. His life flows on smoothly, peacefully, happily, with little of rapids and broken waters, gradually and in the most natural and inevitable way enlarging itself, moving in new and wider channels and with increased volume and force, but never detaching itself and breaking off from its beginnings. It is a spectacle which M. Renan, who has lived this life, takes a gentle pleasure in contemplating. He looks back on it with thankfulness, and also with amusement. It makes a charming and complete picture. No part could be wanting without injuring the effect of the whole. It is the very ideal of the education of the Rousseau school—a child of nature, developing, amid the simplest and humblest circumstances of life, the finest gifts and most delicate graces of faith and reverence and purity—brought up by sages whose wisdom he could not in time help outrunning, but whose piety, sweetness, disinterestedness, and devoted labour left on his mind impressions which nothing could wear out; and at length, when the time came, passing naturally, and without passion or bitterness, from out of their faithful but too narrow discipline into a wider and ampler air, and becoming, as was fit, master and guide to himself, with light which they could not bear, and views of truth greater and deeper than they could conceive. But every stage of the progress, through the virtues of the teachers, and the felicitous disposition of the pupil, exhibits both in exactly the due relations in which each ought to be with the other, with none of the friction of rebellious and refractory temper on one side, or of unintelligent harshness on the other. He has nothing to regret in the schools through which he passed, in the preparations which he made there for the future, in the way in which they shaped his life. He lays down the maxim, "On ne doit jamais écrire que de ce qu'on aime." There is a serene satisfaction diffused through the book, which scarcely anything intervenes to break or disturb; he sees so much poetry in his life, so much content, so much signal and unlooked-for success, that he has little to tell except what is delightful and admirable. And then he is so certain that he is right: he can look down with so much good-humoured superiority on past and present, alike on what he calls "l'effroyable aventure du moyen âge," and on the march of modern society to the dead level of "Americanism." It need not be said that the story is told with all M. Renan's consummate charm of storytelling. All that it wants is depth of real feeling and seriousness—some sense of the greatness of what he has had to give up, not merely of its poetic beauty and tender associations. It hardly seems to occur to him that something more than his easy cheerfulness and his vivid historical imagination is wanted to solve for him the problems of the world, and that his gradual transition from the Catholicism of the seminary to the absolute rejection of the supernatural in religion does not, as he describes it, throw much light on the question of the hopes and destiny of mankind.

The outline of his story is soon told. It is in general like that of many more who in France have broken away from religion. A clever studious boy, a true son of old Brittany—the most melancholy, the most tender, the most ardent, the most devout, not only of all French provinces, but of all regions in Europe—is passed on from the teaching of good, simple, hard-working country priests to the central seminaries, where the leaders of the French clergy are educated. He comes up a raw, eager, ignorant provincial, full of zeal for knowledge, full of reverence and faith, and first goes through the distinguished literary school of St. Nicolas du Chardonnet, of which Dupanloup was the founder and the inspiring soul. Thence he passed under the more strictly professional discipline of St. Sulpice: first at the preparatory philosophical school at Issy, then to study scientific theology in the house of St. Sulpice itself at Paris. At St. Sulpice he showed special aptitudes for the study of Hebrew, in which he was assisted and encouraged by M. le Hir, "the most remarkable person," in his opinion, "whom the

French clergy has produced in our days," a "savant and a saint," who had mastered the results of German criticism as they were found in the works of Gesenius and Ewald. On his faith all this knowledge had not made the faintest impression; but it was this knowledge which broke down M. Renan's, and finally led to his retiring from St. Sulpice. On the one side was the Bible and Catholic theology, carefully, scientifically, and consistently taught at St. Sulpice; on the other were the exegesis and the historical criticism of the German school. He came at length to the conclusion that the two are incompatible; that there was but a choice of alternatives; and purely on the ground of historical criticism, he says, not on any abstract objections to the supernatural, or to miracles, or to Catholic dogma, he gave up revealed religion. He gave it up not without regrets at the distress caused to friends, and at parting with much that was endeared to him by old associations, and by intrinsic beauty and value; but, as far as can be judged, without any serious sense of loss. He spent some time in obscurity, teaching, and studying laboriously, and at length beginning to write. Michel Lévy, the publisher, found him out, and opened to him a literary career, and in due time he became famous. He has had the ambiguous honour of making the Bible an object of such interest to French readers as it never was before, at the cost of teaching them to find in it a reflection of their own characteristic ways of looking at life and the world. It is not an easy thing to do with such a book as the Bible; but he has done it.

As a mere history of a change of convictions, the *Souvenirs* are interesting, but hardly of much importance. They are written with a kind of Epicurean serenity and dignity, avoiding all exaggeration and violence, profuse in every page in the delicacies and also in the reticences of respect, not too serious to exclude the perpetual suggestion of a well-behaved amused irony, not too much alive to the ridiculous and the self-contradictory to forget the attitude of composure due to the theme of the book. He warns his readers at the outset that they must not look for a stupid literalness in his account. "Ce qu'on dit de soi est toujours poésie" —the reflection of states of mind and varying humours, not the exact details of fact. "Tout est vrai dans ce petit volume, mais non de ce genre de vérité qui est requis pour une *Biographie universelle*. Bien des choses ont été mises, afin qu'on sourie; si l'usage l'eût permis, j'aurais dû écrire plus d'une fois à la marge—*cum grano salis.*" It is candid to warn us thus to read a little between the lines; but it is a curious and unconscious disclosure of his characteristic love of a mixture of the misty and the clear. The really pleasant part of it is his account, which takes up half the volume, of Breton ways and feelings half a century ago, an account which exactly tallies with the pictures of them in Souvestre's writings; and the kindliness and justice with which he speaks of his old Catholic and priestly teachers, not only in his boyish days at Tréguier, but in his seminary life in Paris. His account of this seminary life is unique in its picturesque vividness. He describes how, at St. Nicolas, under the fiery and irresistible Dupanloup, whom he speaks of with the reserved courtesy due to a distinguished person whom he much dislikes, his eager eyes were opened to the realities of literature, and to the subtle powers of form and style in writing, which have stood him in such stead, and have been the real secret of his own success.

> Le monde s'ouvrit pour moi. Malgré sa prétention d'être un asile fermé aux bruits du dehors, Saint-Nicolas était à cette époque la maison la plus brillante et la plus mondaine. Paris y entrait à pleins bords par les portes et les fenêtres, Paris tout entier, moins la corruption, je me hâte de le dire, Paris avec ses petitesses et ses grandeurs, ses hardiesses et ses chiffons, sa force révolutionnaire et ses mollesses flasques. Mes vieux prêtres de Bretagne savaient bien mieux les mathématiques et le latin que mes nouveaux maîtres ; mais ils vivaient dans des catacombes sans lumière et sans air. Ici, l'atmosphère du siècle circulait librement. . . . Au bout de quelque temps une chose tout à fait inconnue m'était révélée. Les mots, talent, éclat, réputation eurent un sens pour moi. J'étais perdu pour l'idéal modeste que mes anciens maîtres m'avaient inculqué.

And he describes how Dupanloup brought his pupils perpetually into direct relations with himself and communicated to them something of his own enthusiasm. He gained the power over their hearts which a great general gains over his soldiers. His approval, his interest in a man, were the all-absorbing object, the all-sufficient reward; the one punishment feared was dismissal, always inflicted with courtesy and tact, from the honour and the joy of serving under him :—

Adoré de ses élèves, M. Dupanloup n'était pas toujours agréable à ces collaborateurs. On m'a dit que, plus tard, dans son diocèse, les choses se passèrent de la même manière, qu'il fut toujours plus aimé de ses laïques que de ses prêtres. Il est certain qu'il écrasait tout autour de lui. Mais sa violence même nous attachait; car nous sentions que nous étions son but unique. Ce qu'il était, c'était un éveilleur incomparable ; pour tirer de chacun de ses élèves la somme de ce qu'il pouvait donner, personne ne l'égalait. Chacun de ses deux cents élèves existait distinct dans sa pensée; il était pour chacun d'eux l'excitateur toujours présent, le motif de vivre et de travailler. Il croyait au talent et en faisait la base de la foi. Il répétait souvent que l'homme vaut en proportion de sa faculté d'admirer. Son admiration n'était pas toujours assez éclairée par la science ; mais elle venait d'une grande chaleur d'âme et d'un cœur vraiment possédé de l'amour du beau. . . . Les défauts de l'éducation qu'il donnait étaient les défauts même de son esprit. Il était trop peu rationnel, trop peu scientifique. On eût dit que ses deux cents élèves étaient destinés à être tous poètes, écrivains, orateurs.

St. Nicolas was literary. Issy and St. Sulpice

were severely philosophic and scientific, places of *"fortes études"*; and the writer thinks that they were more to his own taste than the more brilliant literary education given under Dupanloup. In one sense it may be so. They introduced him to exactness of thought and precision of expression, and they widened his horizon of possible and attainable knowledge. He passed, he says, from words to things. But he is a writer who owes so much to the form into which he throws his thoughts, to the grace and brightness and richness of his style, that he probably is a greater debtor to the master whom he admires and dislikes, Dupanloup, than to the modest, reserved, and rather dull Sulpician teachers, whom he loves and reveres and smiles at, whose knowledge of theology was serious, profound, and accurate, and whose characteristic temper was one of moderation and temperate reason, joined to a hatred of display, and a suspicion of all that seemed too clever and too brilliant. But his witness to their excellence, to their absolute self-devotion to their work, to their dislike of extravagance and exaggeration, to their good sense and cultivation, is ungrudging and warm. Of course he thinks them utterly out of date; but on their own ground he recognises that they were men of strength and solidity, the best and most thorough of teachers; the most sincere, the most humble, the most self-forgetting of priests :—

Beaucoup de mes jugements étonnent les gens du monde parcequ'ils n'ont pas vu ce que j'ai vu. J'ai vu à

Saint-Sulpice, associés à des idées étroites, je l'avoue, les miracles que nos races peuvent produire en fait de bonté, de modestie, d'abnégation personelle. Ce qu'il y a de vertu à Saint-Sulpice suffirait pour gouverner un monde, et cela m'a rendu difficile pour ce que j'ai trouvé ailleurs.

M. Renan, as we have said, is very just to his education, and to the men who gave it. He never speaks of them except with respect and gratitude. It is seldom, indeed, that he permits himself anything like open disparagement of the men and the cause which he forsook. The shafts of his irony are reserved for men on his own side, for the radical violences of M. Clémenceau, and for the exaggerated reputation of Auguste Comte, "who has been set up as a man of the highest order of genius, for having said, in bad French, what all scientific thinkers for two hundred years have seen as clearly as himself." He attributes to his ecclesiastical training those excellences in his own temper and principles on which he dwells with much satisfaction and thankfulness. They are, he considers, the result of his Christian and "Sulpician" education, though the root on which they grew is for ever withered and dead. "La foi disparue, la morale reste. . . . C'est par le caractère que je suis resté essentiellement l'élève de mes anciens maîtres." He is proud of these virtues, and at the same time amused at the odd contradictions in which they have sometimes involved him :—

Il me plairait d'expliquer par le détail et de montrer

comment la gageure paradoxale de garder les vertus
cléricales, sans la foi qui leur sert de base et dans un
monde pour lequel elles ne sont pas faites, produisit, en
ce que me concerne, les rencontres les plus divertissantes.
J'aimerais à raconter toutes les aventures que mes vertus
sulpiciennes m'amenèrent, et les tours singuliers qu'elles
m'ont joués. Après soixante ans de vie sérieuse on a le
droit de sourire ; et où trouver une source de rire plus
abondante, plus à portée, plus inoffensive qu'en soi-
même ? Si jamais un auteur comique voulait amuser le
public de mes ridicules, je ne lui demanderais qu'une
chose ; c'est de me prendre pour collaborateur ; je lui
conterais des choses vingt fois plus amusantes que celles
qu'il pourrait inventer.

He dwells especially on four of these virtues which
were, he thinks, graven ineffaceably on his nature at St.
Sulpice. They taught him there not to care for money
or success. They taught him the old-fashioned
French politeness—that beautiful instinct of giving
place to others, which is perishing in the democratic
scramble for the best places, in the omnibus and the
railway as in business and society. It is more curious
to find that he thinks that they taught him to be
modest. Except on the faith of his assertions, the
readers of his book would not naturally have supposed
that he believed himself specially endowed with this
quality; it is at any rate the modesty which, if it
shrinks into retirement from the pretensions of the
crowd, goes along with a high and pitying sense of
superiority, and a self-complacency of which the good

humour never fails. His masters also taught him to value purity. For this he almost makes a sort of deprecating apology. He saw, indeed, "the vanity of this virtue as of all the others"; he admits that it is an unnatural virtue. But he says, "L'homme ne doit jamais se permettre deux hardiesses à la fois. Le libre penseur doit être réglé en ses mœurs." In this doctrine it may be doubted whether he will find many followers. An unnatural virtue, where nature only is recognised as a guide, is more likely to be discredited by his theory than recommended by his example, particularly if the state of opinion in France is such as is described in the following passage—a passage which in England few men, whatever they might think, would have the boldness to state as an acknowledged social phenomenon :—

Le monde, dont les jugements sont rarement tout à fait faux, voit une sorte de ridicule à être vertueux quand on n'y est pas obligé par un devoir professionnel. Le prêtre, ayant pour état d'être chaste, comme le soldat d'être brave, est, d'après ces idées, presque le seul qui puisse sans ridicule tenir à des principes sur lesquels la morale et la mode se livrent les plus étranges combats. Il est hors de doute qu'en ce point, comme en beaucoup d'autres, mes principes cléricaux, conservés dans le siècle, m'ont nui aux yeux du monde.

We have one concluding observation to make. This is a book of which the main interest, after all, depends on the way in which it touches on the question of questions, the truth and reality of the Christian religion. But from first to last it does not show the faintest evidence that the writer ever really knew, or even cared, what religion is. Religion is not only a matter of texts, of scientific criticisms, of historical investigations, of a consistent theology. It is not merely a procession of external facts and events, a spectacle to be looked at from the outside. It is, if it is anything, the most considerable and most universal interest in the complex aggregate of human interests. It grows out of the deepest moral roots, out of the most characteristic and most indestructible spiritual elements, out of wants and needs and aspirations and hopes, without which man, as we know him, would not be man. When a man, in asking whether Christianity is true, leaves out all this side of the matter, when he shows that it has not come before him as a serious and importunate reality, when he shows that he is unaffected by those deep movements and misgivings and anxieties of the soul to which religion corresponds, and treats the whole matter as a question only of erudition and criticism, we may acknowledge him to be an original and acute critic, a brilliant master of historical representation; but he has never yet come face to face with the problems of religion. His love of truth may be unimpeachable, but he does not know what he is talking about. M. Renan speaks of giving up his religion as a man might speak of accepting a new and unpopular physical hypothesis like evolution, or of making up his mind to give up the personality of Homer or the early history of Rome. Such an interior attitude of mind towards religion as is implied, for instance, in Bishop Butler's *Sermons on the Love of God*, or the *De Imitatione*, or Newman's *Parochial Sermons*, seems to him, as far as we can judge, an unknown and unattempted experience. It is easy to deal with a question if you leave out half the factors of it, and those the most difficult and the most serious. It is easy to be clear if you do not choose to take notice of the mysterious, and if you exclude from your consideration as vague and confused all that vast department of human concerns where we at best can only "see through a glass darkly." It is easy to find the world a pleasant and comfortable and not at all perplexing place, if your life has been, as M. Renan describes his own, a "charming promenade" through it; if, as he says, you are blessed with "a good humour not easily disturbed"; and you "have not suffered much"; and "nature has prepared cushions to soften shocks"; and you have "had so much enjoyment in this life that you really have no right to claim any compensation beyond it." That is M. Renan's experience of life—a life of which he looks forward to the perfection in the clearness and security of its possible denials of ancient beliefs, and in the immense development of its positive and experimental knowledge. How would Descartes have rejoiced, he says, if he could have seen some poor treatise on physics or cosmography of our day, and what would we not give to catch a glimpse of such an elementary schoolbook of a hundred years hence.

But that is not at any rate the experience of all the world, nor does it appear likely ever to be within the reach of all the world. There is another aspect of life more familiar than this, an aspect which has presented itself to the vast majority of mankind, the awful view of it which is made tragic by pain and sorrow and moral evil; which, in the way in which religion looks at it, if it is sterner, is also higher and nobler, and is brightened by hope and purposes of love; a view which puts more upon men and requires more from them, but holds before them a destiny better than the perfection here of physical science. To minds which realise all this, it is more inconceivable than any amount of miracle that such a religion as Christianity should have emerged naturally out of the conditions of the first century. They refuse to settle such a question by the short and easy method on which M. Renan relies; they will not consent to put it on questions about the two Isaiahs, or about alleged discrepancies between the Evangelists; they will not think the claims of religion disposed of by M. Renan's canon, over and over again contradicted, that whether there can be or not, there *is* no evidence of the supernatural in the world. To those who measure and feel the true gravity of the issues, it is almost unintelligible to find a man who has been face to face with Christianity all his life treating the deliberate condemnation of it almost gaily and with a light heart, and showing no regrets in having to give it up as a delusion and a dream. It is a poor and meagre end of a life of thought and study to come to the conclusion that the age in which he has lived is, if not one of the greatest, at least "the most amusing of all ages."

XV

LIFE OF FREDERICK ROBERTSON[1]

IF the proof of a successful exhibition of a strongly marked and original character be that it excites and sustains interest throughout, that our tastes are appealed to and our judgments called forth with great strength, that we pass continuously and rapidly, as we read, from deep and genuine admiration to equally deep and genuine dissent and disapprobation, that it allows us to combine a general but irresistible sense of excellence growing upon us through the book with an under-current of real and honest dislike and blame, then this book in a great measure satisfies the condition of success. It is undeniable that in what it shows us of Mr. Robertson there is much to admire, much to sympathise with, much to touch us, a good deal to instruct us. He is set before us, indeed, by the editor, as the ideal of all that a great Christian teacher and spiritual guide, all that a brave and wise and high-souled man, may be con-

[1] *Life and Letters of Frederick W. Robertson.* Edited by Stopford A. Brooke. *Guardian,* 15th November 1865.

ceived to be. We cannot quite accept him as an example of such rare and signal achievement; and the fault of the book is the common one of warm-hearted biographers to wind their own feelings and those of their readers too high about their subject; to talk as if their hero's excellences were unknown till he appeared to display them, and to make up for the imperfect impression resulting from actual facts and qualities by insisting with overstrained emphasis on a particular interpretation of them. The book would be more truthful and more pleasing if the editor's connecting comments were more simply written, and made less pretension to intensity and energy of language. Yet with all drawbacks of what seem to us imperfect taste, an imperfect standard of character, and an imperfect appreciation of what there is in the world beyond a given circle of interests, the book does what a biography ought to do—it shows us a remarkable man, and it gives us the means of forming our own judgment about him. It is not a tame panegyric or a fancy picture.

The main portion of the book consists of Mr. Robertson's own letters, and his own accounts of himself; and we are allowed to see him, in a great degree at least, as he really was. The editor draws a moral, indeed, and tells us what we ought to think about what we see; but we can use our own judgment about that. And, as so often happens in real life, what we see both attracts and repels; it calls forth, successively and in almost equal measure, warm sympathy and admiration, and distinct and hearty disagreement. At least there is nothing of commonplace—of what is commonplace yet in our generation; though there is a good deal that bids fair to become commonplace in the next. It is the record of a genuine spontaneous character, seeking its way, its duty, its perfection, with much sincerity and elevation of purpose, and many anxieties and sorrows, and not, we doubt not, without much of the fruits that come with real self-devotion; a record disclosing a man with great faults and conspicuous blanks in his nature, one with whose principles, taste, or judgment we constantly find ourselves having a vehement quarrel, just after having been charmed and conciliated by some unexpectedly powerful or refined statement of an important truth. We cannot think, and few besides his own friends will think, that he had laid his hand with so sure an accuracy and with so much promise upon the clue which others had lost or bungled over. But there is much to learn in his thoughts and words, and there is not less to learn from his life. It is the life of a man who did not spare himself in fulfilling what he received as his task, who sacrificed much in order to speak his message, as he thought, more worthily and to do his office more effectually, and whose career touches us the more from the shadow of suffering and early death that hangs over its aspirations and activity. A book which fairly shows us such a life is not of less value because it also shows us much that we regret and condemn.

Mr. Robertson was brought up not only in the straitest traditions of the Evangelical school, but in the heat of its controversial warfare. His heart, when he was a boy, was set on entering the army; and one of his most characteristic points through life, shown in many very different forms, was his pugnacity, his keen perception of the "*certaminis gaudia*":—

"There is something of combativeness in me," he writes, "which prevents the whole vigour being drawn out, except when I have an antagonist to deal with, a falsehood to quell, or a wrong to avenge. Never till then does my mind feel quite alive. Could I have chosen my own period of the world to have lived in, and my own type of life, it should be the feudal ages, and the life of a Cid, the redresser of wrongs."

. . . . . .

"On the other hand," writes his biographer, "when he met men who despised Christianity, or who, like the Roman Catholics, held to doctrines which he believed untrue, this very enthusiasm and unconscious excitement swept him sometimes beyond himself. He could not moderate his indignation down to the cool level of ordinary life. Hence he was wanting at this time in the wise tolerance which formed so conspicuous a feature of his maturer manhood. He held to his own views with pertinacity. He believed them to be true; and he almost refused to allow the possibility of the views of others having truth in them also. He was more or less one-sided at this period. With the Roman Catholic religion it was war to the death, not in his later mode of warfare, by showing the truth which lay beneath the error, but by denouncing the error. He seems invariably, with the pugnacity of a young man, to have attacked their faith; and the mode in which this was done was startlingly different from that which afterwards he adopted."

He yielded, after considerable resistance, to the wishes and advice of his friends, that he should prepare for orders. "With a romantic instinct of self-sacrifice," says his biographer, "he resolved to give up the idea of his whole life." This we can quite understand; but with that propensity of biographers to credit their subject with the desirable qualities which it may be supposed that they ought to have, besides those which they really have, the editor proceeds to observe that this would scarcely have happened had not Mr. Robertson's "*characteristic self-distrust* disposed him to believe that he was himself the worst judge of his future profession." This is the way in which the true outline of a character is blurred and confused, in order to say something proper and becoming. Self-distrust was not among the graces or weaknesses of Mr. Robertson's nature, unless indeed we mistake for it the anxiety which even the stoutest heart may feel at a crisis, or the dissatisfaction which the proudest may feel at the interval between attempt and achievement.

He was an undergraduate at Brasenose at the height of the Oxford movement. He was known there, so far as he was known at all, as a keen partisan of the Evangelical school; and though no one then suspected the power which was really in him, his party, not rich in men of strength or promise, made the most of a recruit who showed ability and entered heartily into their watchwords, and, it must be said, their rancour. He was conspicuous among the young men of his standing for the forwardness with which he took his side against "Tractarianism," and the vehemence of his dislike of it, and for the almost ostentatious and defiant prominence which he gave to the convictions and social habits of his school. He expressed his scorn and disgust at the "donnishness," the coldness, the routine, the want of heart, which was all that he could see at Oxford out of the one small circle of his friends. He despised the Oxford course of work, and would have nothing more to do with it than he could help—as he lived to regret afterwards. Yet even then he was in his tastes and the instinctive tendencies of his mind above his party. He was an admiring reader of Wordsworth and Shelley; he felt the strength of Aristotle and Plato; he is said to have appreciated Mr. Newman's preaching, and to have gallantly defended what he admired in him and his friends. His editor, indeed, Mr. Brooke, appears to be a little divided and embarrassed, between his wish to enforce Mr. Robertson's largeness of mind and heart, and his fear of giving countenance to suspicions that he was ever so little inclined to "High Churchism"; between his desire to show that Mr. Robertson estimated the High Church leaders as much as an intelligent man ought, and disliked their system as much as a sound-thinking Christian ought. We should have thought that he need not be so solicitous to "set at rest the question about Mr. Robertson's High Church tendencies." "I hate High Churchism," was one of his latest declarations, when professing his sympathy with individual High Churchmen. One thing, however, is quite clear—that in his early life his partisanship was thoroughgoing and unflinching enough to satisfy the fiercest and most fanatical of their opponents. Such a representation as this is simply misleading :—

The almost fierceness with which he speaks against the Tract school is proof in him of the strength of the attraction it possessed for him, just as afterwards at Brighton his attacks on Evangelicalism are proof of the strength with which he once held to that form of Christianity, and the force of the reaction with which he abandoned it for ever. Out of these two reactions—when their necessary ultra tendencies had been mellowed down by time—emerged at last the clearness and the just balance of principles with which he taught during 1848 and the following years, at Brighton. He had probed both schools of theological thought to their recesses, and had found them wanting. He spoke of what he knew when he protested against both. He spoke also of what he knew when he publicly recognised the Spirit of all good moving in the lives of those whose opinions he believed to be erroneous.

It is absurd to say, because he sometimes spoke of the "danger" he had been in from "Tractarianism," that he had felt in equal degree the "strength of attraction" towards the one school and towards the other, and it is equally absurd to talk of his "having probed both to their recesses." He read, and argued, and discussed the pamphlets of the controversy—the "replies," Mr. Brooke says, with more truth probably than he thought of in using the word—like other undergraduates who took interest in what was going on, and thought themselves fit to choose their side. With his tutor and friend, Mr. Churton, he read Taylor's *Ancient Christianity*, carefully looking out the passages from the Fathers. "I am reading the early Church history with Golightly," he says, "which is a very great advantage, as he has a fund of general information and is a close reader." But we must doubt whether this involved "probing to the recesses" the "Tractarian" side of the question. And we distrust the depth and the judgment, and the impartiality also of a man who is said to have read Newman's sermons continually with delight to the day of his death, and by whom no book was more carefully studied and more highly honoured than *The Christian Year*, and who yet to the last could see nothing better in the Church movement as a whole than, according to the vulgar view of it, a revival of forms partly useful, partly hurtful. It seems to us the great misfortune of his life, and one which exercised its evil influence on him to the end, that, thrown young into the narrowest and weakest of religious schools, he found it at first so congenial to his vehement temperament, that he took so kindly to certain of its more unnatural and ungenerous ways, and thus was cut off from the larger and healthier influences of the society round him. Those were days when older men than he took their side too precipitately; but he found himself encouraged, even as an undergraduate, to dogmatise, to be positive, to hate, to speak evil. He learnt the lesson too well. This is the language of an undergraduate at the end of his university course:—

But I seem this term to have in a measure waked out of a long trance, partly caused by my own gross inconsistencies, and partly by the paralysing effects of this Oxford-delusion heresy, for such it is I feel persuaded. And to know it a man must live here, and he will see the promising and ardent men sinking one after another in a deadly torpor, wrapped up in self-contemplation, dead to their Redeemer, and useless to His Church, under the baneful breath of this accursed upas tree. I say accursed, because I believe that St. Paul would use the same language to Oxford as he did to the Galatian Church, "I would they were even cut off which trouble you"; accursed, because I believe that the curse of God will fall on it. He has denounced it on the Papal heresy, and He is no respecter of persons, to punish the name and not the reality. May He forgive me if I err, and lead me into all truth. But I do not speak as one who has been in no danger, and therefore cannot speak very quietly. It is strange into what ramifications the disbelief of external justification will extend; *we will* make it internal, whether it be by self-mortification, by works of evangelical obedience, or by the sacraments, and that just at the time when we suppose most that we are magnifying the work of the Lord.

Mr. Brooke rather likes to dwell, as it seems to us, in an unreal and disproportionate way, on Mr. Robertson's sufferings, in the latter part of his life, from the bitter and ungenerous attacks of which he was the object. "This is the man," he says in one place, "who was afterwards at Brighton driven into the deepest solitariness of heart, whom God thought fit to surround with slander and misunderstanding." He was, we doubt not, fiercely assailed by the Evangelical party, which he had left, and which he denounced in no gentle language; he was, as we can well believe, "constantly attacked, by some manfully, by others in an underhand manner, and was the victim of innuendoes and slander." We cannot, however, help thinking that Mr. Brooke unconsciously exaggerates the solitariness and want of sympathy which went with all this. Mr. Robertson had, and knew that he had, his ardent and enthusiastic admirers as well as his worrying and untiring opponents. But what we remark is this. It was the measure which he had meted out to others, in the fierceness of his zeal for Evangelicalism, which the Evangelicals afterwards meted out to him. They did not more talk evil of what they knew not and had taken no real pains to understand, than he had done of a body of men as able, as well-instructed, as deep-thinking, as brave, as earnest as himself in their war against sin and worldliness. The stupidity, the perverse ill-nature, the resolute ignorance, the audacious and fanatical application of Scripture condemnations, the reckless judging without a desire to do justice, which he felt and complained of so bitterly when turned against himself, he had sanctioned and largely shared in when the same party which attacked him in the end attacked the earlier revivers of thoughtful and earnest religion. Nor do we find that he ever expressed regret for a vehemence of condemnation which his after-knowledge must have shown him that he had no business to pass, because, even if he afterwards adhered to it, he had originally passed it on utterly false and inadequate grounds. He only became as fierce against the Evangelicals as he had been against the followers of Mr. Newman. He never unlearnt the habit of harsh reprobation which his Evangelical friends had encouraged. He only transferred its full force against themselves.

He left Oxford and began his ministry, first at Winchester, and then at Cheltenham, full of Evangelical *formulae* and Evangelical narrow zeal. It does not appear that, except as an earnest hard-working clergyman, he was in any way distinguished from numbers of the same class, though we are quite willing to believe that even then his preaching, in warmth and vigour, was above the average. But as he, or his biographer, says, he had not yet really begun to think. When he began to think, he did so with the rapidity, the intensity, the impatient fervid vehemence which lay all along at the bottom of his character. His Evangelical views appear to have snapped to pieces and dissolved with a violence and sudden abruptness entirely unaccounted for by anything which these volumes show us. He read Carlyle; but so did many other people. He found the religious world at Cheltenham not so pure as he had imagined it; but this is what must have happened anywhere, and is not enough to account for such a complete revolution of belief. He had a friend deeply read in German philosophy and criticism who is said to have exercised influence on him. Still, we repeat, the steps and processes of the change from the Evangelicalism of Cheltenham to a condition, at first, of almost absolute doubt, are very imperfectly explained :—

These letters were written in 1843. In the following year doubts and questionings began to stir in his mind. He could not get rid of them. They were forced upon him by his reading and his intercourse with men. They grew and tortured him. His teaching in the pulpit altered, and it became painful to him to preach. He was reckoned of the Evangelical school, and he began to feel that his position was becoming a false one. He felt the excellence and earnestness, and gladly recognised the work of the nobler portion of that party, but he felt also that he must separate from it. In his strong reaction from its extreme tendencies, he understood with a shock which upturned his whole inward life for a time, that the system on which he had founded his whole faith and work could never be received by him again. Within its pale, for him, there was henceforward neither life, peace, nor reality. It was not, however, till almost the end of his ministry at Cheltenham that this became clearly manifest to him. It had been growing slowly into a conviction. An outward blow—the sudden ruin of a friendship which he had wrought, as he imagined, for ever into his being—a blow from which he never afterwards wholly recovered—accelerated the inward crisis, and the result was a period of spiritual agony so awful that it not only shook his health to its centre, but smote his spirit down into so profound a darkness that of all his early faiths but one remained, "It must be right to do right."

This seems to have been in 1846, and in the beginning of the next year he had already taken his new line. The explanation does not explain much. We have no right to ask for more than his friends think fit to tell us of this turning-point of his life. But we observe that this deeply important passage is left with but little light and much manifest reticence. That the crisis took place we have his own touching and eloquent words to assure us. It left him also as firm in his altered convictions as he had been in his old ones. What caused it, what were its circumstances and characteristics, and what affected its course and results, we can only guess. But it was decisive and it was speedy. He spent a few months in Germany in the end of 1846, and in the beginning of 1847 the Bishop of Oxford was willing to appoint him to St. Ebbe's. But his stay there was short. Three months afterwards he accepted the chapel at Brighton which he held till his death in August 1853.

He was now the Robertson whom all the world knows, and the change was a most remarkable one. It seems strictly accurate to say that he started at once into a new man—new in all his views and tastes; new in the singular burst of power which at once shows itself in the keen, free, natural language of his letters and his other writings; new in the deep concentrated earnestness of character with which he seemed to grasp his peculiar calling and function. All the conventionalities of his old school, which hung very thick about him even to the end of his Cheltenham life, seem suddenly to drop off, and leave him, without a trace remaining on his mind, in the full use and delight of his new liberty. We cannot say that we are more inclined to agree with him in his later stage than in his earlier. And the rapid transformation of a most dogmatic and zealous Evangelical into an equally positive and enthusiastic "Broad Churchman" does not seem a natural or healthy process, and suggests impatience and self-confidence more than self-command and depth. But we get, without doubt, to a real man—a man whose words have a meaning, and stand for real things; whose language no longer echoes the pale dreary commonplaces of a school, but reveals thoughts which he has thought for himself, and the power of being able "to speak as he will." His mind seems to expand, almost at a bound, to all the manifold variety of interests of which the world is full. His letters on his own doings, on the books and subjects of the day, on the remarks or the circumstances of his friends, his criticism, his satire, his controversial or friendly discussions, are full of energy, versatility, refinement, boldness, and strength; and his remarkable power of clear, picturesque, expressive diction, not unworthy of our foremost masters of English, appears all at once, as it were, full grown. It is difficult to believe, as we read the later portions of his life, that we are reading about the same man who appeared, so short a time before, at the beginning, to promise at best to turn into a popular Evangelical preacher, above the average, perhaps, in taste and power, but not above the average in freedom from cramping and sour prejudices.

Mr. Robertson had hold of some great truths, and he applied them, both in his own thoughts and self-development and in his popular teaching, with great force. He realised two things with a depth and intensity which give an awful life and power to all he said about religion. He realised with singular and pervading keenness that which a greater man than he speaks of as the first and the great discovery of the awakened soul—"the thought of two, and two only, supreme and luminously self-evident beings, himself and the Creator." "Alone with God," expresses the feeling which calmed his own anxieties and animated his religious appeals to others. And he realised with equal earnestness the great truth which is spoken of by Mr. Brooke, though in language which to us has an unpleasant sound, in the following extract:—

Yet, notwithstanding all this—which men called while he lived, and now when he is dead will call, want of a clear and well-defined system of theology—he had a fixed basis for his teaching. It was the Divine-human Life of Christ. It is the fourth principle mentioned in his letter, "that belief in the human character of Christ must be antecedent to belief in His divine origin." He felt that an historical Christianity was absolutely essential; that only through a visible life of the Divinest in the flesh could God become intelligible to men; that Christ was God's idea of our nature realised; that only when we fall back on the glorious portrait of what has been, can we be delivered from despair of Humanity; that in Christ "all the blood of all the nations ran," and all the powers of man were redeemed. Therefore he grasped as the highest truth, on which to rest life and thought, the reality expressed in the words, "the Word was made Flesh." The Incarnation was to him the centre of all history, the blossoming of Humanity. The Life which followed the Incarnation was the explanation of the Life of God, and the only solution of the problem of the Life of man. He did not speak much of loving Christ; his love was fitly mingled with that veneration which makes love perfect; his voice was solemn, and he paused before he spoke His name in common talk; for what that name meant had become the central thought of his intellect and the deepest realisation of his spirit. He had spent a world of study, of reverent meditation, of adoring contemplation, on the Gospel history. Nothing comes forward more frequently in his letters than the way in which he had entered into the human life of Christ. To that everything is referred—by that everything is explained.

In bringing home these great truths to the feelings of those who had lived insensible to them lay the chief value of his preaching. He awakened men to believe that there was freshness and reality in things which they had by use become dulled to. There are no doubt minds which rise to the truth most naturally and freely without the intervention of dogmatic expressions, and to these such expressions, as they are a limit and a warning, are also felt as a clog. Mr. Robertson's early experience had made him suspicious and irritable about dogma as such; and he prided himself on being able to dispense with it, while at the same time preserving the principle and inner truth which it was intended to convey. But in his ostentatious contempt of dogmatic precision and exactness, none but those who have not thought about the matter will see any proof of his strength or wisdom. Dogma, accurate, subtle, scientific, does not prevent a mind of the first order from breathing freshness of feeling, grandeur, originality, and the sense of reality, into the exposition of the truth which it represents. It is no fetter except to those minds which in their impulsiveness, their self-confidence, and their want of adequate grasp and sustained force, most need its salutary restraint. And no man has a right, however eloquent and impressive his speech may be, to talk against dogma till he shows that he does not confound accuracy of statement with conventional formalism. Mr. Robertson lays down the law pretty confidently about the blunders of everybody about him—Tractarian, Evangelical, Dissenter, Romanist, and Rationalist. We must say that the impression of every page of his letters is, that clear and "intuitive" as he was, he had not always understood what he condemned. He was especially satisfied with a view of Baptism which he thought rose above both extremes and took in the truth of both while it avoided their errors. But is it too much to say that a man who, not in the heat of rhetoric, but when preparing candidates for Confirmation, and piquing himself on his freedom from all prejudice, deliberately describes the common Church view of Baptism as implying a "magical" change, and actually illustrates what he means by the stories of magical changes in the *Arabian Nights*—who knowing, or able to read, all that has been said by divines on the subject from the days of Augustine, yet commits himself to the assertion that this is in fact what they hold and teach—is it too much to say that such a man, whatever may be his other gifts, has forfeited all claim to be considered capable of writing and expressing himself with accuracy, truth, and distinctness on theological questions ? And if theological questions are to be dealt with, ought they not to be dealt with accurately, and not loosely ?

But we have lingered too long over these volumes. They are very instructive, sometimes very elevating, almost always very touching. The life which they describe greatly wanted discipline, self-restraint, and the wise and manly fear of overrating one's own novelties. But we see in it a life consecrated to duty, fulfilled with much pain and self-sacrifice, and adorned by warm and deep affections, by vigour and refinement of thought, and earnest love for truth and purity. No one can help feeling his profound and awful sense of things unseen, though in the philosophy by which he sought to connect things seen and things unseen, we cannot say that we can have much confidence. We have only one concluding remark to make, and that is not on him but on his biographer. An exaggerated tone, as we have said, seems to us to pervade the book. There is what seems to us an unhealthy attempt to create in the reader an impression of the exceptional severity of the sufferings of Mr. Robertson's life, of his loneliness, of his persecutions. But in this point much may fairly be pardoned to the affection of a friend. What, however, we can less excuse is the want of good feeling with which Mr. Brooke, in his account of Mr. Robertson's last days, allows himself to give an *ex parte* account of a dispute between Mr. Robertson and the Vicar of Brighton, about the appointment of a curate, and not simply to insinuate, but distinctly declare that this dispute with its result was the fatal stroke which, in his state of ill-health, hastened his death. We say nothing about the rights of the story, for we never heard anything of them but what Mr. Brooke tells us. But there is an appearance of vindictiveness in putting it on record with this particular aspect which nothing in the story itself seems to us to justify. In describing Mr. Robertson's departure from Cheltenham, Mr. Brooke has plainly thought right to use much reticence. He would have done well to have used the same reticence about these quarrels at Brighton.

XVI

LIFE OF BARON BUNSEN[1]

BUNSEN was really one of those persons, more common two centuries ago than now, who could belong as much to an adopted country as to that in which they were born and educated. A German of the Germans, he yet succeeded in also making himself at home in England, in appreciating English interests, in assimilating English thought and traditions, and exercising an important influence at a critical time on one extremely important side of English life and opinion. He was less felicitous in allying the German with the Englishman, perhaps from personal peculiarities of impatience, self-assertion, and haste, than one who has since trodden in his steps and realised more completely and more splendidly some of the great designs which floated before his mind. But few foreigners have gained more fairly, by work and by sympathy, the *droit de cité* in England than Bunsen.

It is a great pity that books must be so long and

[1] *A Memoir of Baron Bunsen.* By his Widow, Baroness Bunsen. *Saturday Review*, 2nd May 1868.

so bulky, and though Bunsen's life was a very full and active one in all matters of intellectual interest, and in some of practical interest also, we cannot help thinking that his biography would have gained by greater exercise of self-denial on the part of his biographer. It is altogether too prolix, and the distinction is not sufficiently observed between what is interesting simply to the Bunsen family and their friends, and what is interesting to the public. One of the points in which biographers, and the present author among the number, make mistakes, is in their use of letters. They never know when to stop in giving correspondence. If we had only one or two letters of a remarkable man, they would be worth printing, even if they were very much like other people's letters. But when we have bundles and letter-books without end to select from, selection, in a work professedly biographical, becomes advisable. We want types and specimens of a man's letters; and when the specimen has been given, we want no more, unless what is given is for its own sake remarkable. A great number of Bunsen's early letters are printed. Some of them are of much interest, showing how early the germs were formed of ideas and plans which occupied his life, and what were the influences by which he was surrounded, and how he comported himself in regard to them. But many more of these letters are what any young man of thought and of an affectionate nature might have written; and we do not want to have it shown us, over and over again, merely that Bunsen was thoughtful and affectionate. A wise and severe economy in this matter would have produced at least the same effect, at much less cost to the reader.

Bunsen was born in 1791, at Corbach, in the little principality of Waldeck, and grew up under the severe and simple training of a frugal German household, and with a solid and vigorous German education. He became in time Heyne's pupil at Göttingen, and very early showed the qualities which distinguished him in his after life—restless eagerness after knowledge and vast powers of labour, combined with large and ambitious, and sometimes vague, ideas, and with depth and fervour of religious sentiment. He entered on life when the reaction against the cold rationalistic theories of the age before him was stimulated by the excitement of the war of liberation; and in his deep and supreme interest in the Bible he kept to the last the stamp which he then received. More interesting than the recollections of a distinguished man's youth by his friends after he has become distinguished—which are seldom quite natural and not always trustworthy—are the contemporary records of the impressions made on *him* in his youth by those who were distinguished men when he was young. In some of Bunsen's letters we have such impressions. Thus he writes of Heyne in 1813:—

Poor and lonely did I arrive in this place [Göttingen]. Heyne received me, guided me, bore with me, encouraged me, showed me in himself the example of a high and noble energy, and indefatigable activity in a calling which was not that to which his merit entitled him. He might have superintended and administered and maintained an entire kingdom without more effort and with yet greater efficiency than the University for which he lived; he was too great for a mere philologer, and in general for a professor of mere learning in the age into which he was cast, and he was more distinguished in every other way than in this. . . . And what has he established or founded at the cost of this exertion of faculties? Learning annihilates itself, and the most perfect is the first submerged; for the next age scales with ease the height which cost the preceding the full vigour of life. Yet two things remain of him and will not perish—the one, the tribute left by his free spirit to the finest productions of the human mind; and what he felt, thought, and has immortalised in many men of excellence gone before. Read his explanations of Tischbein's engravings from Homer, his last preface to Virgil, and especially his oration on the death of Müller, and you will understand what I mean. I speak not of his political instinct, made evident in his survey of the public and private life of the ancients. The other memorial which will subsist of him, more warm in life than the first, is the remembrance of his generosity, to which numbers owe a deep obligation.

And of Schelling, about the same time, whom he had just seen in Munich :—

Schelling before all must be mentioned as having received me well, after his fashion, giving me frequent occasions of becoming acquainted with his philosophical views and judgments, in his own original and peculiar manner. His mode of disputation is rough and angular; his peremptoriness and his paradoxes terrible. Once he undertook to explain animal magnetism, and for this purpose to give an idea of Time, from which resulted that all is present and in existence—the Present as existing in the actual moment; the Future, as existing in a future moment. When I demanded the proof, he referred me to the word *is*, which applies to existence, in the sentence that "this *is* future." Seckendorf, who was present (with him I have become closely acquainted, to my great satisfaction), attempted to draw attention to the confounding the subjective (*i.e.* him who pronounces that sentence) with the objective; or, rather, to point out a simple grammatical misunderstanding—in short, declared the position impossible. "Well, replied Schelling drily, "you have not understood me." Two Professors (his worshippers), who were present, had meanwhile endeavoured by their exclamations, "Only observe, all *is*, all *exists*" (to which the wife of Schelling, a clever woman, assented), to help me into conviction; and a vehement beating the air—for arguing and holding fast by any firm point were out of the question—would have arisen, if I had not contrived to escape by giving a playful turn to the conversation. I am perfectly aware that Schelling *could* have expressed and carried through his real opinion far better—*i.e.* rationally. I tell the anecdote merely to give an idea of his manner in conversation.

At Göttingen he was one of a remarkable set, comprising Lachmann, Lücke, Brandis, and some others, thought as much of at the time as their friends, but who failed to make their way to the front ranks of the world. Like others of his countrymen, Bunsen began to find "that the world's destinies were not without their effect on him," and to feel dissatisfied with the comparatively narrow sphere of even German learning. The thought grew, and took possession of him, of "bringing over, into his knowledge and into his fatherland, the solemn and distant East," and to "draw the East into the study of the entire course of humanity (particularly of European, and more especially of Teutonic humanity)," making Germany the "central point of this study." Vast plans of philological and historical study, involving, as the only means then possible of carrying them out, schemes of wide travel and long sojourn in the East, opened on him. Indian and Persian literature, the instinctive certainty of its connection with the languages and thought of the West, and the imperfection of means of study in Europe, drew him, as many more were drawn at the time, to seek the knowledge which they wanted in foreign and distant lands. With Bunsen, this wide and combined study of philology, history, and philosophy, which has formed one of the characteristic pursuits of our time, was from the first connected with the study of the Bible as its central point. In 1815 came a decisive turning-point in his life—his acquaintance, and the beginning of his close connection, with Niebuhr, at Berlin; and from this time he felt himself a Prussian. "That State in Northern Germany," he writes to Brandis in 1815, "which gladly receives every German, from wheresoever he may come, and considers every one thus entering as a citizen born, is *the true Germany*" :—

That such a State [he proceeds, in the true Bismarckian spirit] should prove inconvenient to others of inferior importance, which persist in continuing their isolated existence, regardless of the will of Providence and of the general good, is of no consequence whatever; nor even does it matter that, in its present management, there are defects and imperfections. . . . We intend to be in Berlin in three weeks; and there (in Prussia) am I resolved to fix my destinies.

After reading Persian for a short time in Paris with De Sacy, and after the failure of a plan of travel with Mr. Astor of New York, Bunsen joined Niebuhr at Florence in the end of 1816, and went on with him to Rome, where Niebuhr was Prussian envoy. There, enjoying Niebuhr's society, "equally sole in his kind with Rome," he took up his abode, and plunged into study. He gave up his plans of Oriental travel, finding he could do all that he wanted without them. Too much a student, as he writes to a friend, to think of marrying, which he could not do "without impairing his whole scheme of mental development," he nevertheless found his fate in an English lady, Miss Waddington, who became his wife. And, finally, when the health of his friend Brandis, Niebuhr's secretary in the Prussian Legation, broke down, Bunsen took his place, and entered on that combined path of study and diplomacy in which he continued for the greater part of his life.

It may be questioned whether Bunsen's career answered altogether successfully to what he proposed to himself, or was in fact all that his friends and he himself thought it; but it was eminently one in which from the first he had laid down for himself a plan of life which he tenaciously followed through many changes and varieties of work, without ever losing sight of the purpose with which he began. He piqued himself on having early seen that a man ought to have an object to which to devote his whole life—" be it a dictionary like Johnson's or a history like Gibbon's "—and on having discerned and chosen his own object. And at an early time of his life in Rome he draws an outline of thought and inquiry, destined to break off into many different labours, in very much the same language in which he might have described it in the last year of his life:—

The consciousness of God in the mind of man, and that which in and through that consciousness He has accomplished, especially in language and religion, this was from the earliest time before my mind. After having awhile fancied to attain my point, sometimes here, sometimes there, at length (it was in the Christmas holidays of 1812, after having gained the prize in November) I made a general and comprehensive plan. I wished to go through and represent heathen antiquity, in its principal phases, in three great periods of the world's history, according to its languages, its religious conceptions, and its political institutions; first of all in the East, where the earliest expressions in each are highly remarkable, although little known; then in the second great epoch, among the Greeks and Romans; thirdly, among the Teutonic nations, who put an end to the Roman Empire.

. . . .

At first I thought of Christianity only as something which every one, like the mother tongue, knows intuitively, and therefore not as the object of a peculiar study. But in January 1816, when I for the last time took into consideration all that belonged to my plan, and wrote it down, I arrived at this conclusion, that as God had caused the conception of Himself to be developed in the mind of man in a twofold manner, the one through revelation to the Jewish people through their patriarchs, the other through reason in the heathen; so also must the inquiry and representation of this development be twofold; and as God had kept these two ways for a length of time independent and separate, so should we, in the course of the examination, separate knowledge from man, and his development from the doctrine of revelation and faith, firmly trusting that God in the end would bring about the union of both. This is now also my firm conviction, that we must not mix them or bring them together forcibly, as many have done with well-meaning zeal but unclear views, and as many in Germany with impure designs are still doing.

The design had its interruptions, both intellectual and practical. The plan was an ambitious one, too ambitious for Bunsen's time and powers, or even probably for our own more advanced stage of knowledge; and Bunsen ever found it hard to resist the attractions of a new object of interest, and did not always exhaust it, though he seldom touched anything without throwing light on it. Thus he was drawn by circumstances to devote a good deal of time, more than he intended, to the mere antiquarianism of Rome. By and by he found himself succeeding Niebuhr as the diplomatic representative of Prussia at Rome. And his attempt to meet the needs of his own strong devotional feelings by giving more warmth and interest to the German services at the embassy, "the congregation on the Capitoline Hill," led him, step by step, to those wider schemes for liturgical reform which influenced so importantly the course of his fortunes. They brought him, a young and unknown man, with little more than Niebuhr's good word, into direct and confidential communication with the King of Prussia, who was then intent on plans of the same kind, and who recognised in Bunsen, after some preliminary jealousy and misgivings, the man most fitted to assist in carrying them out. But though Bunsen, who started with the resolve of being both a student and a scholar, was driven, as he thought against his will, into paths which led him deeper and deeper into public life and diplomacy, his early plans were never laid aside even under the stress of official employment. Perhaps it may be difficult to strike the balance of what they lost or gained by it.

The account of his life at Rome contains much that is interesting. There is the curious mixture of sympathy and antipathy in Bunsen's mind for the place itself; the antipathy of a German, a Protestant, and a free inquirer, for the Roman, the old Catholic, the narrow, timid, traditional spirit which pervaded everything in the great seat of clerical and Papal government; and the sympathy, scarcely less intense, not merely, or in the first place, for the classical aspects of Rome, but for its religious character, as still the central point of Christendom, full of the memorials and the savour of the early days of Christianity, mingling with what its many centuries of history have added to them; and for all that aroused the interest and touched the mind of one deeply busy with two great religious problems—the best forms for Christian worship, and the restoration, if possible, of some organisation and authority in Protestant Germany. For a long time Bunsen, like his master Niebuhr, was on the best terms with Cardinals, Monsignori, and Popes. The Roman services were no objects to him of abhorrence or indifference. He saw, in the midst of accretions, the remains of the more primitive devotion; and the architecture, the art, and the music, to be found only in Rome, were to him inexhaustible sources of delight. As may be supposed, letters like Bunsen's, and the recollections of his biographer, are full of interesting gossip; notices of famous people, and of things that happened in Rome in the days of the Emancipation and Reform Bills, Revolutions of Naples in '20 and France in '30, during the twenty years, from 1818 to 1838, in which the men of the great war and the restorations were going off the scene, and the men of the modern days—Liberals, High Churchmen, Ultramontanes—were coming on. Those twenty years, of course, were not without their changes in Bunsen's own views. The man who had come to Rome, in position a poor and obscure student, had grown into the oracle of a highly cultivated society, whose acquaintance was eagerly sought by every one of importance who lived at Rome or visited it, and into the diplomatic representative of one of the great Powers. The scholar had come to have, not merely theories, but political and ecclesiastical aims. The disciple of Niebuhr, who at one time had seen all things very much as Niebuhr saw them in his sad later days of disgust at revolution and cynical despair of liberty, had come since under the influence of Arnold, and, as his letters to Arnold show, had taken into his own mind much of the more generous and hopeful, though vague, teaching of that equally fervid teacher of liberalism and of religion. These letters are of much interest. They show the dreams and the fears and antipathies of the time; they contain some remarkable anticipations, some equally remarkable miscalculations, and some ideas and proposals which, with our experience, excite our wonder that any one could have imagined them practicable. Every one knows that Bunsen's diplomatic career at Rome ended unfortunately. He was mixed up with the violent proceedings of the Prussian Government in the dispute with the Archbishop of Cologne about marriages between Protestants and Catholics, and he had the misfortune to offend equally both his own Court and that of Rome. It is possible that, as is urged in the biography before us, he was sacrificed to the blunders and the enmities of powers above him. But, for whatever reason, no clear account is given of the matter by his biographer, though a good deal is suggested; and in the absence of intelligible explanations the conclusion is natural that, though he may have been ill-used, he may also have been unequal to his position.

But his ill-success or his ill-usage at Rome was more than compensated by the results to which it may be said to have led. Out of it ultimately came that which gave the decisive character to Bunsen's life—his settlement in London as Prussian Minister. On leaving Rome he came straight to England. He came full of admiration and enthusiasm to "his Ithaca, his island fatherland," and he was flattered and delighted by the welcome he received, and by the power which he perceived in himself, beyond that of most foreigners, to appreciate and enjoy everything English. He liked everything—people, country, and institutions; even, as his biographer writes, our rooks. The zest of his enjoyment was not diminished by his keen sense of what appear to foreigners our characteristic defects—the want of breadth of interest and boldness of speculative thought which accompanies so much energy in public life and so much practical success; and he seems to have felt in himself a more than ordinary fitness to be a connecting link between the two nations—that he had much to teach Englishmen, and that they were worth teaching. He thoroughly sympathised with the earnestness and strong convictions of English religion; but he thought it lamentably destitute of rational grounds, of largeness of idea and of critical insight, enslaved to the letter, and afraid of inquiry. But, with all drawbacks, his visit to England made it a very attractive place to him; and when he was appointed by his Government Envoy to the Swiss Confederation, with strict injunctions "to do nothing," his eyes were often turned towards England. In 1840 the King of Prussia died, and Bunsen's friend and patron, the Crown Prince, became Frederic William IV. He resembled Bunsen in more ways than one; in his ardent religious sentiment, in his eagerness, in his undoubting and not always far-sighted self-confidence and self-assertion, and in a combination of practical vagueness of view and a want of understanding men, with a feverish imperiousness in carrying out a favourite plan. In 1841 he sent Bunsen to England to negotiate the ill-considered and precipitate arrangement for the Jerusalem bishopric; and on the successful conclusion of the negotiation, Bunsen was appointed permanently to be Prussian Minister in London. The manner of appointment was remarkable. The King sent three names to Lord Aberdeen and the English Court, and they selected Bunsen's.

Thus Bunsen, who twenty-five years before had sat down a penniless student, almost in despair at the failure of his hopes as a travelling tutor, in Orgagna's *loggia* at Florence, had risen, in spite of real difficulties and opposition, to a brilliant position in active political life; and the remarkable point is that, whether he was ambitious or not of this kind of advancement—and it would perhaps have been as well on his part to have implied less frequently that he was not—he was all along, above everything, the student and the theologian. What is even more remarkable is that, plunged into the whirl of London public life and society, he continued still to be, more even than the diplomatist, the student and theologian. The Prussian Embassy during the years that he occupied it, from 1841 to 1854, was not an idle place, and Bunsen was not a man to leave important State business to other hands. The French Revolution, the German Revolution, the Frankfort Assembly, the question of the revival of the Empire, the beginnings of the Danish quarrel and of the Crimean war, all fell within that time, and gave the Prussian Minister in such a centre as London plenty to think of, to do, and to write about. Yet all this time was a time of intense and unceasing activity in that field of theological controversy in which Bunsen took such delight. The diplomatist entrusted with the gravest affairs of a great Power in the most critical and difficult times, and fully alive to the interest and responsibility of his charge, also worked harder than most Professors, and was as positive and fiery in his religious theories and antipathies as the keenest and most dogmatic of scholastic disputants. He was busy about Egyptian chronology, about cuneiform writing, about comparative philology; he plunged with characteristic eagerness into English theological war; and such books as his *Church of the Future*, and his writings on Ignatius and Hippolytus, were not the least important of the works which marked the progress of the struggle of opinions here. But they represented only a very small part of the unceasing labour that was going on in the early morning hours in Carlton House Terrace. All this time the foundations were being laid and the materials gathered for books of wider scope and more permanent aim, too vast for him to accomplish even in his later years of leisure. It is an original and instructive picture; for though we boast statesmen who still carry on the great traditions of scholarship, and give room in their minds for the deeper and more solemn problems of religion and philosophy, they are not supposed to be able to carry on simultaneously their public business and their classical or scientific studies, and at any rate they do not attack the latter with the devouring zeal with which Bunsen taxed the efforts of hard-driven secretaries and readers to keep pace with his inexhaustible demands for more and more of the most abstruse materials of knowledge.

The end of his London diplomatic career was, like the end of his Roman one, clouded with something like disgrace; and, like the Roman one, is left here unexplained. But it was for his happiness, probably, that his residence in England came to a close. He had found the poetry of his early notions about England, political and theological at least, gradually changing into prose. He found less and less to like, in what at first most attracted him, in the English Church; he and it, besides knowing one another better, were also changing. He probably increased his sympathies for England, and returned in a measure to his old kindness for it, by looking at it only from a distance. The labour of his later days, as vast and indefatigable as that of his earlier days, was devoted to his great work, which was, as it were, to popularise the Bible and revive interest in it by a change in the method of presenting it and commenting on it. To the last the Bible was the central point of his philosophical as well as his religious thoughts, as it had been in his first beginnings as a student at Göttingen and Rome. After a life of many trials, but of unusual prosperity and enjoyment, he died in the end of 1860. The account of his last days is a very touching one.

We do not pretend to think Bunsen the great and consummate man that, naturally enough, he appears to his friends. We doubt whether he can be classed as a man in the first rank at all. We doubt whether he fully understood his age, and yet it is certain that he was confident and positive that he did understand it better than most men; and an undue confidence of this kind implies considerable defects both of intellect and character. He wanted the patient, cautious, judicial self-distrust which his studies eminently demanded, and of which he might have seen some examples in England. No one can read these volumes without seeing the disproportionate power which first impressions had with him; he was always ready to say that something, which had just happened or come before him, was the greatest or the most complete thing of its kind. Wonderfully active, wonderfully quick and receptive, full of imagination and of the power of combining and constructing, and never wearied out or dispirited, his mind took in large and grand ideas, and developed them with enthusiasm and success, and with all the resources of wide and varied knowledge; but the affluence and ingenuity of his thoughts indisposed him, as it indisposes many other able men, to the prosaic and uninteresting work of calling these thoughts into question, and cross-examining himself upon their grounds and tenableness. He tried too much; the multiplicity of his intellectual interests was too much for him, and he often thought that he was explaining when he was but weaving a wordy tissue, and "darkening counsel" as much as any of the theological sciolists whom he denounced. People, for instance, must, it seems to us, be very easily satisfied who find any fresh light in the attempt, not unfrequent in his letters, to adapt the Lutheran watchword of Justification by faith to modern ideas. He was very rapid, and this rapidity made him hasty and precipitate; it also made him apt to despise other men, and, what was of more consequence, the difficulties of the subject likewise. Others did not always find it easy to understand him; and it may fairly be questioned if he always sufficiently asked whether he understood himself. He was generous and large-spirited in intention, though not always so in fact.

Doubtless so much knowledge, so much honest and unsparing toil, such freshness and quickness of thought, have not been wasted; there will always be much to learn from Bunsen's writings. But his main service has been the moral one of his example; of his ardent and high-souled industry, of his fearlessness in accepting the conclusions of his inquiries, of his untiring faith through many changes and some disappointments that there is a way to reconcile all the truths that interest men—those of religion, and those of nature and history. The sincerity and earnestness with which he attempted this are a lesson to everybody; his success is more difficult to recognise, and it may perhaps be allowable to wish that he had taken more exactly the measure of the great task which he set to himself. His ambition was a high one. He aspired to be the Luther of the new 1517 which he so often dwelt upon, and to construct a theology which, without breaking with the past, should show what Christianity really is, and command the faith and fill the opening thought of the present. It can hardly be said that he succeeded. The Church of the Future still waits its interpreter, to make good its pretensions to throw the ignorant and mistaken Church of the Past into the shade.

XVII

COLERIDGE'S MEMOIR OF KEBLE[1]

Mr. KEBLE has been fortunate in his biographer. There have been since his death various attempts to appreciate a character manifestly of such depth and interest, yet about which outsiders could find so little to say. Professor Shairp, of St. Andrews, two or three years ago gave a charming little sketch, full of heart and insight, and full too of noble modesty and reverence, which deserves to be rescued from the danger of being forgotten into which sketches are apt to fall, both on account of its direct subject, and also for the contemporary evidence which it contains of the impressions made on a perfectly impartial and intelligent observer by the early events of the Oxford movement. The brilliant Dean of Westminster, in *Macmillan's Magazine*, has attempted, with his usual grace and kindliness, to do justice to Keble's character, and has shown how hard he found the task. The paper on Keble forms a pendant to a recent

[1] *A Memoir of the Rev. John Keble.* By the Right Hon. Sir J. T. Coleridge. *Saturday Review*, 20th March 1869.

paper on Dean Milman. The two papers show conspicuously the measure and range of Dr. Stanley's power; what he can comprehend and appreciate in religious earnestness and height, and what he cannot; in what shapes, as in Dean Milman, he can thoroughly sympathise with it and grasp it, and where its phenomena, as in Mr. Keble, simply perplex and baffle him, and carry him out of his depth.

Sir John Coleridge knew Keble probably as long and as intimately as any one; and on the whole, he had the most entire sympathy with his friend's spirit, even where he disagreed with his opinions. He thoroughly understood and valued the real and living unity of a character which mostly revealed itself to the outer world by what seemed jerks and discordant traits. From early youth, through manhood to old age, he had watched and tested and loved that varied play and harmony of soul and mind, which was sometimes tender, sometimes stern, sometimes playful, sometimes eager; abounding with flashes of real genius, and yet always inclining by instinctive preference to things homely and humble; but which was always sound and unselfish and thorough, endeavouring to subject itself to the truth and will of God. To Sir John Coleridge all this was before him habitually as a whole; he could take it in, not by putting piece by piece together, but because he saw it. And besides being an old and affectionate and intelligent friend, he was also a discriminating one. In his circumstances he was as opposite to Keble as any one could be; he was a lawyer and man of the world, whose busy life at Westminster had little in common with the studies or pursuits of the divine and the country parson.

Such an informant presents a picture entirely different in kind from the comments and criticisms of those who can judge only from Mr. Keble's writings and religious line, or from the rare occasions in which he took a public part. These appearances, to many who willingly acknowledge the charm which has drawn to him the admiration and affection of numbers externally most widely at variance with him, do not always agree together. People delight in his poetry who hate his theology. They cannot say too much of the tenderness, the depth, the truth, the quick and delicate spirit of love and purity, which have made his verses the best interpreters and soothers of modern religious feeling; yet, in the religious system from which his poetry springs, they find nothing but what seems to them dry, harsh, narrow, and antiquated. He attracts and he repels; and the attraction and repulsion are equally strong. They see one side, and he is irresistible in his simplicity, humbleness, unworldliness, and ever considerate charity, combined with so much keenness and freshness of thought, and such sure and unfailing truth of feeling. They see another, and he seems to them full of strange unreality, strained, exaggerated, morbid, bristling with a forced yet inflexible intolerance. At one moment he seems the very ideal of a Christian teacher, made to win the sympathy of all hearts; the next moment a barrier rises in the shape of some unpopular doctrine or some display of zealous severity, seeming to be a strange contrast to all that was before, which utterly astonishes and disappoints. Mr. Keble was very little known to the public in general, less so even than others whose names are associated with his; and it is evident that to the public in general he presented a strange assemblage of incoherent and seemingly irreconcilable qualities. His mind seemed to work and act in different directions; and the results at the end seemed to be with wide breaks and interruptions between them. But a book like this enables us to trace back these diverging lines to the centre from which they spring. What seemed to be in such sharp contradiction at the outside is seen to flow naturally from the perfectly homogeneous and consistent character within. Many people will of course except to the character. It is not the type likely to find favour in an age of activity, doubt, and change. But, as it was realised in Mr. Keble, there it is in Sir John Coleridge's pages, perfectly real, perfectly natural, perfectly whole and uniform, with nothing double or incongruous in it, though it unfolded itself in various and opposite ways. And its ideal was simply that which has been consecrated as the saintly character in the Christian Church since the days of St. John—the deepest and most genuine love of all that was good; the deepest and most genuine hatred of all that was believed to be evil.

The picture which Sir John Coleridge puts before us, though deficient in what is striking and brilliant, is a sufficiently remarkable and uncommon one. It is the picture of a man of high cultivation and intellect, in whom religion was not merely something flavouring and elevating life, not merely a great element and object of spiritual activity, but really and unaffectedly the one absorbing interest, and the spring of every thought and purpose. Whether people like such a character or not, and whether or not they may think the religion wrong, or distorted and imperfect, if they would fairly understand the writer of the *Christian Year* they must start from this point. He was a man who, without a particle of the religious cant of any school, without any self-consciousness or pretension or unnatural strain, literally passed his days under the quick and pervading influence, for restraint and for stimulus, of the will and presence of God. With this his whole soul was possessed; its power over him had not to be invoked and stirred up; it acted spontaneously and unnoticed in him; it was dominant in all his activity; it quenched in him aims, and even, it may be, faculties; it continually hampered the free play of his powers and gifts, and made him often seem, to those who had not the key, awkward, unequal, and unintelligible. But for this awful sense of truth and reality unseen, which dwarfed to him all personal thoughts and all present things, he might have been a more finished writer, a more attractive preacher, a less indifferent foster-father to his own works. But it seemed to him a shame, in the presence of all that his thoughts habitually dwelt with, to think of the ordinary objects of authorship, of studying anything of this world for its own sake, of perfecting works of art, of cultivating the subtle forces and spells of language to give attractiveness to his writings. Abruptness, inadequacy, and obscurity of expression were light matters, and gave him little concern, compared with the haunting fear of unreal words. This "seeking first the kingdom of God and His righteousness," as he understood it, was the basis of all that he was; it was really and unaffectedly his governing principle, the root of his affections and his antipathies, just as to other men is the passion for scientific discovery or political life.

But within these limits, and jealously restrained by these conditions, a strongly marked character, exuberant with power and life, and the play of individual qualities, displayed itself. There were two intellectual sides to his mind—one which made him a poet, quickness and delicacy of observation and sympathetic interpretation, the realising and anticipating power of deep feeling and penetrative imagination; the other, at first sight, little related to poetry, a hard-headed, ingenious, prosaic shrewdness and directness of common sense, dealing practically with things as they are and on the whole, very little curious about scientific questions and precision, argumentative in a fashion modelled on Bishop Butler, and full of logical resource, good and, often it must be owned, bad. It was a mind which unfolded first under the plain, manly discipline of an old-fashioned English country parsonage, where the unshowy piety and strong morality and modest theology of the middle age of Anglicanism, the school of Pearson, Bull, and Wilson, were supreme. And from this it came under the new influences of bold and independent thought which were beginning to stir at Oxford; influences which were at first represented by such men as Davison, Copleston, and, above all, Whately; influences which repelled Keble by what he saw of hardness, shallowness, and arrogance, and still more of self-sufficiency and intellectual display and conceit in the prevailing tone of speculation, but which nevertheless powerfully affected him, and of which he showed the traces to the last. Sir John Coleridge is disappointing as to the amount of light which he throws on the process which was going on in Keble's mind during the fifteen years or so between his degree and the *Christian Year;* but there is one touch which refers to this period. Speaking in 1838 of Alexander Knox, and expressing dislike of his position, "as on the top of a high hill, seeing which way different schools tend," and "exercising a royal right of eclecticism over all," he adds:—

I speak the more feelingly because I know I was myself inclined to eclecticism at one time; and if it had not been for my father and my brother, where I should have been now, who can say?

But he was a man who, with a very vigorous and keen intellect, capable of making him a formidable disputant if he had been so minded, may be said not to have cared for his intellect. He used it at need, but he distrusted and undervalued it as an instrument and help. Goodness was to him the one object of desire and reverence; it was really his own measure of what he respected and valued; and where he recognised it, and in whatever shape, grave or gay, he cared not about seeming consistent in somehow or other paying it homage. People who knew him remember how, in this austere judge of heresy, burdened by the ever-pressing conviction of the "decay" of the Church and the distress of a time of change, tenderness, playfulness, considerateness, the restraint of a modesty which could not but judge, yet mistrusted its fitness, marked his ordinary intercourse. Overflowing with affection to his friends, and showing it in all kinds of unconventional and unexpected instances, keeping to the last a kind of youthful freshness as if he had never yet realised that he was not a boy, and shrunk from the formality and donnishness of grown-up life, he was the most refined and thoughtful of gentlemen, and in the midst of the fierce party battles of his day, with all his strong feeling of the tremendous significance of the strife, always a courteous and considerate opponent. Strong words he used, and used deliberately. But those were the days when the weapons of sarcasm and personal attack were freely handled. The leaders of the High Church movement were held up to detestation as the Oxford Malignants, and they certainly showed themselves fully able to give their assailants as good as they brought; yet Mr. Keble, involved in more than one trying personal controversy, feeling as sternly and keenly as any one about public questions, and tried by disappointment and the break up of the strongest ties, never lost his evenness of temper, never appeared in the arena of personal recrimination. In all the prominent part which he took, and in the resolute and sometimes wrathful tone in which he defended what seemed harsh measures, he may have dropped words which to opponents seemed severe ones, but never any which even they could call a scornful one or a sneer.

It was in keeping with all that he was—a mark of imperfection it may be, yet part of the nobleness and love of reality in a man who felt so deeply the weakness and ignorance of man—that he cared so little about the appearances of consistency. Thus, bound as he was by principle to show condemnation when he thought that a sacred cause was invaded, he was always inclining to conciliate his wrath with his affectionateness, and his severity with his consideration of circumstances and his own mistrust of himself. He was, of all men holding strong opinions, one of the most curiously and unexpectedly tolerant, wherever he could contrive to invent an excuse for tolerance, or where long habitual confidence was weighed against disturbing appearances. Sir John Coleridge touches this in the following extract, which is characteristic:—

On questions of this kind especially [University Reform], his principles were uncompromising; if a measure offended against what he thought honest, or violated what he thought sacred, good motives in the framers he would not admit as palliation, nor would he be comforted by an opinion of mine that measures mischievous in their logical consequences were never in the result so mischievous, or beneficial measures so beneficial, as had been foretold. So he writes playfully to me at an earlier time:—

"Hurrell Froude and I took into consideration your opinion that 'there are good men of all parties,' and agreed that it is a bad doctrine for these days; the time being come in which, according to John Miller, 'scoundrels must be called scoundrels'; and, moreover, we have stigmatised the said opinion by the name of the Coleridge Heresy. So hold it any longer at your peril."

I think it fair to set down these which were, in truth, formed opinions, and not random sayings; but it would be most unfair if one concluded from them, written and spoken in the freedom of friendly intercourse, that there was anything sour in his spirit, or harsh and narrow in his practice; when you discussed any of these things with him, the discussion was pretty sure to end, not indeed with any insincere concession of what he thought right and true, but in consideration for individuals and depreciation of himself.

And the same thing comes out in the interesting

letter in which the Solicitor-General describes his last recollections of Keble:—

There was, I am sure, no trace of failing then to be discerned in his apprehension, or judgment, or discourse. He was an old man who had been very ill, who was still physically weak, and who needed care; but he was the same Mr. Keble I had always known, and whom, for aught that appeared, I might hope still to know for many years to come. Little bits of his tenderness, flashes of his fun, glimpses of his austerer side, I seem to recall, but I cannot put them upon paper. . . . Once I remember walking with him just the same short walk, from his house to Sir William's, and our conversation fell upon Charles I., with regard to whose truth and honour I had used some expressions in a review, which had, as I heard, displeased him. I referred to this, and he said it was true. I replied that I was very sorry to displease him by anything I said or thought; but that if the Naseby letters were genuine, I could not think that what I said was at all too strong, and that a man could but do his best to form an honest opinion upon historical evidence, and, if he had to speak, to express that opinion. On this he said, with a tenderness and humility not only most touching, but to me most embarrassing, that "It might be so; what was he to judge of other men; he was old, and things were now looked at very differently; that he knew he had many things to unlearn and learn afresh; and that I must not mind what he had said, for that in truth belief in the heroes of his youth had become part of him." I am afraid these are my words, and not his; and I cannot give his way of speaking, which to any one with a heart, I think, would have been as overcoming as it was to me.

This same carelessness about appearances seems to us to be shown in Keble's theological position in his later years. A more logical, or a more plausible, but a less thoroughly real man might easily have drifted into Romanism. There was much in the circumstances round him, in the admissions which he had made, to lead that way; and his chivalrous readiness to take the beaten or unpopular side would help the tendency. But he was a man who gave great weight to his instinctive perception of what was right and wrong; and he was also a man who, when he felt sure of his duty, did not care a straw about what the world thought of appearances, or required as a satisfaction of seeming consistency. In him was eminently illustrated the characteristic strength and weakness of English religion, which naturally comes out in that form of it which is called Anglicanism; that poor Anglicanism, the butt and laughing-stock of all the clever and high-flying converts to Rome, of all the clever and high-flying Liberals, and of all those poor copyists of the first, far from clever, though very high-flying, who now give themselves out as exclusive heirs of the great name of Catholic; sneered at on all sides as narrow, meagre, shattered, barren; which certainly does not always go to the bottom of questions, and is too much given to "hunting-up" passages for *catenas* of precedents and authorities; but which yet has a strange, obstinate, tenacious moral force in it;

which, without being successful in formulating theories or in solving fallacies, can pierce through pretences and shams; and which in England seems the only shape in which intense religious faith can unfold itself and connect itself with morality and duty, without seeming to wear a peculiar dress of its own, and putting a barrier of self-chosen watchwords and singularities between itself and the rest of the nation.

It seems to us a great advantage to truth to have a character thus exhibited in its unstudied and living completeness, and exhibited directly, as the impression from life was produced on those before whose eyes it drew itself out day by day in word and act, as the occasion presented itself. There is, no doubt, a more vivid and effective way; one in which the Dean of Westminster is a great master, though it is not the method which he followed in what is probably his most perfect work, the *Life of Dr. Arnold*—the method of singling out points, and placing them, if possible, under a concentrated light, and in strong contrast and relief. Thus in Keble's case it is easy, and doubtless to many observers natural and tempting, to put side by side, with a strange mixture of perplexity and repulsion, *The Christian Year*, and the treatise *On Eucharistical Adoration*: to compare even in Keble's poetry, his tone on nature and human life, on the ways of children and the thoughts of death, with that on religious error and ecclesiastical divergences from the Anglican type: and to dwell on the contrast between Keble bearing his great gifts with such sweetness and modesty, and touching with such tenderness and depth the most delicate and the purest of human feelings, and Keble as the editor of Froude's *Remains*, forward against Dr. Hampden, breaking off a friendship of years with Dr. Arnold, stiff against Liberal change and indulgent to ancient folly and error, the eulogist of patristic mysticism and Bishop Wilson's "discipline," and busy in the ecclesiastical agitations and legal wranglings of our later days, about Jerusalem Bishoprics and Courts of Final Appeal and ritual details, about Gorham judgments, *Essays and Reviews* prosecutions, and Colenso scandals. The objection to this method of contrast is that it does not give the whole truth. It does not take notice that, in appreciating a man like Keble, the thing to start from is that his ideal and model and rule of character was neither more nor less than the old Christian one. It was simply what was accepted as right and obvious and indisputable, not by Churchmen only, but by all earnest believers up to our own days. Given certain conditions of Christian faith and duty which he took for granted as much as the ordinary laws of morality, then the man's own individual gifts or temper or leanings displayed themselves. But when people talk of Keble being narrow and rigid and harsh and intolerant, they ought first to recollect that he had been brought up with the ideas common to all whom he ever heard of or knew as religious people. All earnest religious conviction must seem narrow to those who do not share it. It was nothing individual or peculiar, either to him or his friends, to have strong notions about defending what they believed that they had received as the truth; and they were people who knew what they were about, too, and did not take things up at random. In this he was not different from Hooker, or Jeremy Taylor, or Bishop Butler, or Baxter, or Wesley, or Dr. Chalmers; it may be added, that he was not different from Dr. Arnold or Archbishop Whately. It must not be forgotten that till of late years there was always supposed, rightly or wrongly, to be such a thing as false doctrine, and that intolerance of it, within the limits of common justice, was always held as much part of the Christian character as devotion and charity. Men differed widely as to what was false doctrine, but they did not differ much as to there being such a thing, and as to what was to be thought of it. Keble, like other people of his time, took up his system, and really, considering that the ideal which he honestly and earnestly aimed at was the complete system of the Catholic Church, it is an abuse of words to call it, whatever else it may be called, a narrow system. There may be a wider system still, in the future; but it is at least premature to say that a man is narrow because he accepts in good faith the great traditional ideas and doctrines of the Christian Church: for of everything that can yet be called a religious system, in the sense commonly understood, as an embodiment of definite historical revelation, it is not easy to conceive a less narrow one. And, accepting it as the truth, it was dearer to him than life. That he was sensitively alive to whatever threatened or opposed it, and was ready to start up like a soldier, ready to do battle against any odds and to risk any unpopularity or misconstruction, was only the sure and natural result of that deep love and loyalty and thorough soundness of heart with which he loved his friends, but what he believed to be truth and God's will better than his friends. But it is idle and shallow to confuse the real narrowness which springs from a harsh temper or a cramped and self-sufficient intellect, and which is quite compatible with the widest theoretical latitude, and the inevitable appearance of narrowness and severity which must always be one side which a man of strong convictions and earnest purpose turns to those whose strong convictions and earnest purpose are opposite to his.

Mr. Keble, saintly as was his character, if ever there was such a character, belonged, as we all do, to his day and generation. The aspect of things and the thoughts of men change; enlarging, we are always apt to think, but perhaps really also contracting in some directions where they once were larger. In Mr. Keble, the service which he rendered to his time consisted, not merely, as it is sometimes thought, in soothing and refining it, but in bracing it. He was the preacher and example of manly hardness, simplicity, purpose in the religious character. It may be that his hatred of evil—of hollowness, impurity, self-will, conceit, ostentation—was greater than was always his perception of various and mingled good, or his comprehension of those middle things and states which are so much before us now. But the service cannot be overrated, to all parties, of the protest which his life and all his words were against dangers which were threatening all parties, and not least the Liberal party—the danger of shallowness and superficial flippancy; the danger of showy sentiment and insincerity, of worldly indifference to high duties and calls. With the one great exception of Arnold—Keble's once sympathetic friend, though afterwards parted from him—the religious Liberals of our time have little reason to look back with satisfaction to the leaders, able and vigorous as some of them were, who represented their cause then. They owe to Keble, as much as do those who are more identified with his theology, the inestimable service of having interpreted religion by a genuine life, corresponding in its thoroughness and unsparing, unpretending devotedness, as well as in its subtle vividness of feeling, to the great object which religion professes to contemplate.

XVIII

MAURICE'S THEOLOGICAL ESSAYS[1]

THE purpose of this volume of essays is to consider the views entertained by Unitarians of what are looked upon by Christians generally as fundamental truths; to examine what force there is in Unitarian objections, and what mistakes are involved in the popular notions and representations of those fundamental truths; and so, without entering into controversy, for which Mr. Maurice declares himself entirely indisposed, and in the utility of which he entirely disbelieves, to open the way for a deeper and truer, and more serious review, by all parties, of either the differences or the misunderstandings which keep them asunder. It is a work, the writer considers, as important as any which he has undertaken: "No labour I have been engaged in has occupied me so much, or interested me more deeply;" and with his estimate of his subject we are not disposed to disagree.

We always rise from the perusal of one of Mr.

---

[1] *Theological Essays.* By F. D. Maurice. *Guardian*, 7th September 1853.

Maurice's books with the feeling that he has shown us one great excellence, and taught us one great lesson. He has shown us an example of serious love of truth, and an earnest sense of its importance, and of his own responsibility in speaking of it. Most readers, whatever else they may think, must have their feeling of the wide and living interest of a theological or moral subject quickened by Mr. Maurice's thoughts on it. This is the excellence. The lesson is this—to look into the meaning of our familiar words, and to try to use them with a real meaning. Not that Mr. Maurice always shows us how; but it is difficult for conscience to escape being continually reminded of the duty. And it is in these two things that the value of Mr. Maurice's writings mainly consists. The enforcing of them has been, to our mind, his chief "mission," and his most valuable contribution to the needs of his generation.

In this volume they are exhibited, as in his former ones; and in this he shows also, as he has shown before, his earnest desire to find a way whereby, without compromising truth or surrendering sacred convictions of the heart, serious men of very different sides might be glad to find themselves in some points mistaken, in order that they might find themselves at one. This philosophy, not of comprehension but of conciliation, the craving after which has awakened in the Church, whenever mental energy has been quickened, the philosophy in which Clement of Alexandria and Origen, and, we may add, St. Augus tine, made many earnest essays, is certainly no unworthy aim for the theologian of our days. He would, indeed, deserve largely of the Church who should show us a solid and safe way to it.

But while we are far from denouncing or suspecting the wish or the design, we are bound to watch jealously and criticise narrowly the execution. For we all know what such plans have come to before now. And it is for the interest of all serious and earnest people on all sides, that there should be no needless and additional confusion introduced into theology—such confusion as is but too likely to follow, when a design of conciliation, with the aim of which so many, for good reasons or bad ones, are sure to sympathise, is carried out by hands that are not equal to it. With the fullest sense of the serious truthfulness of those who differ from us, of the real force of many of their objections and criticisms on our proceedings, our friends, and our ideas, it is far better to hold our peace, than from impatience at what we feel to be the vulnerable point of our own side, to rush into explanations before we are sure of our power adequately to explain.

And to this charge it seems to us that Mr. Maurice is open. There is sense and manliness in his disclaimer of proselytism; and there is a meaning in which we can agree with his account of truth. "If I could persuade all Dissenters," he says, "to become members of my Church to-morrow, I should be very sorry to do it. I believe the chances are they might leave it the next day. I do not wish to make them think as I think. But I want that they and I should be what we pretend to be, and then I doubt not we should find that there is a common ground for us all far beneath our thinkings. For truth I hold not to be that which every man troweth, but to be that which lies at the bottom of all men's trowings, that in which those trowings have their only meeting-point." He would make as clear as can be that deep substructure, and leave the sight of it to work its natural effect on the honest heart. A noble aim; but surely requiring, if anything can, the clear eye, the steady hand, the heart as calm as earnest. Surely a work in which the greatest exactness and precision, as well as largeness of thought, would not be too much. For if we but take away the "trowings" without coming down to the central foundation, or lose ourselves, and mistake a new "trowing" of our own for it, it is hardly a sufficient degree of blame to say that we have done no good.

And in these qualities of exactness and precision it does seem to us that Mr. Maurice is, for his purpose, fatally deficient. His criticisms are often acute, his thrusts on each side often very home ones, and but too full of truth; his suggestions often full of thought and instruction; his balancings and contrasts of errors and truths, if sometimes too artificial, yet generally striking. But when we come to seek for the reconciling truth, which one side has overlaid and distorted, and the other ignorantly shrunk back from, but which, when placed in its real light and fairly seen, is to attract the love and homage of both, we seem—not to grasp a shadow—Mr. Maurice is too earnest and real a believer for that—but to be very much where we were, except that a cloud of words surrounds us. His positive statements seem like a running protest against being obliged to commit himself and come to the point; like a continual assertion of the hopelessness and uselessness of a definite form of speaking about the matter in hand. Take, for instance, the following short statement :—

"My object," he says, speaking of the words which he has taken as the subject of his essays, "has been to examine the language with which we are most familiar, and which has been open to most objections, especially from Unitarians. Respecting the Conception I have been purposely silent; not because I have any doubt about that article, or am indifferent to it, but because I believe the word '*miraculous*,' which we *ordinarily connect with it, suggests an untrue meaning; because I think the truth is conveyed to us most safely in the simple language of the Evangelists;* and because that language taken in connection with the rest of their story, offers itself, I suspect, to a majority of those who have taken in the idea of an Incarnation, as the *only natural and rational* account of the method by which the eternal Son of God could have taken human flesh."

Now, would not Mr. Maurice have done better if he had enounced the definite meaning, or shade of meaning, which he considers short of, or different

from, our *ordinary* meaning of *miraculous*, as applied
to this subject, and yet the same as that suggested
by the Gospel account? We have no doubt what
Mr. Maurice does believe on this sacred subject.
But we are puzzled by what he means to disavow,
as an "*untrue meaning*" of the word *miraculous*, as
applied to what he believes. And the Unitarians
whom he addresses must, we think, be puzzled too.

We have quoted this passage because it is a short
one, and therefore a convenient one for a short
notice like this. But the same tormenting indistinct-
ness pervades the attempts generally to get a meaning or a position, which shall be substantially and in
its living force the same as the popular and orthodox
article, yet convict it of confusion or formalism;
and which shall give to the Unitarian what he aims
at by his negation of the popular article, without
leaving him any longer a reason for denying it. The
essay on Inspiration is an instance of this. Mr.
Maurice says very truly, that it is necessary to face
the fact that important questions are asked on the
subject, very widely, and by serious people; that
popular notions are loose and vague about it; that it
is a dangerous thing to take refuge in a hard theory,
if it is an inconsistent and inadequate one; that if
doubts do grow up, they are hardly to be driven
away by assertions. He accepts the challenge to
state his own view of Inspiration, and devotes many
pages to doing so. In these pages are many true
and striking things. So far as we understand, there

is not a statement that we should contradict. But we have searched in vain for a passage which might give, in Mr. Maurice's words, a distinct answer to the question of friend or opponent, What do you mean by the "Inspiration of the Bible?" Mr. Maurice tells us a most important truth—that that same Great Person by whose "holy inspiration" all true Christians still hope to be taught, inspired the prophets. He protests against making it necessary to say that there is a *generic* difference between one kind of Inspiration and the other, or "setting up the Bible as a book which encloses all that may be lawfully called Inspiration." He looks on the Bible as a link—a great one, yet a link, joining on to what is before and what comes after—in God's method of teaching man His truth. He cares little about phrases like "verbal inspiration" and "plenary inspiration"—"forms of speech which are pretty toys for those that have leisure to play with them; and if they are not made so hard as to do mischief, the use of them should not be checked. But they do not belong to business." He bids us, instead, give men "the Book of Life," and "have courage to tell them that there is a Spirit with them who will guide them into all truth." Great and salutary lessons. But we must say that they have been long in the world, and, it must be said, are as liable to be misunderstood as any other "popular" notions on the subject. If there is nothing more to say on the subject—if it is one where, though we see and are sure of a truth, yet we must confess it to be behind a veil, as yet indistinct and not to be grasped, let us manfully say so, and wait till God reveal even this unto us. But it is not a wise or a right course to raise expectations of being able to say something, not perhaps new, but satisfactory, when the questions which are really being asked, which are the professed occasion of the answer, remain, in their intellectual difficulty, entirely unresolved. Mr. Maurice is no trifler; when he throws hard words about,—when at the close of this essay he paints to himself the disappointment of some "Unitarian listener, who had hoped that Mr. Maurice was going to join him in cursing his enemies, and found that he had blessed them these three times," —he ought to consider whether the result has not been, and very naturally, to leave both parties more convinced than before of the hollowness of all professions to enter into, and give weight to, the difficulties and the claims of opposite sides.

Mr. Maurice has not done justice, as it seems to us, in this case, to the difficulty of the Unitarian. In other cases he makes free with the common belief of Christendom, and claims sacrifices which are as needless as they are unwarrantable. If there is a belief rooted in the minds of Christians, it is that of a future judgment. If there is an expectation which Scripture and the Creed sanction in the plainest words, it is that this present world is to have an end, and that then, a time now future, Christ will judge quick and dead. Say as much as can be said of the difficulty of conceiving such a thing, it really amounts to no more than the difficulty of conceiving what will happen, and how we shall be dealt with, when this familiar world passes away. And this belief in a "*final* judgment, *unlike any other that has ever been in the world*," Mr. Maurice would have us regard as a misinterpretation of Bible and Creed—a "dream" which St. Paul would never "allow us" to entertain, but would "compel" us instead "to look upon every one of what we rightly call 'God's judgments' as *essentially resembling it in kind and principle.*" "Our eagerness to deny this," he continues, "to make out an altogether peculiar and unprecedented judgment at the end of the world, has obliged us first *to practise the most violent outrages upon the language of Scripture*, insisting that words cannot really mean what, according to all ordinary rules of construction, they must mean." It really must be said that the "outrage," if so it is to be called, is not on the side of the popular belief. And why does this belief seem untenable to Mr. Maurice? Because it seems inconsistent to him with a truth which he states and enforces with no less earnestness than reason, that Christ is every moment judging us—that His tribunal is one before which we in our inmost "being are standing now—and that the time will come when we shall know that it is so, and when all that has concealed the Judge from us shall be taken away." Doubtless Christ is always with us—always seeing us—always judging us. Doubtless "everywhere" in Scripture the idea is kept before us of judgment in its fullest, largest, most natural sense, as "importing" not merely passing sentence, and awarding reward or penalty, but "discrimination and discovery. Everywhere that discrimination or discovery is supposed to be exercised over the man himself, over his internal character, over his meaning and will." Granted, also, that men have, in their attempts to figure to themselves the "great assize," sometimes made strange work, and shown how carnal their thoughts are, both in what they expected, and in the influence they allowed it to have over them. But what of all this? Correct these gross ideas, but leave the words of Scripture in their literal meaning, and do not say that all those who receive them as the announcement of what is to be, under conditions now inconceivable to man, *must* understand "the substitution of a mere external trial or examination" for the inward and daily trial of our hearts, as a mere display of "earthly pomp and ceremonial"—a resumption by Christ "of earthly conditions"; or that, because they believe that at "some distant unknown period they shall be brought into the presence of One who is now" not "far from them," but out of sight —how, or in what manner they know not—therefore they *must* suppose that He "is not now fulfilling the office of a Judge, whatever else may be committed to Him."

Mr. Maurice is aiming at a high object. He would reconcile the old and the new. He would disencumber what is popular of what is vulgar, confused, sectarian, and preserve and illustrate it by disencumbering it. He calls on us not to be afraid of the depths and heights, the freedom and largeness, the "spirit and the truth," of our own theology. It is a warning and a call which every age wants. We sympathise with his aim, with much of his positive teaching, with some of his aversions and some of his fears. We do not respect him the less for not being afraid of being called hard names. But certainly such a writer has need, in no common degree, of conforming himself to that wise maxim, which holds in writing as well as in art—" Know what you want to do, then do it."

FREDERICK DENISON MAURICE[1]

THIS Easter week we have lost a man about whom opinions and feelings were much divided, who was by many of the best and most thoughtful among us looked on as the noblest and greatest of recent English teachers, and who certainly had that rare gift of inspiring enthusiasm and trust among honest and powerful minds in search of guidance, which belongs to none but to men of a very high order. Professor Maurice has ended a life of the severest and most unceasing toil, still working to the utmost that failing bodily strength allowed—still to the last in harness. The general public, though his name is familiar to them, probably little measure the deep and passionate affection with which he was regarded by the circle of his friends and by those whose thoughts and purposes he had moulded; or the feeling which his loss causes in them of a blank, great and not to be filled up, not only personally for themselves, but in the agencies which are working

[1] *Saturday Review*, 6th April 1872.

most hopefully in English society. But even those who knew him least, and only from the outside, and whose points of view least coincided with his, must feel that there has been, now that we look back on his course, something singularly touching and even pathetic in the combination shown in all that he did, of high courage and spirit, and of unwearied faith and vigour, with the deepest humility and with the sincerest disinterestedness and abnegation, which never allowed him to seek anything great for himself, and, in fact, distinguished and honoured as he was, never found it. For the sake of his generation we may regret that he did not receive the public recognition and honour which were assuredly his due; but in truth his was one of those careers which, for their own completeness and consistency, gain rather than lose by escaping the distractions and false lights of what is called preferment.

The two features which strike us at the moment as characteristic of Mr. Maurice as a writer and teacher, besides the vast range both of his reading and thought, and the singularly personal tone and language of all that he wrote, are, first, the combination in him of the most profound and intense religiousness with the most boundless claim and exercise of intellectual liberty; and next, the value which he set, exemplifying his estimate in his own long and laborious course, on processes and efforts, as compared with conclusions and definite results, in that pursuit of truth which was to him the most sacred of duties. There is no want of earnest and fervent religion among us, intelligent, well-informed, deliberate, as well as of religion, to which these terms can hardly be applied. And there is also no want of the boldest and most daring freedom of investigation and judgment. But what Mr. Maurice seemed to see himself, and what he endeavoured to impress on others, was that religion and liberty are no natural enemies, but that the deepest and most absorbing forms of historical and traditional religion draw strength and seriousness of meaning, and binding obligation, from an alliance, frank and unconditional, with what seem to many the risks, the perilous risks and chances, of freedom.

It was a position open to obvious and formidable criticism; but against this criticism is to be set the fact, that in a long and energetic life, in which amidst great trials and changes there was a singular uniformity and consistency of character maintained, he did unite the two—the most devout Christianity with the most fearless and unshrinking boldness in facing the latest announcements and possibilities of modern thought. That he always satisfactorily explained his point of view to others is more than can be said; but he certainly satisfied numbers of keen and anxious thinkers, who were discontented and disheartened both by religion as it is presented by our great schools and parties, and by science as its principles and consequences are expounded by the leading philosophical authorities of the day. The other point to which we have adverted partly explains the influence which he had with such minds. He had no system to formulate or to teach. He was singularly ready to accept, as adequate expressions of those truths in whose existence he so persistently believed, the old consecrated forms in which simpler times had attempted to express them. He believed that these truths are wider and vaster than the human mind which is to be made wiser and better by them. And his aim was to reach up to an ever more exact, and real, and harmonious hold of these truths, which in their essential greatness he felt to be above him; to reach to it in life as much as in thought. And so to the end he was ever striving, not so much to find new truths as to find the heart and core of old ones, the truth of the truth, the inner life and significance of the letter, of which he was always loth to refuse the traditional form. In these efforts at unfolding and harmonising there was considerable uniformity; no one could mistake Mr. Maurice's manner of presenting the meaning and bearing of an article of the Creed for the manner of any one else; but the result of this way of working, in the effect of the things which he said, and in his relations to different bodies of opinion and thought both in the Church and in society, was to give the appearance of great and important changes in his teaching and his general point of view, as life went on. This governing thought of his, of the immeasurably transcendent compass and height of all truths compared with the human mind and spirit which was to bow to them and to gain life and elevation by accepting them, explains the curious and at present almost unique combination in him, of deep reverence for the old language of dogmatic theology, and an energetic maintenance of its fitness and value, with dissatisfaction, equally deep and impartially universal, at the interpretations put on this dogmatic language by modern theological schools, and at the modes in which its meaning is applied by them both in directing thought and influencing practice. This habit of distinguishing sharply and peremptorily between dogmatic language and the popular reading of it at any given time is conspicuous in his earliest as in his latest handling of these subjects; in the pamphlet of 1835, *Subscription no Bondage*, explaining and defending the old practice at Oxford; and in the papers and letters, which have appeared from him in periodicals, on the Athanasian Creed, and which are, we suppose, almost his last writings.

The world at large thought Mr. Maurice obscure and misty, and was, as was natural, impatient of such faults. The charge was, no doubt, more than partially true; and nothing but such genuine strength and comprehensive power as his could have prevented it from being a fatal one to his weight and authority. But it is not uninstructive to remember what was very much at the root of it. It had its origin, not altogether, but certainly in a great degree, in two of his moral characteristics. One was his stubborn, conscientious determination, at any cost of awkwardness, or apparent inconsistency, or imperfection of statement, to say out what he had to say, neither more nor less, just as he thought it, and just as he felt it, with the most fastidious care for truthful accuracy of meaning. He never would suffer what he considered either the connection or the balance and adjustment of varied and complementary truths to be sacrificed to force or point of expression; and he had to choose sometimes, as all people have, between a blurred, clumsy, and ineffective picture and a consciously incomplete and untrue one. His choice never wavered; and as the artist's aim was high, and his skill not always equally at his command, he preferred the imperfection which left him the consciousness of honesty. The other cause which threw a degree of haze round his writings was the personal shape into which he was so fond of throwing his views. He shrunk from their enunciation as arguments and conclusions which claimed on their own account and by their own title the deference of all who read them; and he submitted them as what he himself had found and had been granted to see—the lessons and convictions of his own experience. Sympathy is, no doubt, a great bond among all men; but, after all, men's experience and their points of view are not all alike, and when we are asked to see with another's eyes, it is not always easy. Mr. Maurice's desire to give the simplest and most real form to his thoughts as they arose in his own mind contributed more often than he supposed to prevent others from entering into his meaning. He asked them to put themselves in his place. He did not sufficiently put himself in theirs.

But he has taught us great lessons, of the sacredness, the largeness, and, it may be added, the difficulty of truth; lessons of sympathy with one another, of true humility and self-conquest in the busy and unceasing activity of the intellectual faculties. He has left no school and no system, but he has left a spirit and an example. We speak of him here only as those who knew him as all the world knew him; but those who were his friends are never tired of speaking of his grand simplicity of character, of his tenderness and delicacy, of the irresistible spell of lovableness which won all within its reach. They remember how he spoke, and how he read; the tones of a voice of singularly piercing clearness, which was itself a power of interpretation, which revealed his own soul and went straight to the hearts of hearers. He has taken his full share in the controversies of our days, and there must be many opinions both about the line which he took, and even sometimes about the temper in which he carried on debate. But it is nothing but the plainest justice to say that he was a philosopher, a theologian, and, we may add, a prophet, of whom, for his great gifts, and, still more, for his noble and pure use of them, the modern English Church may well be proud.

XX

SIR RICHARD CHURCH[1]

GENERAL SIR RICHARD CHURCH died last week at Athens. Many English travellers in the East find their way to Athens; most of them must have heard his name repeated there as the name of one closely associated with the later fortunes of the Greek nation, and linking the present with times now distant; some of them may have seen him, and may remember the slight wiry form which seemed to bear years so lightly, the keen eye and grisled moustache and soldierly bearing, and perhaps the antique and ceremonious courtesy, stately yet cordial, recalling a type of manners long past, with which he welcomed those who had a claim on his attentions or friendly offices. Five and forty years ago his name was much in men's mouths. He was prominent in a band of distinguished men, who represented a new enthusiasm in Europe. Less by what they were able to do than by their character and their unreserved self-devotion and

[1] *Guardian*, 26th March 1873.

sacrifice, they profoundly affected public opinion, and disarmed the jealousy of absolutist courts and governments in favour of a national movement, which, whether disappointment may have followed its success, was one of the most just and salutary of revolutions—the deliverance of a Christian nation from the hopeless tyranny of the Turks.

He was one of the few remaining survivors of the generation which had taken part in the great French war and in the great changes resulting from it—changes which have in time given way to vaster alterations, and been eclipsed by them. He began his military life as a boy-ensign in one of the regiments forming part of the expedition which, under Sir Ralph Abercromby, drove the French out of Egypt in 1801; and on the shores of the Mediterranean, where his career began, it was for the most part continued and finished. His genius led him to the more irregular and romantic forms of military service; he had the gift of personal influence, and the power of fascinating and attaching to himself, with extraordinary loyalty, the people of the South. His adventurous temper, his sympathetic nature, his chivalrous courtesy, his thorough trustworthiness and sincerity, his generosity, his high spirit of nobleness and honour, won for him, from Italians and Greeks, not only that deep respect which was no unusual tribute from them to English honesty and strength and power of command, but that love, and that affectionate and almost tender veneration, for which strong and resolute Englishmen have not always cared from races of whose characteristic faults they were impatient.

His early promise in the regular service was brilliant; as a young staff-officer, and by a staff-officer's qualities of sagacity, activity, and decision, he did distinguished service at Maida; and had he followed the movement which made Spain the great battle-ground for English soldiers, he had every prospect of earning a high place among those who fought under Wellington. But he clung to the Mediterranean. He was employed in raising and organising those foreign auxiliary corps which it was thought were necessary to eke out the comparatively scanty numbers of the English armies, and to keep up threatening demonstrations on the outskirts of the French Empire. It was in this service that his connection with the Greek people was first formed, and his deep and increasing interest in its welfare created. He was commissioned to form first one, and then a second, regiment of Greek irregulars; and from the Ionian Islands, from the mainland of Albania, from the Morea, chiefs and bands, accustomed to the mountain warfare, half patriotic, half predatory, carried on by the more energetic Greek highlanders against the Turks, flocked to the English standards. The operations in which they were engaged were desultory, and of no great account in the general result of the gigantic contest; but they made Colonel Church's name familiar to the Greek population, who were hoping, amid the general confusion, for an escape from the tyranny of the Turks. But his connection with Greece was for some time delayed. His peculiar qualifications pointed him out as a fit man to be a medium of communication between the English Government and the foreign armies which were operating on the outside of the circle within which the decisive struggle was carried on against Napoleon; and he was the English Military Commissioner attached to the Austrian armies in Italy in 1814 and 1815.

At the Peace, his eagerness for daring and adventurous enterprise was tempted by great offers from the Neapolitan Government. The war had left brigandage, allied to a fierce spirit of revolutionary freemasonry, all-powerful in the south of Italy; and a stern and resolute, yet perfectly honest and just hand, was needed to put it down. He accepted the commission; he was reckless of conspiracy and threats of assassination; he was known to be no sanguinary and merciless lover of severity, but he was known also to be fearless and inexorable against crime; and, not without some terrible examples, yet with complete success, he delivered the south of Italy from the scourge. But his thoughts had always been turned towards Greece; at last the call came, and he threw himself with all his hopes and all his fortunes into a struggle which more than any other that history can show engaged at the time the interest of Europe. His first efforts resulted in a disastrous defeat against overwhelming odds, for which, as is natural, he has been severely criticised; his critics have shown less quickness in perceiving the qualities which he displayed after it—his unshaken, silent fortitude, the power with which he kept together and saved the wrecks of his shattered and disheartened volunteer army, the confidence in himself with which he inspired them, the skill with which he extricated them from their dangers in the face of a strong and formidable enemy, the humanity which he strove so earnestly by word and example to infuse into the barbarous warfare customary between Greeks and Turks, the tenacity with which he clung to the fastnesses of Western Greece, obtaining by his perseverance from the diplomacy of Europe a more favourable line of boundary for the new nation which it at length recognised. To this cause he gave up everything; personal risks cannot be counted; but he threw away all prospects in England; he made no bargains; he sacrificed freely to the necessities of the struggle any pecuniary resource that he could command, neither requiring nor receiving any repayment. He threw in his lot with the people for whom he had surrendered everything, in order to take part in their deliverance. Since his arrival in Greece in 1827 he has never turned his face westwards. He took the part which is perhaps the only becoming and justifiable one for the citizen of one State who permits himself to take arms, even in the cause of independence, for another; having fought for the

Greeks, he lived with them, and shared, for good and for evil, their fortunes.

For more than forty years he has resided at Athens under the shadow of the great rock of the Acropolis. Distinguished by all the honours the Greek nation could bestow, military or political, he has lived in modest retirement, only on great emergencies taking any prominent part in the political questions of Greece, but always throwing his influence on the side of right and honesty. The course of things in Greece was not always what an educated Englishman could wish it to be. But whatever his judgment, or, on occasion, his action might be, there never could be a question, with his friends any more than with his opponents—enemies he could scarcely be said to have—as to the straightforwardness, the pure motives, the unsullied honour of anything that he did or anything that he advised. The Greeks saw among them one deeply sympathising with all that they cared for, commanding, if he had pleased to work for it, considerable influence out of Greece, the intimate friend of a Minister like Sir Edmund Lyons, yet keeping free from the temptation to make that use of influence which seems so natural to politicians in a place like Athens; thinking much of Greece and of the interests of his friends there, but thinking as much of truth and justice and conscience; hating intrigue and trick, and shaming by his indignant rebuke any proposal of underhand courses that might be risked in his presence.

The course of things, the change of ideas and of men, threw him more and more out of any forward and prominent place in the affairs of Greece. But his presence in Athens was felt everywhere. There was a man who had given up everything for Greece and sought nothing in return. His blameless unselfishness, his noble elevation of character, were a warning and a rebuke to the faults which have done so much mischief to the progress of the nation; and yet every Greek in Athens knew that no one among them was more jealous of the honour of the nation or more anxious for its good. To a new political society, freshly exposed to the temptations of party struggles for power, no greater service can be rendered than a public life absolutely clear from any suspicion of self-seeking, governed uninterruptedly and long by public spirit, public ends, and a strong sense of duty. Such a service General Church has rendered to his adopted country. During his residence among them for nearly half a century they have become familiar, not in word, but in living reality, with some of the best things which the West has to impart to the East. They have had among them an example of English principle, English truth, English high-souled disinterestedness, and that noble English faith which, in a great cause, would rather hope in vain than not hope at all. They have learned to venerate all this, and, some of them, to love it.

XXI

DEATH OF BISHOP WILBERFORCE[1]

THE beautiful summer weather which came on us at the beginning of this week gives by contrast a strange and terrible point to the calamity, the announcement of which sent such a shock through the whole country on Monday last. Summer days in all their brilliance seemed come at last, after a long waiting which made them the more delightful. But as people came down to breakfast on that morning, or as they gathered at railway stations on their way to business, the almost incredible tidings met them that the Bishop of Winchester was dead; that he had been killed by a fall from his horse. In a moment, by the most trivial of accidents, one of the foremost and most stirring men of our generation had passed away from the scene in which his part was so large a one. With everything calm and peaceful round him, in the midst of the keen but tranquil enjoyment of a summer evening ride with a friend through some of the most charming scenery in England, looking forward to meeting

[1] *Guardian*, 23rd July 1873.

another friend, and to the pleasure which a quiet Sunday brings to hard-worked men in fine weather, and a pleasant country house, the blow fell. The moment before, as Lord Granville remarks, he had given expression to the fulness of his enjoyment. He was rejoicing in the fine weather, he was keenly noticing the beauty of the scenery at every point of the way; with his characteristic love of trees he was noticing the different kinds and the soils which suited them; especially he was greatly pleased with his horse. There comes a slight dip in the smooth turf; the horse stumbles and recovers himself unhurt; but in that short interval of time all has vanished, all things earthly, from that quick eye and that sensitive and sympathetic mind. It is indeed tragic. He is said to have thought with distress of a lingering end. He was spared it. He died as a soldier dies.

A shock like this brings with it also a shock of new knowledge and appreciation of things. We are made to feel with a new force what it is that we have lost, and to understand more exactly what is the proportion of what we have lost to what we still retain. To friends and opponents the Bishop of Winchester could not but be, under any circumstances, a person of the greatest importance. But few of us, probably, measured fully and accurately the place which he filled among us. We are better aware of it now when he has been taken away from us. Living among us, and acting before us from day to day, the object of each day's observation and criticism, under each day's varying circumstances and feelings, within our reach always if we wanted to see him or to hear him, he was presented to our thoughts in that partial disclosure, and that everyday homeliness, which as often disguise the true and complete significance of a character, as they give substance and reality to our conceptions of it. As the man's course moves on, we are apt to lose in our successive judgments of the separate steps of it—it may be steps of great immediate interest—our sense of its connection and tendency, of the true measure of it as a whole, of the degree in which character is growing and rising, or, on the other hand, falling or standing still. The Bishop of Winchester had many admirers—many who deeply loved and trusted him—many who, in the face of a good deal of suspicion and hostile comment, stoutly insisted on the high estimate which they had formed of him. But even among them, and certainly in the more indifferent public, there were few who had rightly made it clear to their own minds what he had really grown to be both in the Church and the country.

For it is obvious, at the first glance now that he is gone, that there is no one who can fill the place which he filled. It seems to us beyond dispute that he has been the greatest Bishop the English Church has seen for a century and a half. We do not say the greatest man, but the greatest Bishop; the one among the leaders of the English Church who most adequately understood the relations of his office, not only to the Church, but to his times and his country, and who most adequately fulfilled his own conception of them. We are very far from saying this because of his exuberant outfit of powers and gifts; because of his versatility, his sympathetic nature, his eager interest in all that interested his fellows, his inexhaustible and ready resources of thought and speech, of strong and practical good sense, of brilliant or persuasive or pathetic eloquence. In all this he had equals and rivals, though perhaps he had not many in the completeness and balance of his powers. Nor do we say anything of those gifts, partly of the intellect, but also of the soul and temper and character, by which he was able at once to charm without tiring the most refined and fastidious society, to draw to him the hearts of hard-working and anxious clergymen, and to enchain the attention of the dullest and most ignorant of rustic congregations. All these are, as it seems to us, the subordinate, and not the most interesting, parts of what he was; they were on the surface and attracted notice, and the parts were often mistaken for the whole. Nor do we forget what often offended even equitable judges, disliking all appearance of management and mere adroitness—or what was often objected against his proceedings by opponents at least as unscrupulous as they wished him to be thought. We are far from thinking that his long career was free from either mistakes or faults; it is not likely that a course steered amid such formidable and perplexing difficulties, and steered with such boldness and such little attempt to evade them, should not offer repeated occasions not only for ill-natured, but for grave and serious objections.

But looking over that long course of his Episcopate, from 1845 to the present year, we see in him, in an eminent and unique degree, two things. He had a distinct and statesmanlike idea of Church policy; and he had a new idea of the functions of a Bishop, and of what a Bishop might do and ought to do. And these two ideas he steadily kept in view and acted upon with increasing clearness in his purpose and unflagging energy in action. He grasped in all its nobleness and fulness and height the conception of the Church as a great religious society of Divine origin, with many sides and functions, with diversified gifts and ever new relations to altering times, but essentially, and above all things, a religious society. To serve that society, to call forth in it the consciousness of its calling and its responsibilities, to strengthen and put new life into its organisation, to infuse ardour and enthusiasm and unity into its efforts, to encourage and foster everything that harmonised with its principle and purpose, to watch against the counteracting influences of self-willed or ignorant narrowness, to adjust its substantial rights and its increasing activity to the new exigencies of political changes, to elicit from the Church all that could command the respect and win the sympathy and confidence of Englishmen, and make its presence recognised as a supreme blessing by those whom nothing but what was great and real in its benefits would satisfy—this was the aim from which, however perplexed or wavering or inconsistent he may have been at times, he never really swerved. In the breadth and largeness of his principle, in the freedom and variety of its practical applications, in the distinctness of his purposes and the intensity of his convictions, he was an example of high statesmanship common in no age of the Church, and in no branch of it. And all this rested on the most profound personal religion as its foundation, a religion which became in time one of very definite doctrinal preferences, but of wide sympathies, and which was always of very exacting claims for the undivided work and efforts of a lifetime.

When he became Bishop he very soon revolutionised the old notion of a Bishop's duties. He threw himself without any regard to increasing trouble and labour on the great power of personal influence. In every corner of his diocese he made himself known and felt; in all that interested its clergy or its people he took his part more and more. He went forth to meet men; he made himself their guest and companion as well as their guide and chief; he was more often to be found moving about his diocese than he was to be found at his own home at Cuddesdon. The whole tone of communication between Bishop and people rose at once in freedom and in spiritual elevation and earnestness; it was at once less formal and more solemnly practical. He never spared his personal presence; always ready to show himself, always ready to bring the rarer and more impressive rites of the Church, such as Ordination, within the view of people at a distance from his Palace or Cathedral, he was never more at his ease than in a crowd of new faces, and never exhausted and worn out in what he had to say to fresh listeners. Gathering men about him at one time; turning them to account, assigning them tasks, pressing the willing, shaming the indolent or the reluctant, at another; travelling about with the rapidity and system of an officer inspecting his positions, he infused into the diocese a spirit and zeal which nothing but such labour and sympathy could give, and bound it together by the bands of a strong and wise organisation.

What he did was but a very obvious carrying out of the idea of the Episcopal office; but it had not seemed necessary once, and his merit was that he saw both that it was necessary and practicable. It is he who set the standard of what is now expected, and is more or less familiar, in all Bishops. And as he began so he went on to the last. He never flagged, he never grew tired of the continual and varied intercourse which he kept up with his clergy and people. To the last he worked his diocese as much as possible not from a distance, but from local points which brought him into closer communication with his flock. London, with its great interests and its great attractions, social and political, never kept away one who was so keenly alive to them, and so prominent in all that was eventful in his time, from attending to the necessities and claims of his rural parishes. What his work was to the very last, how much there was in him of unabated force, of far-seeing judgment, of noble boldness and earnestness, of power over the souls and minds of men in many ways divided, a letter from Dr. Monsell[1] in our columns shows.

[1] ... The shock that the sudden announcement of an event so solemn must ever give, was tenfold great to one who, like myself, had been, during the past week, closely associated with him in anxious deliberations as to the best means of meeting the various difficulties and dangers with which the Church is at present surrounded.

He had gathered round him, as was his annual wont, his Archdeacons and Rural Deans, to deliberate for the Church's interests; and in his opening address, and conduct of a most important meeting, never had he shone out more clearly in intellectual vigour, in theological soundness, in moral boldness, in Christian gentleness and love.

... He spoke upon the gravest questions of the day—questions which require more than they generally receive, delicate handling. He divided from the evil of things, which some in the spirit of party condemn wholesale, the hidden good which lies wrapt up in them, and which it would be sin as well as folly to sweep away. He made every man who heard him feel the blessing of having in the Church such a veteran leader, and drew forth from more than one there the openly expressed hope that as he had in bygone days been the bold and cautious controller of an earlier movement in the right direction, so now he would save to the Church some of her precious things which rude men would sweep away, and help her to regain what is essential to her spiritual existence without risking the sacredness of private life, the purity of private thoughts, the sense of direct responsibility between God

He had a great and all-important place in a very critical moment, to which he brought a seriousness of purpose, a power and ripeness of counsel, and a fearlessness distinctly growing up to the last. It is difficult to see who will bend the bow which he has dropped.

and the soul, which are some of the most distinctive characteristics of our dear Church of England.

From his council chamber in Winchester House I went direct with him to the greater council chamber of St. Stephen's to hear him there vindicate the rights and privileges of his order, and beat back the assaults of those who, in high places, think that by a speech in, or a vote of, either house they can fashion the Church as they please. Never did he speak with more point and power; and never did he seem to have won more surely the entire sympathy of the house.

To gather in overwhelming numbers round him in the evening his London clergy and their families, to meet them all with the kind cordiality of a real father and friend, to run on far into the middle of the night in this laborious endeavour to please—was "the last effort of his toilsome day."

XXII

RETIREMENT OF THE PROVOST OF ORIEL[1]

DR. HAWKINS, the Provost of Oriel, has resigned the Provostship. He has held it from 1828, within four years of half a century. The time during which he has presided over his college has been one of the most eventful periods in the history of the University; it has been a time of revolt against custom, of reform, of keen conflict, of deep changes; and in all connected with these he has borne a part, second to none in prominence, in importance, and we must add, in dignity. No name of equal distinction has disappeared from the list of Heads of Houses since the venerable President of Magdalen passed away. But Dr. Routh, though he watched with the keenest intelligence, and not without sympathy, all that went on in the days into which his life had been prolonged, watched it with the habits and thoughts of days long departed; he had survived from the days of Bishop

[1] *Guardian*, 4th November 1874.

Horne and Dr. Parr far into our new and strange century, to which he did not belong, and he excited its interest as a still living example of what men were before the French Revolution. The eminence of the Provost of Oriel is of another kind. He calls forth interest because among all recent generations of Oxford men, and in all their restless and exciting movements, he has been a foremost figure. He belongs to modern Oxford, its daring attempts, its fierce struggles, its successes, and its failures. He was a man of whom not only every one heard, but whom every one saw; for he was much in public, and his unsparing sense of public duty made him regularly present in his place at Council, at Convocation, at the University Church, at College chapel. The outward look of Oxford will be altered by the disappearance in its ceremonies and gatherings of his familiar form and countenance.

He would anywhere have been a remarkable man. His active and independent mind, with its keen, discriminating, practical intelligence, was formed and disciplined amid that company of distinguished scholars and writers who, at Oxford, in the second decade of the century were revolted by the scandalous inertness and self-indulgence of the place, with its magnificent resources squandered and wasted, its stupid orthodoxy of routine, its insensibility to the questions and the dangers rising all round; men such as Keble, Arnold, Davison, Copleston, Whately. These men, different as they were from one another, all represented the awakening but still imperfect consciousness that a University life ought to be something higher than one of literary idleness, given up to the frivolities of mere elegant scholarship, and to be crowned at last by comfortable preferment; that there was much difficult work to be seriously thought about and done, and that men were placed at Oxford under heavy responsibilities to use their thoughts and their leisure for the direct service of their generation. Clever fops and dull pedants joined in sneering at this new activity and inquisitiveness of mind, and this grave interest and employment of intellect on questions and in methods outside the customary line of University studies and prejudices; but the men were too powerful, and their work too genuine and effective, and too much in harmony with the temper and tendencies of the time, to be stopped by impertinence and obstructiveness. Dr. Hawkins was one of those who made the Oriel Common-room a place of keen discussion and brilliant conversation, and, for those days, of bold speculation; while the College itself reflected something of the vigour and accomplishments of the Common-room. Dr. Newman, in the *Apologia*, has told us, in touching terms of acknowledgment, what Dr. Hawkins was when, fifty years ago, the two minds first came into close contact, and what intellectual services he believed Dr. Hawkins had rendered him. He tells us, too, how Dr. Hawkins had profoundly impressed him by a work in which, with characteristic independence and guarded caution equally characteristic, he cuts across popular prejudices and confusions of thought, and shows himself original in discerning and stating an obvious truth which had escaped other people—his work on *Unauthoritative Tradition*. His logical acuteness, his habits of disciplined accuracy, abhorrent and impatient of all looseness of thinking and expression, his conscientious efforts after substantial reality in his sharpest distinctions, his capacity for taking trouble, his serious and strong sense of the debt involved in the possession of intellectual power —all this would have made him eminent, whatever the times in which he lived.

But the times in which we live and what they bring with them mould most of us; and the times shaped the course of the Provost of Oriel, and turned his activity into a channel of obstinate and prolonged antagonism, of resistance and protest, most conscientious but most uncompromising, against two great successive movements, both of which he condemned as unbalanced and recoiled from as revolutionary—the Tractarian first, and then the Liberal movement in Oxford. Of the former, it is not perhaps too much to say that he was in Oxford, at least, the ablest and most hurtful opponent. From his counsels, from his guarded and measured attacks, from the power given him by a partial agreement against popular fallacies with parts of its views, from his severe and unflinching determination, it received its heaviest blows and suffered its greatest losses.

He detested what he held to be its anti-Liberal temper, and its dogmatic assertions; he resented its taking out of his hands a province of theology which he and Whately had made their own, that relating to the Church; he thought its tone of feeling and its imaginative and poetical side exaggerated or childish; and he could not conceive of its position except as involving palpable dishonesty. No one probably guided with such clear and self-possessed purpose that policy of extreme measures, which contributed to bring about, if it did not itself cause, the break-up of 1845. Then succeeded the great Liberal tide with its demands for extensive and immediate change, its anti-ecclesiastical spirit, its scarcely disguised scepticism, its daring philosophical and critical enterprises. By degrees it became clear that the impatience and intolerance which had purged the University of so many Churchmen had, after all, left the Church movement itself untouched, to assume by degrees proportions scarcely dreamed of when it began; but that what the defeat of the Tractarians really had done was, to leave the University at the mercy of Liberals to whom what had been called Liberalism in the days of Whately was mere blind and stagnant Conservatism.

One war was no sooner over than the Provost of Oriel found another even more formidable on his hands. The most dauntless and most unshaken of combatants, he faced his new antagonists with the same determination, the same unshrinking sense of duty with which he had fought his old ones. He used the high authority and influence which his position and his character justly gave him, to resist or to control, as far as he could, the sweeping changes which, while bringing new life into Oxford, have done so much to break up her connection of centuries with the Church. He boldly confronted the new spirit of denial and unbelief. He wrote, he preached, he published, as he had done against other adversaries, always with measured and dignified argument, but not shrinking from plain-spoken severity of condemnation. Never sparing himself labour when he thought duty called, he did not avail himself of the privilege of advancing years to leave the war to be carried on by younger champions.

It is impossible for those who may at times have found themselves most strongly, and perhaps most painfully, opposed to him, not to admire and revere one who, through so long a career has, in what he held to be his duty to the Church and to religion, fought so hard, encountered such troubles, given up so many friendships and so much ease, and who, while a combatant to the last, undiscouraged by odds and sometimes by ill-success, has brought to the weariness and disappointment of old age an increasing gentleness and kindliness of spirit, which is one of the rarest tokens and rewards of patient and genuine self-discipline. A man who has set himself steadily and undismayed to stem and bring to reason the two most powerful currents of conviction and feeling which have agitated his times, leaves an impressive example of zeal and fearlessness, even to those against whom he has contended. What is the upshot which has come of these efforts, and whether the controversies of the moment have not in his case, as in others, diverted and absorbed faculties which might have been turned to calmer and more permanent tasks, we do not inquire.

Perhaps a life of combat never does all that the combatant thinks it ought to accomplish, or compensates for the sacrifices it entails. In the case of the Provost of Oriel, he had, with all his great and noble qualities, one remarkable want, which visibly impaired his influence and his persuasiveness. He was out of sympathy with the rising aspirations and tendencies of the time on the two opposite sides; he was suspicious and impatient of them. He was so sensible of their weak points, the logical difficulties which they brought with them, their precipitate and untested assumptions, the extravagance and unsoundness of character which often seemed inseparable from them, that he seldom did justice to them viewed in their complete aspect, or was even alive to what was powerful and formidable in the depth, the complexity, and the seriousness of the convictions and enthusiasm which carried them onwards. In truth, for a man of his singular activity and reach of mind, he was curiously indifferent to much that most interested his contemporaries in thought and literature; he did not understand it, and he undervalued it as if it belonged merely to the passing fashions of the hour.

This long career is now over. Warfare is always a rude trade, and men on all sides who have had to engage in it must feel at the end how much there is to be forgiven and needing forgiveness; how much now appears harsh, unfair, violent, which once appeared only necessary and just. A hard hitter like the Provost of Oriel must often have left behind the remembrance of his blows. But we venture to say that, even in those who suffered from them, he has left remembrances of another and better sort. He has left the recollection of a pure, consistent, laborious life, elevated in its aim and standard, and marked by high public spirit and a rigid and exacting sense of duty. In times when it was wanted, he set in his position in the University an example of modest and sober simplicity of living; and no one who ever knew him can doubt the constant presence, in all his thoughts, of the greatness of things unseen, or his equally constant reference of all that he did to the account which he was one day to give at his Lord's judgment-seat. We trust that he may be spared to enjoy the rest which a weaker or less conscientious man would have claimed long ago.

XXIII

MARK PATTISON[1]

THE Rector of Lincoln, who died at Harrogate this day week, was a man about whom judgments are more than usually likely to be biassed by prepossessions more or less unconscious, and only intelligible to the mind of the judge. There are those who are in danger of dealing with him too severely. There are also those whose temptation will be to magnify and possibly exaggerate his gifts and acquirements—great as they undoubtedly were,—the use that he made of them, and the place which he filled among his contemporaries. One set of people finds it not easy to forget that he had been at one time closer than most young men of his generation to the great religious leaders whom they are accustomed to revere; that he was of a nature fully to understand and appreciate both their intellectual greatness and their moral and spiritual height; that he had shared to the full their ideas and hopes; that they, too, had measured his depth of character, and grasp, and breadth, and

[1] *Guardian*, 6th August 1884.

subtlety of mind; and that the keenest judge among them of men and of intellect had picked him out as one of the most original and powerful of a number of very able contemporaries. Those who remember this cannot easily pardon the lengths of dislike and bitterness to which in after life Pattison allowed himself to be carried against the cause which once had his hearty allegiance, and in which, if he had discovered, as he thought, its mistakes and its weakness, he had once recognised with all his soul the nobler side. And on the other hand, the partisans of the opposite movement, into whose interests he so disastrously, as it seems to us, and so unreservedly threw himself, naturally welcomed and made the most of such an accession to their strength, and such an unquestionable addition to their literary fame. To have detached such a man from the convictions which he had so professedly and so earnestly embraced, and to have enlisted him as their determined and implacable antagonist—to be able to point to him in the maturity and strength of his powers as one who, having known its best aspects, had deliberately despaired of religion, and had turned against its representatives the scorn and hatred of a passionate nature, whose fires burned all the more fiercely under its cold crust of reserve and sarcasm—this was a triumph of no common order; and it might conceivably blind those who could rejoice in it to the comparative value of qualities which, at any rate, were very rare and remarkable ones.

Pattison was a man who, in many ways, did not do himself justice. As a young man, his was a severe and unhopeful mind, and the tendency to despond was increased by circumstances. There was something in the quality of his unquestionable ability which kept him for long out of the ordinary prizes of an Oxford career; in the class list, in the higher competition for Fellowships, he was not successful. There are those who long remembered the earnest pleading of the Latin letters which it was the custom to send in when a man stood for a Fellowship, and in which Pattison set forth his ardent longing for knowledge, and his narrow and unprosperous condition as a poor student. He always came very near; indeed, he more than once won the vote of the best judges; but he just missed the prize. To the bitter public disappointments of 1845 were added the vexations caused by private injustice and ill-treatment. He turned fiercely on those who, as he thought, had wronged him, and he began to distrust men, and to be on the watch for proofs of hollowness and selfishness in the world and in the Church. Yet at this time, when people were hearing of his bitter and unsparing sayings in Oxford, he was from time to time preaching in village churches, and preaching sermons which both his educated and his simple hearers thought unlike those of ordinary men in their force, reality, and earnestness. But with age and conflict the disposition to harsh and merciless judgments strengthened and became characteristic. This, however, should be remembered: where he revered he revered with genuine and unstinted reverence; where he saw goodness in which he believed he gave it ungrudging honour. He had real pleasure in recognising height and purity of character, and true intellectual force, and he maintained his admiration when the course of things had placed wide intervals between him and those to whom it had been given. His early friendships, where they could be retained, he did retain warmly and generously even to the last; he seemed almost to draw a line between them and other things in the world. The truth, indeed, was that beneath that icy and often cruel irony there was at bottom a most warm and affectionate nature, yearning for sympathy, longing for high and worthy objects, which, from the misfortunes especially of his early days, never found room to expand and unfold itself. Let him see and feel that anything was real—character, purpose, cause—and at any rate it was sure of his respect, probably of his interest. But the doubt whether it was real was always ready to present itself to his critical and suspicious mind; and these doubts grew with his years.

People have often not given Pattison credit for the love that was in him for what was good and true; it is not to be wondered at, but the observation has to be made. On the other hand, a panegyric, like that which we reprint from the *Times*, sets too high an estimate on his intellectual qualities, and on the position which they gave him. He was full of the passion for knowledge; he was very learned, very acute in his judgment on what his learning brought before him, very versatile, very shrewd, very subtle; too full of the truth of his subject to care about seeming to be original; but, especially in his poetical criticisms, often full of that best kind of originality which consists in seeing and pointing out novelty in what is most familiar and trite. But, not merely as a practical but as a speculative writer, he was apt to be too much under the empire and pressure of the one idea which at the moment occupied and interested his mind. He could not resist it; it came to him with exclusive and overmastering force; he did not care to attend to what limited it or conflicted with it. And thus, with all the force and sagacity of his University theories, they were not always self-consistent, and they were often one-sided and exaggerated. He was not a leader whom men could follow, however much they might rejoice at the blows which he might happen to deal, sometimes unexpectedly, at things which they disliked. And this holds of more serious things than even University reform and reconstruction.

And next, though every competent reader must do justice to Pattison's distinction as a man of letters, as a writer of English prose, and as a critic of what is noble and excellent and what is base and poor in literature, there is a curious want of completeness, a frequent crudity and hardness, a want, which is sometimes a surprising want, of good sense and good taste, which form unwelcome blemishes in his work, and just put it down below the line of first-rate excellence which it ought to occupy. Morally, in that love of reality, and of all that is high and noble in character, which certainly marked him, he was much better than many suppose, who know only the strength of his animosities and the bitterness of his sarcasm. Intellectually, in reach, and fulness, and solidity of mental power, it may be doubted whether he was so great as it has recently been the fashion to rate him.

XXIV

PATTISON'S ESSAYS[1]

THIS is a very interesting but a very melancholy collection of papers. They are the remains of the work of a man of first-rate intellect, whose powers, naturally of a high order, had been diligently and wisely cultivated, whose mind was furnished in a very rare degree with all that reading, wide and critical, could give, and which embraced in the circle of its interest all that is important to human life and society. Mr. Pattison had no vulgar standard of what knowledge is, and what goodness is. He was high, sincere, exacting, even austere, in his estimates of either; and when he was satisfied he paid honour with sometimes unexpected frankness and warmth. But from some unfortunate element in his temperament, or from the effect upon it of untoward and unkindly circumstances at those critical epochs of

[1] *Essays by the late Mark Pattison, sometime Rector of Lincoln College.* Collected and arranged by Henry Nettleship, M.A., Corpus Professor of Latin in the University of Oxford. *Guardian,* 1st May 1889

mental life, when character is taking its bent for good and all, he was a man in whose judgment severity—and severity expressing itself in angry scorn—was very apt to outrun justice. Longing for sympathy and not ill-fitted for it, capable of rare exertions in helping those whom he could help, he passed through life with a reputation for cynicism which, while he certainly exhibited it, he no less certainly would, if he had known how, have escaped from. People could easily tell what would incur his dislike and opposition, what would provoke his slow, bitter, merciless sarcasm; it was never easy to tell what would satisfy him, what would attract his approval, when he could be tempted to see the good side of a thing. It must not be forgotten that he had gone through a trial to which few men are equal. He had passed from the extreme ranks and the strong convictions of the Oxford movement—convictions of which the translation of Aquinas's *Catena Aurea*, still printed in the list of his works, is a memorial—to the frankest form of Liberal thought. As he himself writes, we cannot give up early beliefs, much less the deep and deliberate convictions of manhood, without some shock to the character. In his case the change certainly worked. It made him hate what he had left, and all that was like it, with the bitterness of one who has been imposed upon, and has been led to commit himself to what he now feels to be absurd and contemptible, and the bitterness of this disappointment gave an edge to all his work. There seems through all his criticism, powerful as it is, a tone of harshness, a readiness to take the worst construction, a sad consciousness of distrust and suspicion of all things round him, which greatly weakens the effect of his judgment. If a man will only look for the worst side, he will only find the worst side; but we feel that we act reasonably by not accepting such a teacher as our guide, however ably he may state his case. There is a want of equitableness and fairness in his stern and sometimes cruel condemnations; and yet not religion only, but the wisest wisdom of the world tells of the indispensable value of this equitableness, this old Greek virtue of ἐπιείκεια, in our views of men and things. It is not religion only, but common sense which says that "sweetness and light," kindliness, indulgence, sympathy, are necessary for moral and spiritual health. Scorn, indignation, keenly stinging sarcasm, doubtless have their place in a world in which untruth and baseness abound and flourish; but to live on these is poison, at least to oneself.

These fierce antipathies warped his judgment in strange and unexpected ways. Among these papers is a striking one on Calvin. If any character in history might be expected to have little attraction for him it is Calvin. Dogmatist, persecutor, tyrant, the proud and relentless fanatic, who more than any one consecrated harsh narrowness in religion by cruel theories about God, what was there to recommend him to a lover of liberty who had no patience for ecclesiastical pretensions of any kind, and who tells us that

Calvin's "sins against human liberty are of the deepest dye"? For if Laud chastised his adversaries with whips, Calvin chastised his with scorpions. Perhaps it is unreasonable to be suprised, yet we are taken by surprise, when we find a thinker like Mr. Pattison drawn by strong sympathy to Calvin and setting him up among the heroes and liberators of humanity. Mr. Pattison is usually fair in details, that is, he does not suppress bad deeds or qualities in those whom he approves, or good deeds or qualities in those whom he hates: it is in his general judgments that his failing comes out. He makes no attempt to excuse the notorious features of Calvin's rule at Geneva; but Mr. Pattison reads into his character a purpose and a grandeur which place him far above any other man of his day. To recommend him to our very different ways of thinking, Mr. Pattison has the courage to allege that his interest in dogmatic theology was a subordinate matter, and that the "renovation of character," the "moral purification of humanity," was the great guiding idea of him who taught that out of the mass of human kind only a predestined remnant could possibly be saved. It is a singular interpretation of the mind of the author of the *Institutes* :—

The distinction of Calvin as a Reformer is not to be sought in the doctrine which now bears his name, or in any doctrinal peculiarity. His great merit lies *in his comparative neglect of dogma. He seized the idea of reformation as a real renovation of human character.* The moral purification of humanity as the original idea of Christianity is the guiding idea of his system. . . . He swept away at once the sacramental machinery of material media of salvation which the middle-age Church had provided in such abundance, and which Luther frowned upon, but did not reject. He was not satisfied to go back only to the historical origin of Christianity, but would found human virtue on the eternal antemundane will of God.

Again :—

Calvin thought neither of fame or fortune. The narrowness of his views and the disinterestedness of his soul alike precluded him from regarding Geneva as a stage for the gratification of personal ambition. This abegnation of self was one great part of his success.

And then Mr. Pattison goes on to describe in detail how, governed and possessed by one idea, and by a theory, to oppose which was "moral depravity," he proceeded to establish his intolerable system of discipline, based on dogmatic grounds—meddlesome, inquisitorial, petty, cruel—over the interior of every household in Geneva. What is there fascinating, or even imposing, in such a character? It is the common case of political and religious bigots, whether Jacobin, or Puritan, or Jesuit, poor in thought and sympathy and strong in will, fixing their yoke on a society, till the plague becomes unbearable. He seeks nothing for himself and, forsooth, he makes sacrifices. But he gets what he wants, his idea carried out; and self-sacrifice is of what we care for, and not of what we do not care for. And to keep up this supposed character of high moral purpose, we are told of Calvin's "comparative neglect of dogma," of his seizing the idea of a "real reformation of human character," a "moral purification of humanity," as the guiding idea of his system. Can anything be more unhistorical than to suggest that the father and source of all Western Puritan theology "neglected dogma," and was more of a moralist than a divine? It is not even true that he "swept away at once the sacramental machinery" of mediæval and Lutheran teaching; Calvin writes of the Eucharist in terms which would astonish some of his later followers. But what is the reason why Mr. Pattison attributes to the historical Calvin so much that does not belong to him, and, in spite of so much that repels, is yet induced to credit him with such great qualities? The reason is to be found in the intense antipathy with which Mr. Pattison regarded what he calls "the Catholic reaction" over Europe, and in the fact that undoubtedly Calvin's system and influence was the great force which resisted both what was bad and false in it, and also what was good, true, generous, humane. Calvinism opposed the "Catholic reaction" point-blank, and that was enough to win sympathy for it, even from Mr. Pattison.

The truth is that what Popery is to the average Protestant, and what Protestant heresy is to the average Roman Catholic, the "Catholic reaction," the

"Catholic revival" in the sixteenth and seventeenth centuries and in our own, is to Mr. Pattison's final judgment. It was not only a conspiracy against human liberty, but it brought with it the degradation and ruin of genuine learning. It is the all-sufficing cause and explanation of the mischief and evil doings which he has to set before us. Yet after the violence, the ignorance, the injustice, the inconsistencies of that great ecclesiastical revolution which we call by the vague name of Reformation, a "Catholic reaction" was inevitable. It was not conceivable that common sense and certain knowledge would submit for ever to be overcrowed by the dogmas and assertions of the new teachers. Like other powerful and wide and strongly marked movements, like the Reformation which it combated, it was a very mixed thing. It produced some great evils and led to some great crimes. It started that fatal religious militia, the Jesuit order, which, notwithstanding much heroic self-sacrifice, has formed a permanent bar to all possible reunion of Christendom, has fastened its yoke on the Papacy itself, and has taught the Church, as a systematic doctrine, to put its trust in the worst expedients of human policy. The religious wars in France and Germany, the relentless massacres of the Low Countries and the St. Bartholomew, the consecration of treason and conspiracy, were, without doubt, closely connected with the "Catholic reaction." But if this great awakening and stimulating influence raised new temptations to human passion and wickedness, it was not only in the service of evil that this new zeal was displayed. The Council of Trent, whatever its faults, and it had many, was itself a real reformation. The "Catholic revival" meant the rekindling of earnest religion and care for a good life in thousands of souls. If it produced the Jesuits, it as truly produced Port Royal and the Benedictines. Europe would be indeed greatly the poorer if it wanted some of the most conspicuous products of the Catholic revival.

It is Mr. Pattison's great misfortune that through obvious faults of temper he has missed the success which naturally might have seemed assured to him, of dealing with these subjects in a large and dispassionate way. Scholar, thinker, student as he is, conversant with all literature, familiar with books and names which many well-read persons have never heard of, he has his bitter prejudices, like the rest of us, Protestants or Catholics; and what he hates is continually forcing itself into his mind. He tells, with great and pathetic force, the terrible story of the judicial murder of Calas at Toulouse, and of Voltaire's noble and successful efforts to bring the truth to light, and to repair, as far as could be repaired, its infamous injustice. It is a story which shows to what frightful lengths fanaticism may go in leading astray even the tribunals of justice. But unhappily the story can be paralleled in all times of the world's history; and though the Toulouse mob and Judges were Catholics, their wickedness is no more a proof against the Catholic revival than Titus Oates and the George Gordon riots are against Protestantism, or the Jacobin tribunals against Republican justice. But Mr. Pattison cannot conclude his account without an application. Here you have an example of what the Catholic revival does. It first breaks Calas on the wheel; and then, because Voltaire took up his cause, it makes modern Frenchmen, if they are Catholics, believe that Calas deserved it:—

It is part of that general Catholic revival which has been working for some years, and which like a fog is spreading over the face of opinion. . . . The memory of Calas had been vindicated by Voltaire and the Encyclopedists. That was quite enough for the Catholics. . . . It is the characteristic of Catholicism that it supersedes reason, and prejudges all matters by the application of fixed principles.

It is no use that M. Coquerel flatters himself that he has set the matter at rest. He flatters himself in vain; he ought to know his Catholic countrymen better:—

We have little doubt that as long as the Catholic religion shall last their little manuals of falsified history will continue to repeat that Jean Calas murdered his son because he had become a convert to the Catholic faith.

Are little manuals of falsified history confined only to one set of people? Is not John Foxe still proof against the assaults of Dr. Maitland? The habit of *à priori* judgments as to historical facts is, as

Mr. Pattison truly says, "fatal to truth and integrity." It is most mischievous when it assumes a philosophic gravity and warps the criticism of a distinguished scholar.

This fixed habit of mind is the more provoking because, putting aside the obtrusive and impertinent injustice to which it leads, Mr. Pattison's critical work is of so high a character. His extensive and accurate reading, the sound common sense with which he uses his reading, and the modesty and absence of affectation and display which seem to be a law of his writing, place him very high. Perhaps he believes too much in books and learning, in the power which they exert, and what they can do to enable men to reach the higher conquests of moral and religious truth—perhaps he forgets, in the amplitude of his literary resources, that behind the records of thought and feeling there are the living mind and thought themselves, still clothed with their own proper force and energy, and working in defiance of our attempts to classify, to judge, or to explain: that there are the real needs, the real destinies of mankind, and the questions on which they depend—of which books are a measure indeed, but an imperfect one. As an instance, we might cite his "Essay on the Theology of Germany"—elaborate, learned, extravagant in its praise and in its scorn, full of the satisfaction of a man in possession of a startling and little known subject, but with the contradictions of a man who in spite of his theories believes more than his theories. But, as a student who deals with books and what books can teach, it is a pleasure to follow him; his work is never slovenly or superficial; the reader feels that he is in the hands of a man who thoroughly knows what he is talking about, and both from conscience and from disposition is anxious above all to be accurate and discriminative. If he fails, as he often seems to us to do, in the justice and balance of his appreciation of the phenomena before him, if his statements and generalisations are crude and extravagant, it is that passion and deep aversions have overpowered the natural accuracy of his faculty of judgment.

The feature which is characteristic in all his work is his profound value for learning, the learning of books, of documents, of all literature. He is a thinker, a clear and powerful one; he is a philosopher, who has explored the problems of abstract science with intelligence and interest, and fully recognises their importance; he has taken the measure of the political and social questions which the progress of civilisation has done so little to solve; he is at home with the whole range of literature, keen and true in observation and criticism; he has strongly marked views about education, and he took a leading part in the great changes which have revolutionised Oxford. He is all this; but beyond and more than all this he is a devotee of learning, as other men are of science or politics, deeply penetrated with its importance, keenly alive to the neglect of it, full of faith in the services which it can render to mankind, fiercely indignant at what degrades, or supplants, or enfeebles it. Learning, with the severe and bracing discipline without which it is impossible, learning embracing all efforts of human intellect—those which are warning beacons as well those which have elevated and enlightened the human mind—is the thing which attracts and satisfies him as nothing else does; not mere soulless erudition, but a great supply and command of varied facts, marshalled and turned to account by an intelligence which knows their use. The absence of learning, or the danger to learning, is the keynote of a powerful but acrid survey of the history and prospects of the Anglican Church, for which, in spite of its one-sidedness and unfairness, Churchmen may find not a little which it will be useful to lay to heart. Dissatisfaction with the University system, in its provision for the encouragement of learning and for strengthening and protecting its higher interests, is the stimulus to his essay on Oxford studies, which is animated with the idea of the University as a true home of real learning, and is full of the hopes, the animosities, and, it may be added, the disappointments of a revolutionary time. He exults over the destruction of the old order; but his ideal is too high, he is too shrewd an observer, too thorough and well-trained a judge of what learning really means, to be quite satisfied with the new.

The same devotion to learning shows itself in a feature of his literary work, which is almost characteristic—the delight which he takes in telling the detailed story of the life of some of the famous working scholars of the sixteenth and seventeenth centuries. These men, whose names are known to the modern world chiefly in notes to classical authors, or occasionally in some impertinent sneer, he likes to contemplate as if they were alive. To him they are men with individual differences, each with a character and fortunes of his own, sharers to the full in the struggles and vicissitudes of life. He can appreciate their enormous learning, their unwearied labour, their sense of honour in their profession; and the editor of texts, the collator of various readings and emendations, the annotator who to us perhaps seems but a learned pedant appears to him as a man of sound and philosophic thought, of enthusiasm for truth and light—perhaps of genius—a man, too, with human affections and interests, with a history not devoid of romance. There is something touching in Mr. Pattison's affection for those old scholars, to whom the world has done scant justice. His own chief literary venture was the life of one of the greatest of them, Isaac Casaubon. We have in these volumes sketches, not so elaborate, of several others, the younger Scaliger, Muretus, Huet, and the great French printers, the Stephenses; and in these sketches we are also introduced to a number of their contemporaries, with characteristic observations on them, implying an extensive and first-hand knowledge of what they were, and an acquaintance with what was going on in the scholar world of the day. The most important of these sketches is the account of Justus Scaliger. There is first a review article, very vigorous and animated. But Mr. Pattison had intended a companion volume to his Casaubon; and of this, which was never completed, we have some fragments, not equal in force and compactness to the original sketch. But sketch and fragments together present a very vivid picture of this remarkable person, whose temper and extravagant vanity his biographer admits, but who was undoubtedly a marvel both of knowledge and of the power to use it, and to whom we owe the beginning of order and system in chronology. Scaliger was to Mr. Pattison the type of the real greatness of the scholar, a greatness not the less real that the world could hardly understand it. He certainly leaves Scaliger before us, with his strange ways of working, his hold of the ancient languages as if they were mother tongues, his pride and slashing sarcasm, and his absurd claim of princely descent, with lineaments not soon forgotten; but it is amusing to meet once more, in all seriousness, Mr. Pattison's *bête noire* of the Catholic reaction, in the quarrels between Scaliger and some shallow but clever and scurrilous Jesuits, whom he had provoked by exposing the False Decretals and the False Dionysius, and who revenged themselves by wounding him in his most sensitive part, his claim to descent from the Princes of Verona. Doubtless the religious difference envenomed the dispute, but it did not need the "Catholic reaction" to account for such ignoble wrangles in those days.

These remains show what a historian of literature we have lost in Mr. Pattison. He was certainly capable of doing much more than the specimens of work which he has left behind; but what he has left is of high value. Wherever the disturbing and embittering elements are away, it is hard to say which is the more admirable, the patient and sagacious way in which he has collected and mastered his facts, or the wise and careful judgment which he passes on them. We hear of people being spoilt by their prepossessions, their party, their prejudices, the necessities of their political and ecclesiastical position; Mr. Pattison is a warning that a man may claim the utmost independence, and yet be maimed in his power of being just and reasonable by other things than party. As it is, he has left us a collection of interesting and valuable studies, disastrously and indelibly disfigured by an implacable bitterness, in which he but too plainly found the greatest satisfaction.

Mr. Pattison used in his later years to give an occasional lecture to a London audience. One of the latest was one addressed, we believe, to a class of working people on poetry, in which he dwelt on its healing and consoling power. It was full of Mr. Pattison's clearness and directness of thought, and made a considerable impression on some who only knew it from an abstract in the newspapers; and it was challenged by a working-man in the *Pall Mall Gazette*, who urged against it with some power the argument of despair. Perhaps the lecture was not written; but if it was, and our recollection of it is at all accurate, it was not unworthy of a place in this collection.

XXV

BISHOP FRAZER[1]

EVERY one must be deeply touched by the Bishop of Manchester's sudden, and, to most of us, unexpected death; those not the least who, unhappily, found themselves in opposition to him in many important matters. For, in spite of much that many people must wish otherwise in his career as Bishop, it was really a very remarkable one. Its leading motive was high and genuine public spirit, and a generous wish to be in full and frank sympathy with all the vast masses of his diocese; to put himself on a level with them, as man with man, in all their interests, to meet them fearlessly and heartily, to raise their standard of justice and large-heartedness by showing them that in their life of toil he shared the obligation and the burden of labour, and felt bound by his place to be as unsparing and unselfish a worker as any of his

[1] *Guardian*, 28th October 1885.

flock. Indeed, he was as original as Bishop Wilberforce, though in a different direction, in introducing a new type and ideal of Episcopal work, and a great deal of his ideal he realised. It is characteristic of him that one of his first acts was to remove the Episcopal residence from a mansion and park in the country to a house in Manchester. There can be no doubt that he was thoroughly in touch with the working classes in Lancashire, in a degree to which no other Bishop, not even Bishop Wilberforce, had reached. There was that in the frankness and boldness of his address which disarmed their keen suspicion of a Bishop's inevitable assumption of superiority, and put them at their ease with him. He was always ready to meet them, and to speak off-hand and unconventionally, and as they speak, not always with a due foresight of consequences or qualifications. If he did sometimes in this way get into a scrape, he did not much mind it, and they liked him the better for it. He was perfectly fearless in his dealings with them; in their disputes, in which he often was invited to take a part, he took the part which seemed to him the right one, whether or not it might be the unpopular one. Very decided, very confident in his opinions and the expression of them, there yet was apparent a curious and almost touching consciousness of a deficiency in some of the qualities — knowledge, leisure, capacity for the deeper and subtler tasks of thought—necessary to give a strong speaker the sense of being on sure ground. But he trusted to his manly common sense; and this, with the populations with which he had to deal, served him well, at least in the main and most characteristic part of his work.

And for his success in this part of his work—in making the crowds in Manchester feel that their Bishop was a man like themselves, quite alive to their wants and claims and feelings, and not so unlike them in his broad and strong utterances—his Episcopate deserves full recognition and honour. He set an example which we may hope to see followed and improved upon. But unfortunately there was also a less successful side. He was a Bishop, an overseer of a flock of many ways of life and thought, a fellow-worker with them, sympathetic, laborious, warm-hearted. But he was also a Bishop of the Church of Christ, an institution with its own history, its great truths to keep and deliver, its characteristic differences from the world which it is sent to correct and to raise to higher levels than those of time and nature. There is no reason why this side of the Episcopal office should not be joined to that in which Bishop Frazer so signally excelled. But for this part of it he was not well qualified, and much in his performance of it must be thought of with regret. The great features of Christian truth had deeply impressed him; and to its lofty moral call he responded with conviction and earnestness. But an acquaintance with what he has to interpret and guard which may suffice for a layman is not enough for a

Bishop; and knowledge, the knowledge belonging to his profession, the deeper and more varied knowledge which makes a man competent to speak as a theologian, Bishop Frazer did not possess. He rather disbelieved in it, and thought it useless, or, it might be, mischievous. He resented its intrusion into spheres where he could only see the need of the simplest and least abstruse language. But facts are not what we may wish them, but what they are; and questions, if they are asked, may have to be answered, with toil, it may be, and difficulty, like the questions, assuredly not always capable of easy and transparent statement, of mathematical or physical science; and unless Christianity is a dream and its history one vast delusion, such facts and such questions have made what we call theology. But to the Bishop's practical mind they were without interest, and he could not see how they could touch and influence living religion. And did not care to know about them; he was impatient, and even scornful, when stress was laid on them; he was intolerant when he thought they competed with the immediate realities of religion. And this want of knowledge and of respect for knowledge was a serious deficiency. It gave sometimes a tone of thoughtless flippancy to his otherwise earnest language. And as he was not averse to controversy, or, at any rate, found himself often involved in it, he was betrayed sometimes into assertions and contradictions of the most astounding inaccuracy, which seriously weakened his authority when he was called upon to accept the responsibility of exerting it.

Partly for this reason, partly from a certain vivacity of temper, he certainly showed himself, in spite of his popular qualities, less equal than many others of his brethren to the task of appeasing and assuaging religious strife. The difficulties in Manchester were not greater than in other dioceses; there was not anything peculiar in them; there was nothing but what a patient and generous arbiter, with due knowledge of the subject, might have kept from breaking out into perilous scandals. Unhappily he failed; and though he believed that he had only done his duty, his failure was a source of deep distress to himself and to others. But now that he has passed away, it is but bare justice to say that no one worked up more conscientiously to his own standard. He gave himself, when he was consecrated, ten or twelve years of work, and then he hoped for retirement. He has had fifteen, and has fallen at his post. And to the last, the qualities which gave his character such a charm in his earlier time had not disappeared. There seemed to be always something of the boy about him, in his simplicity, his confiding candour and frankness with his friends, his warm-hearted and kindly welcome, his mixture of humility with a sense of power. Those who can remember him in his younger days still see, in spite of all the storms and troubles of his later ones, the image of the undergraduate and the young bachelor, who years ago made a start of such brilliant promise, and who has fulfilled so much of it, if not all. These things at any rate lasted to the end—his high and exacting sense of public duty, and his unchanging affection for his old friends.

XXVI

NEWMAN'S "APOLOGIA"[1]

WE have not noticed before Dr. Newman's *Apologia*, which has been coming out lately in weekly numbers, because we wished, when we spoke of it, to speak of it as a whole. The special circumstances out of which it arose may have prescribed the mode of publication. It may have been thought more suitable, in point of form, to answer a pamphlet by a series of pamphlets rather than at once by a set octavo of several hundred pages. But the real subject which Dr. Newman has been led to handle is one which will continue to be of the deepest interest long after the controversy which suggested it is forgotten. The real subject is the part played in the great Church movement by him who was the leading mind in it; and it was unsatisfactory to speak of this till all was said, and we could look on the whole course described. Such a subject might have well excused a deliberate and leisurely volume to itself; perhaps in this way we

[1] *Apologia pro Vitâ Suâ.* By John Henry Newman, D.D. *Guardian*, 22nd June 1864.

should have gained, in the laying out and concentration of the narrative, and in what helps to bring it as a whole before our thoughts. But a man's account of himself is never so fresh and natural as when it is called out by the spur and pressure of an accidental and instant necessity, and is directed to a purpose and quickened by feelings which belong to immediate and passing circumstances. The traces of hurried work are of light account when they are the guarantees that a man is not sitting down to draw a picture of himself, but stating his case in sad and deep earnest out of the very fulness of his heart.

The aim of the book is to give a minute and open account of the steps and changes by which Dr. Newman passed from the English Church to the Roman. The history of a change of opinion has often been written from the most opposite points of view; but in one respect this book seems to stand alone. Let it be remembered what it is, the narrative and the justification of a great conversion; of a change involving an entire reversal of views, judgments, approvals, and condemnations; a change which, with all ordinary men, involves a reversal, at least as great, of their sympathies and aversions, of what they tolerate and speak kindly of. Let it be considered what changes of feeling most changes of religion compel and consecrate; how men, commonly and very naturally, look back on what they have left and think they have escaped from, with the aversion of a captive to his prison; how they usually exaggerate and make absolute their divergence from what they think has betrayed, fooled, and degraded them; how easily they are tempted to visit on it and on those who still cling to it their own mistakes and faults. Let it be remembered that there was here to be told not only the history of a change, but the history of a deep disappointment, of the failure of a great design, of the breakdown of hopes the most promising and the most absorbing; and this, not in the silence of a man's study, but in the fever and contention of a great struggle wrought up to the highest pitch of passion and fierceness, bringing with it on all sides and leaving behind it, when over, the deep sense of wrong. It is no history of a mere intellectual movement, or of a passage from strong belief to a weakened and impaired one, to uncertainty, or vagueness, or indifference; it is not the account of a change by a man who is half sorry for his change, and speaks less hostilely of what he has left because he feels less friendly towards what he has joined. There is no reserved thought to be discerned in the background of disappointment or a wish to go back again to where he once was. It is a book which describes how a man, zealous and impatient for truth, thought he had found it in one Church, then thought that his finding was a delusion, and sought for it and believed he had gained it in another. What it shows us is no serene readjustment of abstract doctrines, but the wreck and overturning of trust and conviction and the practical grounds of life, accompanied with everything to provoke, embitter, and exasperate. It need not be said that what Dr. Newman holds he is ready to carry out to the end, or that he can speak severely of men and systems.

Let all this be remembered, and also that there is an opposition between what he was and what he is, which is usually viewed as irreconcilable, and which, on the ordinary assumptions about it, is so; and we venture to say that there is not another instance to be quoted, of the history of a conversion, in which he who tells his conversion has so retained his self-possession, his temper, his mastery over his own real judgment and thoughts, his ancient and legitimate sympathies, his superiority to the natural and inevitable temptations of so altered a position; which is so generous to what he feels to be strong and good in what he has nevertheless abandoned, so fearless about letting his whole case come out, so careless about putting himself in the right in detail; which is so calm, and kindly, and measured, with such a quiet effortless freedom from the stings of old conflicts, which bears so few traces of that bitterness and antipathy which generally—and we need hardly wonder at it—follows the decisive breaking with that on which a man's heart was stayed, and for which he would once have died.

There is another thing to be said, and we venture to say it out plainly, because Dr. Newman himself has shown that he knows quite well what he has been doing. While he has written what will command the sympathy and the reverence of every one, however irreconcilably opposed to him, to whom a great and noble aim and the trials of a desperate and self-sacrificing struggle to compass it are objects of admiration and honour, it is undeniable that ill-nature or vindictiveness or stupidity will find ample materials of his own providing to turn against him. Those who know Dr. Newman's powers and are acquainted with his career, and know to what it led him, and yet persist in the charge of insincerity and dishonesty against one who probably has made the greatest sacrifice of our generation to his convictions of truth, will be able to pick up from his own narrative much that they would not otherwise have known, to confirm and point the old familiar views cherished by dislike or narrowness. This is inevitable when a man takes the resolution of laying himself open so unreservedly, and with so little care as to what his readers think of what he tells them, so that they will be persuaded that he was ever, even from his boyhood, deeply conscious of the part which he was performing in the sight of his Maker. Those who smile at the belief of a deep and religious mind in the mysterious interventions and indications of Providence in the guidance of human life, will open their eyes at the feeling which leads him to tell the story of his earliest recollections of Roman Catholic peculiarities, and of the cross imprinted on his exercise-book. Those who think that everything about religion and their own view of religion is such plain sailing, so palpable and manifest, that all who are not fools or knaves must be of their own opinion, will find plenty to wonder at in the confessions of awful perplexity which equally before and after his change Dr. Newman makes. Those who have never doubted, who can no more imagine the practical difficulties accompanying a great change of belief than they can imagine a change of belief itself, will meet with much that to them will seem beyond pardon, in the actual events of a change, involving such issues and such interests, made so deliberately and cautiously, with such hesitation and reluctance, and in so long a time; they will be able to point to many moments in it when it will be easy to say that more or less ought to have been said, more or less ought to have been done. Much more will those who are on the side of doubt, who acquiesce in, or who desire the overthrow of existing hopes and beliefs, rejoice in such a frank avowal of the difficulties of religion and the perplexities of so earnest a believer, and make much of their having driven such a man to an alternative so obnoxious and so monstrous to most Englishmen. It is a book full of minor premisses, to which many opposite majors will be fitted. But whatever may be thought of many details, the effect and lesson of the whole will not be lost on minds of any generosity, on whatever side they may be; they will be touched with the confiding nobleness which has kept back nothing, which has stated its case with its weak points and its strong, and with full consciousness of what was weak as well as of what was strong, which has surrendered its whole course of conduct, just as it has been, to be scrutinised, canvassed, and judged. What we carry away from following such a history is something far higher and more solemn than any controversial inferences; and it seems almost like a desecration to make, as we say, capital out of it, to strengthen mere argument, to confirm a theory, or to damage an opponent.

The truth, in fact, is, that the interest is personal much more than controversial. Those who read it as a whole, and try to grasp the effect of all its portions compared together and gathered into one, will, it seems to us, find it hard to bend into a decisive triumph for any of the great antagonist systems which appear in collision. There can be no doubt of the perfect conviction with which Dr. Newman has taken his side for good. But while he states the effect of arguments on his own mind, he leaves the arguments in themselves as they were, and touches on them, not for the sake of what they are worth, but to explain the movements and events of his own course. Not from any studied impartiality, which is foreign to his character, but from his strong and keen sense of what is real and his determined efforts to bring it out, he avoids the temptation—as it seems to us, who still believe that he was more right once than he is now—to do injustice to his former self and his former position. At any rate, the arguments to be drawn from this narrative, for or against England, or for or against Rome, seem to us very evenly balanced. Of course, such a history has its moral. But the moral is not the ordinary vulgar one of the history of a religious change. It is not the supplement or disguise of a polemical argument. It is the deep want and necessity in our age of the Church, even to the most intensely religious and devoted minds, of a sound and secure intellectual basis for the faith which they value more than life and all things. We hope that we are strong enough to afford to judge fairly of such a spectacle, and to lay to heart its warnings, even though the particular results seem to go against what we think most right. It is a mortification and a trial to the English Church to have seen her finest mind carried away and lost to her, but it is a mortification which more confident and peremptory systems than hers have had to undergo; the parting was not without its compensations if only it brought home so keenly to many the awfulness and the seriousness of truth; and surely never did any man break so utterly with a Church, who left so many sympathies behind him and took so many with him, who continued to feel so kindly and with such large-hearted justice to those from whom his changed position separated him in this world for ever.

The *Apologia* is the history of a great battle against Liberalism, understanding by Liberalism the tendencies of modern thought to destroy the basis of revealed religion, and ultimately of all that can be called religion at all. The question which he professedly addresses himself to set at rest, that of his honesty, is comparatively of slight concern to those who knew him, except so far that they must be interested that others, who did not know him, should not be led to do a revolting injustice. The real interest is to see how one who felt so keenly the claims both of what is new and what is old, who, with such deep and unusual love and trust for antiquity, took in with quick sympathy, and in its most subtle and most redoubtable shapes, the intellectual movement of modern times, could continue to feel the force of both, and how he would attempt to harmonise them. Two things are prominent in the whole history. One is the fact of religion, early and deeply implanted in the writer's mind, absorbing and governing it without rival throughout. He speaks of an "inward conversion" at the age of fifteen, "of which I was conscious, and of which I am still more certain than that I have hands and feet." It was the religion of dogma and of a definite creed which made him "rest in the thought of two, and two only, supreme and luminously self-evident beings, myself and my Creator"—which completed itself with the idea of a visible Church and its sacramental system. Religion, in this aspect of it, runs unchanged from end to end of the scene of change :—

I have changed in many things; in this I have not. From the age of fifteen dogma has been the fundamental principle of my religion; I know no other religion. I cannot enter into the idea of any other sort of religion; religion, as a mere sentiment, is to me a dream and a mockery. As well can there be filial love without the fact of a father, as devotion without the fact of a Supreme Being. What I held in 1816 I held in 1833, and I hold in 1864. Please God I shall hold it to the end. Even when I was under Dr. Whately's influence I had no temptation to be less zealous for the dogmas of the faith.

The other thing is the haunting necessity, in an age of thought and innovation, of a philosophy of religion, equally deep, equally comprehensive and thorough, with the invading powers which it was wanted to counteract; a philosophy, not on paper or in theory, but answering to and vouched for by the facts of real life. In the English Church he found, we think that we may venture to say, the religion which to him was life, but not the philosophy which he wanted. The *Apologia* is the narrative of his search for it. Two strongly marked lines of thought are traceable all through, one modern in its scope and sphere, the other ancient. The leading subject of his modern thought is the contest with liberal unbelief; contrasted with this was his strong interest in Christian antiquity, his deep attachment to the creed, the history, and the moral temper of the early Church. The one line of thought made him, and even now makes him, sympathise with Anglicanism, which is in the same boat with him, holds the same principle of the unity and continuity of revealed truth, and is doing the same work, though, as he came to think in the end, feebly and hopelessly. The other, more and more, carried him away from Anglicanism; and the contrast and opposition between it and the ancient Church, in organisation, in usage, and in that general tone of feeling which quickens and gives significance and expression to forms, overpowered more and more the sense of affinity, derived from the identity of creeds and sacraments and leading points of Church polity, and from the success with which the best and greatest Anglican writers had appropriated and assimilated the theology of the Fathers. But though he urges the force of ecclesiastical precedents in a startling way, as in the account which he gives of the effect of the history of the Monophysites on his view of the tenableness of the Anglican theory, absolutely putting out of consideration the enormous difference of circumstances between the cases which are compared, and giving the instance in question a force and importance which seem to be in singular contrast with the general breadth and largeness of his reasoning, it was not the halting of an ecclesiastical theory which dissatisfied him with the English Church.

Anglicanism was not daring enough for him. With his ideas of the coming dangers and conflicts, he wanted something bold and thoroughgoing, wide-reaching in its aims, resolute in its language, claiming and venturing much. Anglicanism was not that. It had given up as impracticable much that the Church had once attempted. It did not pretend to rise so high, to answer such great questions, to lay down such precise definitions. Wisely modest, or timidly uncertain—mindful of the unalterable limits of our human condition, *we* say; forgetful, *he* thought, or doubting, or distrustful, of the gifts and promises of a supernatural dispensation—it certainly gave no such complete and decisive account of the condition and difficulties of religion and the world, as had been done once, and as there were some who did still. There were problems which it did not profess to solve; there were assertions which others boldly risked, and which it shrunk from making; there were demands which it ventured not to put forward. Again, it was not refined enough for him; it had little taste for the higher forms of the saintly ideal; it wanted the austere and high-strung virtues; it was contented, for the most part, with the domestic type of excellence, in which goodness merged itself in the interests and business of the common world, and, working in them, took no care to disengage itself or mark itself off, as something distinct from them and above them. Above all, Anglicanism was too limited; it was local, insular, national; its theory was made for its special circumstances; and he describes in a remarkable passage how, in contrast with this, there rung in his ears continually the proud self-assertion of the other side, *Securus judicat orbis terrarum*. What he wanted, what it was the aim of his life to find, was a great and effective engine against Liberalism; for years he tried, with eager but failing hope, to find it in the theology and working of the English Church;

when he made up his mind that Anglicanism was not strong enough for the task, he left it for a system which had one strong power; which claimed to be able to shut up dangerous thought.

Very sorrowful, indeed, is the history, told so openly, so simply, so touchingly, of the once promising advance, of the great breakdown. And yet, to those who still cling to what he left, regret is not the only feeling. For he has the nobleness and the generosity to say what he *did* find in the English Church, as well as what he did not find. He has given her up for good, but he tells and he shows, with no grudging frankness, what are the fruits of her discipline. "So I went on for years, up to 1841. It was, in a human point of view, the happiest time of my life. . . . I did not suppose that such sunshine would last, though I knew not what would be its termination. It was the time of plenty, and during its seven years I tried to lay up as much as I could for the dearth which was to follow it." He explains and defends what to us seem the fatal marks against Rome; but he lets us see with what force, and for how long, they kept alive his own resistance to an attraction which to him was so overwhelming. And he is at no pains to conceal—it seems even to console him to show—what a pang and wrench it cost him to break from that home under whose shadow his spiritual growth had increased. He has condemned us unreservedly; but there must, at any rate, be some wonderful power and charm about that which he loved with a love which is not yet extinguished; else how could he write of the past as he does? He has shown that he can understand, though he is unable to approve, that others should feel that power still.

Dr. Newman has stated, with his accustomed force and philosophical refinement, what he considers the true idea of that infallibility, which he looks upon as the only power in the world which can make head against and balance Liberalism—which "can withstand and baffle the fierce energy of passion, and the all-corroding, all-dissolving scepticism of the intellect in religious inquiries;" which he considers "as a provision, adapted by the mercy of the Creator, to preserve religion in the world, and to restrain that freedom of thought which is one of the greatest of our natural gifts, from its own suicidal excesses." He says, as indeed is true, that it is "a tremendous power," though he argues that, in fact, its use is most wisely and beneficially limited. And doubtless, whatever the difficulty of its proof may be, and to us this proof seems simply beyond possibility, it is no mere power upon paper. It acts and leaves its mark; it binds fast and overthrows for good. But when, put at its highest, it is confronted with the "giant evil" which it is supposed to be sent into the world to repel, we can only say that, to a looker-on, its failure seems as manifest as the existence of the claim to use it. It no more does its work, in the sense of *succeeding* and triumphing, than the less magnificent "Establishments" do. It keeps *some* check—it fails on a large scale and against the real strain and pinch of the mischief; and they, too, keep *some* check, and are not more fairly beaten than it is, in "making a stand against the wild living intellect of man."

Without infallibility, it is said, men will turn freethinkers and heretics; but don't they, *with* it? and what is the good of the engine if it will not do its work? And if it is said that this is the fault of human nature, which resists what provokes and checks it, still that very thing, which infallibility was intended to counteract, goes on equally, whether it comes into play or not. Meanwhile, truth does stay in the world, the truth that there has been among us a Divine Person, of whom the Church throughout Christendom is the representative, memorial, and the repeater of His message; doubtless, the means of knowledge are really guarded; yet we seem to receive that message as we receive the witness of moral truth; and it would not be contrary to the analogy of things here if we had often got to it at last through mistakes. But when it is reached, there it is, strong in its own power; and it is difficult to think that if it is not strong enough in itself to stand, it can be protected by a claim of infallibility. A future, of which infallibility is the only hope and safeguard, seems to us indeed a prospect of the deepest gloom.

Dr. Newman, in a very remarkable passage, describes the look and attitude of invading Liberalism, and tells us why he is not forward in the conflict. "It seemed to be a time of all others in which Christians had a call to be patient, in which they had no other way of helping those who were alarmed than that of exhorting them to have a little faith and fortitude, and 'to beware,' as the poet says, 'of dangerous steps.'" And he interprets "recent acts of the highest Catholic authority" as meaning that there is nothing to do just now but to sit still and trust. Well; but the *Christian Year* will do that much for us, just as well.

People who talk glibly of the fearless pursuit of truth may here see a real example of a life given to it—an example all the more solemn and impressive if they think that the pursuit was in vain. It is easy to declaim about it, and to be eloquent about lies and sophistries; but it is shallow to forget that truth has its difficulties. To hear some people talk, it might be thought that truth was a thing to be made out and expressed at will, under any circumstances, at any time, amid any complexities of facts or principles, by half an hour's choosing to be attentive, candid, logical, and resolute; as if there was not a chance of losing what perhaps you have, as well as of gaining what you think you need. If they would look about them, if they would look into themselves, they would recognise that Truth is an awful and formidable goddess to all men and to all systems; that all have their weak points where virtually, more or less consciously, more or less dexterously, they shrink from meeting her eye; that even when we make sacrifice of everything for her sake, we find that she still encounters us with claims, seemingly inconsistent with all that she has forced us to embrace—with appearances which not only convict us of mistake, but seem to oblige us to be tolerant of what we cannot really assent to.

She gives herself freely to the earnest and true-hearted inquirer; but to those who presume on the easiness of her service, she has a side of strong irony. You common-sense men, she seems to say, who see no difficulties in the world, you little know on what shaky ground you stand, and how easily you might be reduced to absurdity. You critical and logical intellects, who silence all comers and cannot be answered, and can show everybody to be in the wrong —into what monstrous and manifest paradoxes are you not betrayed, blind to the humble facts which upset your generalisations, not even seeing that dulness itself can pronounce you mistaken!

In the presence of such a narrative as this, sober men will think more seriously than ever about charging their most extreme opponents with dishonesty and disregard to truth.

As we said before, this history seems to us to leave the theological question just where it was. The objections to Rome, which Dr. Newman felt so strongly once, but which yielded to other considerations, we feel as strongly still. The substantial points of the English theory, which broke down to his mind, seem to us as substantial and trustworthy as before. He failed, but we believe that, in spite of everything, England is the better for his having made his trial. Even Liberalism owes to the movement of which he was the soul much of what makes it now such a contrast, in largeness of mind and warmth, to the dry, repulsive, narrow, material Liberalism of the Reform era. He, and he mainly, has been the source, often unrecognised and unsuspected, of depth and richness and beauty, and the strong passion for what is genuine and real, in our religious teaching. Other men, other preachers, have taken up his thoughts and decked them out, and had the credit of being greater than their master.

In looking back on the various turns and vicissitudes of his English course, we, who inherit the fruits of that glorious failure, should speak respectfully and considerately where we do not agree with him, and with deep gratitude—all the more that now so much lies between us—where we do. But the review makes us feel more than ever that the English Church, whose sturdy strength he underrated, and whose irregular theories provoked him, was fully worthy of the interest and the labours of the leader who despaired of her. Anglicanism has so far outlived its revolutions, early and late ones, has marched on in a distinct path, has developed a theology, has consolidated an organisation, has formed a character and tone, has been the organ of a living spirit. The "magnetic storms" of thought which sweep over the world may be destructive and dangerous to it, as much as, but not more than, to other bodies which claim to be Churches and to represent the message of God. But there is nothing to make us think that, in the trials which may be in store, the English Church will fail while others hold their own.

XXVII

DR. NEWMAN ON THE "EIRENICON"[1]

DR. PUSEY'S Appeal has received more than one answer. These answers, from the Roman Catholic side, are—what it was plain that they would be—assurances to him that he looks at the question from an entirely mistaken point of view; that it is, of course, very right and good of him to wish for peace and union, but that there is only one way of peace and union—unconditional submission. He may have peace and union for himself at any moment, if he will; so may the English Church, or the Greek Church, or any other religious body, organised or unorganised.

The way is always open; there is no need to write long books or make elaborate proposals about union. Union means becoming Catholic; becoming Catholic means acknowledging the exclusive claims of the Pope or the Roman Church. In the long controversy one party has never for an instant wavered in the assertion that it could not, and never would, be in the wrong. The way to close the controversy, and the only one,

[1] *The Times*, 31st March 1866.

is to admit that Dr. Pusey shall have any amount of assurance and proof that the Roman position and Roman doctrine and practice are the right ones.

His misapprehensions shall be corrected; his ignorance of what is Roman theology fully, and at any length, enlightened. There is no desire to shrink from the fullest and most patient argument in its favour, and he may call it, if he likes, explanation. But there is only one practical issue to what he has proposed—not to stand bargaining for impossible conditions, but thankfully and humbly to join himself to the true Church while he may. It is only the way in which the answer is given that varies. Here characteristic differences appear. The authorities of the Roman Catholic Church swell out to increased magnificence, and nothing can exceed the suavity and the compassionate scorn with which they point out the transparent absurdity and the audacity of such proposals. The Holy Office at Rome has not, it may be, yet heard of Dr. Pusey; it may regret, perhaps, that it did not wait for so distinguished a mark for its censure; but its attention has been drawn to some smaller offenders of the same way of thinking, and it has been induced to open all the floodgates of its sonorous and antiquated verbiage to sweep away and annihilate a poor little London periodical—"*ephemeridem cui titulus,* '*The Union Review.*'" The Archbishop of Westminster, not deigning to name Dr. Pusey, has seized the opportunity to reiterate emphatically, in stately periods and with a polished sarcasm, his boundless contempt for the foolish people who dare to come "with swords wreathed in myrtle" between the Catholic Church and "her mission to the great people of England." On the other hand, there have been not a few Roman Catholics who have listened with interest and sympathy to what Dr. Pusey had to say, and, though obviously they had but one answer to give, have given it with a sense of the real condition and history of the Christian world, and with the respect due to a serious attempt to look evils in the face. But there is only one person on the Roman Catholic side whose reflections on the subject English readers in general would much care to know. Anybody could tell beforehand what Archbishop Manning would say; but people could not feel so certain what Dr. Newman might say.

Dr. Newman has given his answer; and his answer is, of course, in effect the same as that of the rest of his co-religionists. He offers not the faintest encouragement to Dr. Pusey's sanguine hopes. If it is possible to conceive that one side could move in the matter, it is absolutely certain that the other would be inflexible. Any such dealing on equal terms with the heresy and schism of centuries is not to be thought of; no one need affect surprise at the refusal. What Dr. Pusey asks is, in fact, to pull the foundation out from under the whole structure of Roman Catholic pretensions. Dr. Newman does not waste words to show that the plan of the *Eirenicon* is impossible. He evidently assumes that it is so, and we agree with him. But there are different ways of dispelling a generous dream, and telling a serious man who is in earnest that he is mistaken. Dr. Newman does justice, as he ought to do, to feelings and views which none can enter into better than he, whatever he may think of them now. He does justice to the understanding and honesty, as well as the high aims, of an old friend, once his comrade in difficult and trying times, though now long parted from him by profound differences, and to the motives which prompted so venturous an attempt as the *Eirenicon* to provoke public discussion on the reunion of Christendom. He is capable of measuring the real state of the facts, and the mischiefs and evils for which a remedy is wanted, by a more living rule than the suppositions and consequences of a cut-and-dried theory. Rightly or wrongly he argues—at least, he gives us something to think of. Perhaps not the least of his merit is that he writes simply and easily in choice and varied English, instead of pompously ringing the changes on a set of *formulae* which beg the question, and dinning into our ears the most extravagant assertions of foreign ecclesiastical arrogance. We may not always think him fair, or a sound reasoner, but he is conciliatory, temperate, and often fearlessly candid. He addresses readers who will challenge and examine what he says, not those whose minds are cowed and beaten down before audacity in proportion to its coolness, and whom paradox, the more extreme the better, fascinates and drags captive. To his old friend he is courteous, respectful, sympathetic; where the occasion makes it fitting, affectionate, even playful, as men are who can afford to let their real feelings come out, and have not to keep up appearances. Unflinching he is in maintaining his present position as the upholder of the exclusive claims of the Roman Church to represent the Catholic Church of the Creeds; but he has the good sense and good feeling to remember that he once shared the views of those whom he now controverts, and that their present feelings about the divisions of Christendom were once his own. Such language as the following is plain, intelligible, and manly. Of course, he has his own position, and must see things according to it. But he recognises the right of conscience in those who, having gone a long way with him, find that they can go no further, and he pays a compliment, becoming as from himself, and not without foundation in fact, to the singular influence which, from whatever cause, Dr. Pusey's position gives him, and which, we may add, imposes on him, in more ways than one, very grave responsibilities:—

You, more than any one else alive, have been the present and untiring agent by whom a great work has been effected in it; and, far more than is usual, you have received in your lifetime, as well as merited, the confidence of your brethren. You cannot speak merely for yourself; your antecedents, your existing influence, are a pledge to us that what you may determine will be the determination of a multitude. Numbers, too, for whom you cannot properly be said to speak, will be moved by your authority or your arguments; and numbers, again, who are of a school more recent than your own, and who are only not your followers because they have outstripped you in their free speeches and demonstrative acts in our behalf, will, for the occasion, accept you as their spokesman. There is no one anywhere—among ourselves, in your own body, or, I suppose, in the Greek Church—who can affect so vast a circle of men, so virtuous, so able, so learned, so zealous, as come, more or less, under your influence; and I cannot pay them all a greater compliment than to tell them they ought all to be Catholics, nor do them a more affectionate service than to pray that they may one day become such. . . .

I recollect well what an outcast I seemed to myself when I took down from the shelves of my library the volumes of St. Athanasius or St. Basil, and set myself to study them; and how, on the contrary, when at length I was brought into Catholicism, I kissed them with delight, with a feeling that in them I had more than all that I had lost, and, as though I were directly addressing the glorious saints who bequeathed them to the Church, I said to the inanimate pages, "You are now mine, and I am now yours, beyond any mistake." Such, I conceive, would be the joy of the persons I speak of if they could wake up one morning and find themselves possessed by right of Catholic traditions and hopes, without violence to their own sense of duty; and certainly I am the last man to say that such violence is in any case lawful, that the claims of conscience are not paramount, or that any one may overleap what he deliberately holds to be God's command, in order to make his path easier for him or his heart lighter.

I am the last man to quarrel with this jealous deference to the voice of our conscience, whatever judgment others may form of us in consequence, for this reason, because their case, as it at present stands, has as you know been my own. You recollect well what hard things were said against us twenty-five years ago which we knew in our hearts we did not deserve. Hence, I am now in the position of the fugitive Queen in the well-known passage, who, "*haud ignara mali*" herself, had learned to sympathise with those who were inheritors of her past wanderings.

Dr. Newman's hopes, and what most of his countrymen consider the hopes of truth and religion, are not the same. His wish is, of course, that his friend should follow him; a wish in which there is not the slightest reason to think that he will be gratified. But differently as we must feel as to the result, we cannot help sharing the evident amusement with which Dr. Newman recalls a few of the compliments which were lavished on him by some of his present co-religionists when he was trying to do them justice, and was even on the way to join them. He reprints with sly and mischievous exactness a string of those glib phrases of controversial dislike and suspicion which are common to all parties, and which were applied to him by "priests, good men, whose zeal outstripped their knowledge, and who in consequence spoke confidently, when they would have been wiser had they suspended their adverse judgment of those whom they were soon to welcome as brothers in communion." It is a trifle, but it strikes us as characteristic. Dr. Newman is one of the very few who have carried into his present communion, to a certain degree at least, an English habit of not letting off the blunders and follies of his own side, and of daring to think that a cause is better served by outspoken independence of judgment than by fulsome, unmitigated puffing. It might be well if even in him there were a little more of this habit. But, so far as it goes, it is the difference between him and most of those who are leaders on his side. Indirectly he warns eager controversialists that they are not always the wisest and the most judicious and far-seeing of men; and we cannot quarrel with him, however little we may like the occasion, for the entertainment which he feels in inflicting on his present brethren what they once judged and said of him, and in reminding them that their proficiency in polemical rhetoric did not save them from betraying the shallowness of their estimate and the shortness of their foresight.

When he comes to discuss the *Eirenicon*, Dr. Newman begins with a complaint which seems to us altogether unreasonable. He seems to think it hard that Dr. Pusey should talk of peace and reunion, and yet speak so strongly of what he considers the great corruptions of the Roman Church. In ordinary controversy, says Dr. Newman, we know what we are about and what to expect; "'*Caedimur, et totidem plagis consumimus hostem.*' We give you a sharp cut and you return it. . . . But we at least have not professed to be composing an *Eirenicon*, when we treated you as foes." Like Archbishop Manning, Dr. Newman is reminded "of the sword wreathed in myrtle;" but Dr. Pusey, he says, has improved on the ancient device,—"Excuse me, you discharge your olive-branch as if from a catapult."

This is, no doubt, exactly what Dr. Pusey has done. Going much further than the great majority of his countrymen will go with him in admissions in favour of the Roman Catholic Church, he has pointed out with a distinctness and force, never, perhaps, exceeded, what is the impassable barrier which, as long as it lasts, makes every hope of union idle. The practical argument against Rome is stated by him in a shape which comes home to the consciences of all, whatever their theological training and leanings, who have been brought up in English ways and ideas of religion. But why should he not? He is desirous of union—the reunion of the whole of Christendom. He gives full credit to the Roman communion— much more credit than most of his brethren think him justified in giving—for what is either defensible or excellent in it. Dr. Newman must be perfectly aware that Dr. Pusey has gone to the very outside of what our public feeling in England will bear in favour of efforts for reconciliation, and he nowhere shows any sign that he is thinking of unconditional submission. How, then, can he be expected to mince matters and speak smoothly when he comes to what he regards as the real knot of the difficulty, the real and fatal bar to all possibility of a mutual understanding? If his charges are untrue or exaggerated in detail or colouring, that is another matter; but the whole of his pleading for peace presupposes that there are great and serious obstacles to it in what is practically taught and authorised in the Roman Church; and it is rather hard to blame him for "not making the best of things," and raising difficulties in the way of the very object which he seeks, because he states the truth about these obstacles. We are afraid that we must be of Dr. Newman's opinion that the *Eirenicon* is not calculated to lead, in our time at least, to what it aims at—the reunion of Christendom; but this arises from the real obstacles themselves, not from Dr. Pusey's way of stating them. There may be no way to peace, but surely if there is, though it implies giving full weight to your sympathies, and to the points on which you may give way, it also involves the possibility of speaking out plainly, and also of being listened to, on the points on which you really disagree. Does Dr. Newman think that all Dr. Pusey felt he had to do was to conciliate Roman Catholics? Does it follow, because objections are intemperately and unfairly urged on the Protestant side, that therefore they are not felt quite as much in earnest by sober and tolerant people, and that they may not be stated in their real force without giving occasion for the remark that this is reviving the old cruel war against Rome, and rekindling a fierce style of polemics which is now out of date? And how is Dr. Pusey to state these objections if, when he goes into them, not in a vague declamatory way, but showing his respect and seriousness by his guarded and full and definite manner of proof, he is to be met by the charge that he does not show sufficient consideration? All this may be a reason for thinking it vain to write an Eirenicon at all. But if one is to be attempted, it certainly will not do to make it a book of compliments. Its first condition is that if it makes light of lesser difficulties it should speak plainly about greater ones.

But this is, after all, a matter of feeling. No doubt, as Dr. Newman says, people are not pleased or conciliated by elaborate proofs that they are guilty of something very wrong or foolish. What is of more interest is to know the effect on a man like Dr. Newman of such a display of the prevailing tendency of religious thought and devotion in his communion as Dr. Pusey has given from Roman Catholic writers. And it is plain that, whoever else is satisfied with them, these tendencies are not entirely satisfactory to Dr. Newman. That rage for foreign ideas and foreign usages which has come over a section of his friends, the loudest and perhaps the ablest section of them, has no charms for him. He asserts resolutely and rather sternly his right to have an opinion of his own, and declines to commit himself, or to allow that his cause is committed, to a school of teaching which happens for the moment to have the talk to itself; and he endeavours at great length to present a view of the teaching of his Church which shall be free, if not from all Dr. Pusey's objections, yet from a certain number of them, which to Dr. Newman himself appear grave.

After disclaiming or correcting certain alleged admissions of his own, on which Dr. Pusey had placed a construction too favourable to the Anglican Church, Dr. Newman comes to a passage which seems to rouse him. A convert, says Dr. Pusey, must take things as he finds them in his new communion, and it would be unbecoming in him to criticise. This statement gives Dr. Newman the opportunity of saying that, except with large qualifications, he does not accept it for himself. Of course, he says, there are considerations of modesty, of becomingness, of regard to the feelings of others with equal or greater claims than himself, which bind a convert as they bind any one who has just gained admission into a society of his fellow men. He has no business "to pick and choose," and to set himself up as a judge of everything in his new position. But though every man of sense who thought he had reason for so great a change would be generous and loyal in accepting his new religion as a whole, in time he comes "to have a right to speak as well as to hear;" and for this right, both generally and in his own case, he stands up very resolutely:—

Also, in course of time a new generation rises round him, and there is no reason why he should not know as much, and decide questions with as true an instinct, as those who perhaps number fewer years than he does Easter communions. He has mastered the fact and the nature of the differences of theologian from theologian, school from school, nation from nation, era from era. He knows that there is much of what may be called fashion in opinions and practices, according to the circumstances of time and place, according to current politics, the character of the Pope of the day, or the chief Prelates of a particular country; and that fashions change. His experience tells him that sometimes what is denounced in one place as a great offence, or preached up as a first principle, has in another nation been immemorially regarded in just a contrary sense, or has made no sensation at all, one way or the other, when brought before public opinion; and that loud talkers, in the Church as elsewhere, are apt to carry all before them, while quiet and conscientious persons commonly have to give way. He perceives that, in matters which happen to be in debate, ecclesiastical authority watches the state of opinion and the direction and course of controversy, and decides accordingly; so that in certain cases to keep back his own judgment on a point is to be disloyal to his superiors.

So far generally; now in particular as to myself. After twenty years of Catholic life, I feel no delicacy in giving my opinion on any point when there is a call for me, — and the only reason why I have not done so sooner or more often than I have, is that there has been no call. I have now reluctantly come to the conclusion that your Volume *is* a call. Certainly, in many instances in which theologian differs from theologian, and country from country, I have a definite judgment of my own; I can say so without offence to any one, for the very reason that from the nature of the case it is impossible to agree with all of them. I prefer English habits of belief and devotion to foreign, from the same causes, and by the same right, which justifies foreigners in preferring their own. In following those of my people, I show less singularity, and create less disturbance than if I made a flourish with what is novel and exotic. And in this line of conduct I am but availing myself of the teaching which I fell in with on becoming a Catholic; and it is a pleasure to me to think that what I hold now, and would transmit after me if I could, is only what I received then.

He observes that when he first joined the Roman Catholic Church the utmost delicacy was observed in giving him advice; and the only warning which he can recollect was from the Vicar-General of the London district, who cautioned him against books of devotion of the Italian school, which were then just coming into England, and recommended him to get, as safe guides, the works of Bishop Hay. Bishop Hay's name is thus, probably for the first time, introduced to the general English public. It is difficult to forbear a smile at the great Oxford teacher, the master of religious thought and feeling to thousands, being gravely set to learn his lesson of a more perfect devotion, how to meditate and how to pray, from "the works of Bishop Hay"; it is hardly more easy to forbear a smile at his recording it. But Bishop

Hay was a sort of symbol, and represents, he says, English as opposed to foreign habits of thought; and to these English habits he not only gives his preference, but he maintains that they are more truly those of the whole Roman Catholic body in England than the more showy and extreme doctrines of a newer school. Dr. Pusey does wrong, he says, in taking this new school as the true exponent of Roman Catholic ideas. That it is popular he admits, but its popularity is to be accounted for by personal qualifications in its leaders for gaining the ear of the world, without supposing that they speak for their body.

Though I am a convert, then, I think I have a right to speak out; and that the more because other converts have spoken for a long time, while I have not spoken; and with still more reason may I speak without offence in the case of your present criticisms of us, considering that in the charges you bring the only two English writers you quote in evidence are both of them converts, younger in age than myself. I put aside the Archbishop of course, because of his office. These two authors are worthy of all consideration, at once from their character and from their ability. In their respective lines they are perhaps without equals at this particular time; and they deserve the influence they possess. One is still in the vigour of his powers; the other has departed amid the tears of hundreds. It is pleasant to praise them for their real qualifications; but why do you rest on them as authorities? Because the one was "a popular writer"; but is there not sufficient reason for this in the fact of his remarkable gifts, of his poetical fancy, his engaging frankness, his playful wit, his affectionateness, his sensitive piety, without supposing that the wide diffusion of his works arises out of his particular sentiments about the Blessed Virgin? And as to our other friend, do not his energy, acuteness, and theological reading, displayed on the vantage ground of the historic *Dublin Review*, fully account for the sensation he has produced, without supposing that any great number of our body go his lengths in their view of the Pope's infallibility? Our silence as regards their writings is very intelligible; it is not agreeable to protest, in the sight of the world, against the writings of men in our own communion whom we love and respect. But the plain fact is this—they came to the Church, and have thereby saved their souls; but they are in no sense spokesmen for English Catholics, and they must not stand in the place of those who have a real title to such an office.

And he appeals from them, as authorities, to a list of much more sober and modest writers, though, it may be, the names of all of them are not familiar to the public. He enumerates as the "chief authors of the passing generation," "Cardinal Wiseman, Dr. Ullathorne, Dr. Lingard, Mr. Tierney, Dr. Oliver, Dr. Rock, Dr. Waterworth, Dr. Husenbeth, Mr. Flanagan." If these well-practised and circumspect veterans in the ancient controversy are not original and brilliant, at least they are safe; and Dr. Newman will not allow the flighty intellectualism which takes more hold of modern readers to usurp their place, and for himself he sturdily and bluffly declines to give up his old standing-ground for any one:—

I cannot, then, without remonstrance, allow you to identify the doctrine of our Oxford friends in question, on the two subjects I have mentioned, with the present spirit or the prospective creed of Catholics; or to assume, as you do, that because they are thorough-going and relentless in their statements, therefore they are the harbingers of a new age, when to show a deference for Antiquity will be thought little else than a mistake. For myself, hopeless as you consider it, I am not ashamed still to take my stand upon the Fathers, and do not mean to budge. The history of their time is not yet an old almanac to me. Of course I maintain the value and authority of the "Schola," as one of the *loci theologici;* still I sympathise with Petavius in preferring to its "contentious and subtle theology" that "more elegant and fruitful teaching which is moulded after the image of erudite antiquity." The Fathers made me a Catholic, and I am not going to kick down the ladder by which I ascended into the Church. It is a ladder quite as serviceable for that purpose now as it was twenty years ago. Though I hold, as you remark, a process of development in Apostolic truth as time goes on, such development does not supersede the Fathers, but explains and completes them.

Is he right in saying that he is not responsible as a Roman Catholic for the extravagances that Dr. Pusey dwells upon? He is, it seems to us, and he is not. No doubt the Roman Catholic system is in practice a wide one, and he has a right, which we are glad to see that he is disposed to exercise, to maintain the claims of moderation and soberness, and to decline to submit his judgment to the fashionable theories of the hour. A stand made for independence and good sense against the pressure of an exacting and overbearing dogmatism is a good thing for everybody, though made in a camp with which we have nothing to do. He goes far enough, indeed, as it is. Still, it is something that a great writer, of whose genius and religious feeling Englishmen will one day be even prouder than they are now, should disconnect himself from the extreme follies of his party, and attempt to represent what is the nobler and more elevated side of the system to which he has attached himself. But it seems to us much more difficult for him to release his cause from complicity with the doctrines which he dislikes and fears. We have no doubt that he is not alone, and that there are numbers of his English brethren who are provoked and ashamed at the self-complacent arrogance and childish folly shown in exaggerating and caricaturing doctrines which are, in the eyes of most Englishmen, extravagant enough in themselves. But the question is whether he or the innovators represent the true character and tendencies of their religious system. It must be remembered that with a jealous and touchy Government, like that of the Roman Church, which professes the duty and boasts of the power to put down all dangerous ideas and language, mere tolerance means much. Dr. Newman speaks as an Englishman when he writes thus:—

This is specially the case with great ideas. You

may stifle them; or you may refuse them elbow-room; or you may torment them with your continual meddling; or you may let them have free course and range, and be content, instead of anticipating their excesses, to expose and restrain those excesses after they have occurred. But you have only this alternative; and for myself, I prefer much, wherever it is possible, to be first generous and then just; to grant full liberty of thought, and to call it to account when abused.

But that has never been the principle of his Church. At least, the liberty which it has allowed has been a most one-sided liberty. It has been the liberty to go any length in developing the favourite opinions about the power of the Pope, or some popular form of devotion; but as to other ideas, not so congenial, "great" ones and little ones too, the lists of the Roman Index bear witness to the sensitive vigilance which took alarm even at remote danger. And those whose pride it is that they are ever ready and able to stop all going astray must be held responsible for the going astray which they do not stop, especially when it coincides with what they wish and like.

But these extreme writers do not dream of tolerance. They stoutly and boldly maintain that they but interpret in the only natural and consistent manner the mind of their Church; and no public or official contradiction meets them. There may be a disapproving opinion in their own body, but it does not show itself. The disclaimer of even such a man as Dr. Newman is in the highest degree guarded and qualified. They are the people who can excite attention and gain a hearing, though it be an adverse one. They have the power to make themselves the most prominent and accredited representatives of their creed, and, if thoroughgoing boldness and ability are apt to attract the growth of thought and conviction, they are those who are likely to mould its future form. Sober prudent people may prefer the caution of Dr. Newman's "chief authors," but to the world outside most of these will be little more than names, and the advanced party, which talks most strongly about the Pope's infallibility and devotion to St. Mary, has this to say for itself. Popular feeling everywhere in the Roman communion appears to go with it, and authority both in Rome and in England shelters and sanctions it. Nothing can be more clearly and forcibly stated than the following assertions of the unimpeachable claim of "dominant opinions" in the Roman Catholic system by the highest Roman Catholic authority in England. "It is an ill-advised overture of peace," writes Archbishop Manning,

to assail the popular, prevalent, and dominant opinions, devotions, and doctrines of the Catholic Church with hostile criticism. . . . The presence and assistance of the Holy Ghost, which secures the Church within the sphere of faith and morals, invests it also with instincts and a discernment which preside over its worship and doctrines, its practices and customs. We may be sure that whatever is prevalent in the Church, under the eye of its public authority, practised by the people, and not censured by its pastors, is at least conformable to faith and innocent as to morals. Whosoever rises up to condemn such practices and opinions thereby convicts himself of the private spirit which is the root of heresy. But if it be ill-advised to assail the mind of the Church, it is still more so to oppose its visible Head. There can be no doubt that the Sovereign Pontiff has declared the same opinion as to the temporal power as that which is censured in others, and that he defined the Immaculate Conception, and that he believes in his own infallibility. If these things be our reproach, we share it with the Vicar of Jesus Christ. They are not our private opinions, nor the tenets of a school, but the mind of the Pontiff, as they were of his predecessors, as they will be of those who come after him.—Archbishop Manning's *Pastoral*, pp. 64-66, 1866.

To maintain his liberty against extreme opinions generally is one of Dr. Newman's objects in writing his letter; the other is to state distinctly what he holds and what he does not hold, as regards the subject on which Dr. Pusey's appeal has naturally made so deep an impression :—

I do so, because you say, as I myself have said in former years, that "That vast system as to the Blessed Virgin . . . to all of us has been the special *crux* of the Roman system" (p. 101). Here, I say, as on other points, the Fathers are enough for me. I do not wish to say more than they, and will not say less. You, I know, will profess the same; and thus we can join issue on a clear and broad principle, and may hope to come to some intelligible result. We are to have a treatise on the subject of Our Lady soon from the pen of the Most Rev. Prelate; but that cannot interfere with such a mere argument from the Fathers as that to which I shall confine myself here. Nor, indeed, as regards that argument itself, do I profess to be offering you any new matter, any facts which have not been used by others,—by great divines, as Petavius, by living writers, nay, by myself on other occasions. I write afresh, nevertheless, and that for three reasons—first, because I wish to contribute to the accurate statement and the full exposition of the argument in question; next, because I may gain a more patient hearing than has sometimes been granted to better men than myself; lastly, because there just now seems a call on me, under my circumstances, to avow plainly what I do and what I do not hold about the Blessed Virgin, that others may know, did they come to stand where I stand, what they would and what they would not be bound to hold concerning her.

If this "vast system" is a *crux* to any one, we cannot think that even Dr. Newman's explanation will make it easier. He himself recoils, as any Englishman of sense and common feeling must, at the wild extravagances into which this devotion has run. But he accepts and defends, on the most precarious grounds, the whole system of thought out of which they have sprung by no very violent process of growth. He cannot, of course, stop short of accepting the definition of the Immaculate Conception as an article of faith, and, though he emphatically condemns, with a warmth and energy of which no one can doubt the sincerity, a number of revolting consequences drawn from the theology of which that dogma is the expression, he is obliged to defend everything up to that. For a professed disciple of the Fathers this is not easy. If anything is certain, it is that the place which the Blessed Virgin occupies in the Roman Catholic system—popular or authoritative, if it is possible fairly to urge such a distinction in a system which boasts of all-embracing authority— is something perfectly different from anything known in the first four centuries. In all the voluminous writings on theology which remain from them we may look in vain for any traces of that feeling which finds words in the common hymn, "*Ave, maris Stella,*" and which makes her fill so large a space in the teaching and devotion of the Roman Church. Dr. Newman attempts to meet this difficulty by a distinction. The doctrine, he says, was there, the same then as now; it is only the feelings, behaviour, and usages, the practical consequences naturally springing from the doctrine, which have varied or grown:—

I fully grant that the *devotion* towards the Blessed Virgin has increased among Catholics with the progress of centuries. I do not allow that the *doctrine* concerning her has undergone a growth, for I believe it has been in substance one and the same from the beginning.

There is, doubtless, such a distinction, though

whether available for Dr. Newman's purpose is another matter. But when we recollect that modern "doctrine," besides defining the Immaculate Conception, places her next in glory to the Throne of God, and makes her the Queen of Heaven, and the all-prevailing intercessor with her Son, the assertion as to "doctrine" is a bold one. It rests, as it seems to us, simply on Dr. Newman identifying his own inferences from the language of the ancient writers whom he quotes with the language itself. They say a certain thing—that Mary is the "second Eve." Dr. Newman, with all the theology and all the controversies of eighteen centuries in his mind, deduces from this statement a number of refined consequences as to her sinlessness, and greatness, and reward, which seem to him to flow from it, and says that it means all these consequences. Mr. Ruskin somewhere quotes the language of an "eminent Academician," who remarks, in answer to some criticism on a picture, "that if you look for curves, you will see curves; and if you look for angles, you will see angles." So it is here. The very dogma of the Immaculate Conception itself Dr. Newman sees indissolubly involved in the "rudimentary teaching" which insists on the parallelism between Eve and Mary :—

Was not Mary as fully endowed as Eve? . . . If Eve was (as Bishop Bull and others maintain) raised above human nature by that indwelling moral gift which we call grace, is it rash to say that Mary had a greater grace?... And if Eve had this supernatural inward gift given her from the moment of her personal existence, is it possible to deny that Mary, too, had this gift from the very first moment of her personal existence? I do not know how to resist this inference:—well, this is simply and literally the doctrine of the Immaculate Conception. I say the doctrine of the Immaculate Conception is in its substance this, and nothing more or less than this (putting aside the question of degrees of grace), and it really does seem to me bound up in that doctrine of the Fathers, that Mary is the second Eve.

It seems obvious to remark that the Fathers are not even alleged to have themselves drawn this irresistible inference; and next, that even if it be drawn, there is a long interval between it and the elevation of the Mother of Jesus Christ to the place to which modern Roman doctrine raises her. Possibly, the Fathers might have said, as many people will say now, that, in a matter of this kind, it is idle to draw inferences when we are, in reality, utterly without the knowledge to make them worth anything. At any rate, if they had drawn them, we should have found some traces of it in their writings, and we find none. We find abundance of poetical addresses and rhetorical amplification, which makes it all the more remarkable that the plain dogmatic view of her position, which is accepted by the Roman Church, does not appear in them. We only find a "rudimentary doctrine," which, naturally enough, gives the Blessed Virgin a very high and sacred place in the economy of the Incarnation. But how does the doctrine, as it is found in even their rhetorical passages, go a step beyond what would be accepted by any sober reader of the New Testament? They speak of what she was; they do not presume to say what she is. What Protestant could have the slightest difficulty in saying not only what Justin says, and Tertullian copies from him, and Irenaeus enlarges upon, but what Dr. Newman himself says of her awful and solitary dignity, always excepting the groundless assumption which, from her office in this world takes for granted, first her sinlessness, and then a still higher office in the next? We do not think that, as a matter of literary criticism, Dr. Newman is fair in his argument from the Fathers. He lays great stress on Justin Martyr, Tertullian, and Irenaeus, as three independent witnesses from different parts of the world; whereas it is obvious that Tertullian at any rate copies almost literally from Justin Martyr, and it is impossible to compare a mere incidental point of rhetorical, or, if it be so, argumentative illustration, occurring once or twice in a long treatise, with a doctrine, such as that of the Incarnation itself, on which the whole treatise is built, and of which it is full. The wonder is, indeed, that the Fathers, considering how much they wrote, said so little of her; scarcely less is it a wonder, then, that the New Testament says so little, but from this little the only reason which would prevent a Protestant reader of the New Testament from accepting the highest statement of her historical dignity is the reaction from the development of them into the consequences which have been notorious for centuries in the unreformed Churches. Protestants, left to themselves, are certainly not prone to undervalue the saints of Scripture; it has been the presence of the great system of popular worship confronting them which has tied their tongues in this matter. Yet Anglican theologians like Mr. Keble, popular poets like Wordsworth, broad Churchmen like Mr. Robertson, have said things which even Roman Catholics might quote as expressions of their feeling. But Dr. Newman must know that many things may be put, and put most truly, into the form of poetical expression which will not bear hardening into a dogma. A Protestant may accept and even amplify the ideas suggested by Scripture about the Blessed Virgin; but he may feel that he cannot tell how the Redeemer was preserved from sinful taint; what was the grace bestowed on His mother; or what was the reward and prerogative which ensued to her. But it is just these questions which the Roman doctrine undertakes to answer without a shadow of doubt, and which Dr. Newman implies that the theology of the Fathers answered as unambiguously.

But from what has happened in the history of religion, we do not think that Protestants in general who do not shrink from high language about Abraham, Moses, or David, would find anything unnatural or objectionable in the language of the early Christian writers about the Mother of our Lord, though possibly it might not be their own; but the interval from this language to that certain knowledge of her present office in the economy of grace which is implied in what Dr. Newman considers the "doctrine" about her is a very long one. The step to the modern "devotion" in its most chastened form is longer still. We cannot follow the subtle train of argument which says that because the "doctrine" of the second century called her the "second Eve," therefore the devotion which sets her upon the altars of Christendom in the nineteenth is a right development of the doctrine. What is wanted is not the internal thread of the process, but the proof and confirmation from without that it was the right process; and this link is just what is wanting, except on a supposition which begs the question. It is conceivable that this step from "doctrine" to "devotion" may have been a mistake. It is conceivable that the "doctrine" may have been held in the highest form without leading to the devotion; for Dr. Newman, of course, thinks that Athanasius and Augustine held "the doctrine," yet, as he says, "we have no proof that Athanasius himself had any special devotion to the Blessed Virgin," and in another place he repeats his doubts whether St. Chrysostom or St. Athanasius invoked her; "nay," he adds, "I should like to know whether St. Augustine, in all his voluminous writings, invokes her once." What has to be shown is, that this step was not a mistake; that it was inevitable and legitimate.

"This being the faith of the Fathers about the Blessed Virgin," says Dr. Newman, "we need not wonder that it should in no long time be transmuted into devotion." The Fathers expressed a historical fact about her in the term Θεοτόκος; therefore, argues the later view, she is the source of our present grace now. It is the *rationale* of this inference, which is not an immediate or obvious one, which is wanted. And Dr. Newman gives it us in the words of Bishop Butler:—

Christianity is eminently an objective religion. For the most part it tells us of persons and facts in simple words, and leaves the announcement to produce its effect on such hearts as are prepared to receive it. This, at least, is its general character; and Butler recognises it as such in his *Analogy*, when speaking of the Second and Third Persons of the Holy Trinity:—"The internal worship," he says, "to the Son and Holy Ghost is no farther matter of pure revealed command than as the relations they stand in to us are matters of pure revelation; but the relations being known, the obligations to such internal worship are *obligations of reason arising out of those relations themselves.*"

We acknowledge the pertinency of the quotation. So true is it that "the relations being known," the obligations of worship arise of themselves from these relations, that if the present relation of the Blessed

Virgin to mankind has always been considered to be what modern Roman theology considers it, it is simply inconceivable that devotion to her should not have been universal long before St. Athanasius and St. Augustine; and equally inconceivable, to take Dr. Newman's remarkable illustration, that if the real position of St. Joseph is next to her, it should have been reserved for the nineteenth century, if not, indeed, to find it out, at least to acknowledge it; but the whole question is about the fact of the "relations" themselves. If we believe that the Second and Third Persons are God, we do not want to be told to worship them. But such a relation as Dr. Newman supposes in the case of the Blessed Virgin does not flow of itself from the idea contained, for instance, in the word Θεοτόκος, and even if it did, we should still want to be told, in the case of a creature, and remembering the known jealousy of religion of even the semblance of creature worship, what *are* the "religious regards," which, not flowing from the nature of the case, but needing to be distinctly authorised, are right and binding.

The question is of a dogmatic and a popular system. We most fully admit that, with Dr. Newman or any other of the numberless well-trained and excellent men in the Roman Church, the homage to the Mother does not interfere with the absolutely different honour rendered to the Son. We readily acknowledge the elevating and refining beauty of that character, of which the Virgin Mother is the type, and the services which that ideal has rendered to mankind, though we must emphatically say that a man need not be a Roman Catholic to feel and to express the charm of that moral beauty. But here we have a doctrine as definite and precise as any doctrine can be, and a great system of popular devotion, giving a character to a great religious communion. Dr. Newman is not merely developing and illustrating an idea: he is asserting a definite revealed fact about the unseen world, and defending its consequences in a very concrete and practical shape. And the real point is what proof has he given us that this is a revealed fact; that it is so, and that we have the means of knowing it? He has given us certain language of the early writers, which he says is a tradition, though it is only what any Protestant might have been led to by reading his Bible. But between that language, taken at its highest, and the belief and practice which his Church maintains, there is a great gap. The "Second Eve," the Θεοτόκος, are names of high dignity; but enlarge upon them as we may, there is between them and the modern "Regina Coeli" an interval which nothing but direct divine revelation can possibly fill; and of this divine revelation the only evidence is the fact that there is the doctrine. So awful and central an article of belief needs corresponding proof. In Dr. Newman's eloquent pages we have much collateral thought on the subject—sometimes instinct with his delicacy of perception and depth of feeling, sometimes strangely over-refined and irrelevant, but always fresh and instructive, whether to teach or to warn. The one thing which is missing in them is direct proof.

He does not satisfy us, but he does greatly interest us in his way of dealing with the practical consequences of his doctrine, in the manifold development of devotion in his communion. What he tells us reveals two things. By this devotion he is at once greatly attracted, and he is deeply shocked. No one can doubt the enthusiasm with which he has thrown himself into that devotion, an enthusiasm which, if it was at one time more vehement and defiant than it is now, is still a most intense element in his religious convictions. Nor do we feel entitled to say that in him it interferes with religious ideas and feelings of a higher order, which we are accustomed to suppose imperilled by it. It leads him, indeed, to say things which astonish us, not so much by their extreme language as by the absence, as it seems to us, of any ground to say them at all. It forces him into a championship for statements, in defending which the utmost that can be done is to frame ingenious pleas, or to send back a vigorous retort. It tempts him at times to depart from his generally broad and fair way of viewing things, as when he meets the charge that the Son is forgotten for the Mother, not merely by a denial, but by the rejoinder that when the Mother is not honoured as the Roman Church honours her the honour of the Son fails. It would have been better not to have reprinted the following extract from a former work, even though it were singled out for approval by the late Cardinal. The italics are his own:—

I have spoken more on this subject in my *Essay on Development*, p. 438, "Nor does it avail to object that, in this contrast of devotional exercises, the human is sure to supplant the Divine, from the infirmity of our nature; for, I repeat, the question is one of fact, whether it has done so. And next, it must be asked, *whether the character of Protestant devotion towards Our Lord has been that of worship at all;* and not rather such as we pay to an excellent human being. . . . Carnal minds will ever create a carnal worship for themselves, and to forbid them the service of the saints will have no tendency to teach them the worship of God. Moreover, . . . great and constant as is the devotion which the Catholic pays to St. Mary, it has a special province, and *has far more connection with the public services and the festive aspect of Christianity*, and with certain extraordinary offices which she holds, *than with what is strictly personal and primary in religion.*" Our late Cardinal, on my reception, singled out to me this last sentence, for the expression of his especial approbation.

Can Dr. Newman defend the first of these two assertions, when he remembers such books of popular Protestant devotion as Wesley's Hymns, or the German hymn-books of which we have examples in the well-known *Lyra Germanica*? Can he deny the second when he remembers the exercises of the

"Mois de Marie" in French churches, or if he has heard a fervid and earnest preacher at the end of them urge on a church full of young people, fresh from Confirmation and first Communion, a special and personal self-dedication to the great patroness for protection amid the daily trials of life, in much the same terms as in an English Church they might be exhorted to commit themselves to the Redeemer of mankind? Right or wrong, such devotion is not a matter of the "festive aspect" of religion, but most eminently of what is "personal and primary" in it; and surely of such a character is a vast proportion of the popular devotion here spoken of.

But for himself, no doubt, he has accepted this *cultus* on its most elevated and refined side. He himself makes the distinction, and says that there is "a healthy" and an "artificial" form of it; a devotion which does not shock "solid piety and Christian good sense; I cannot help calling this the English style." And when other sides are presented to him, he feels what any educated Englishman who allows his English feelings play is apt to feel about them. What is more, he has the boldness to say so. He makes all kinds of reserves to save the credit of those with whom he cannot sympathise. He speaks of the privileges of Saints; the peculiarities of national temperament; the distinctions between popular language and that used by scholastic writers, or otherwise marked by circumstances; the special characters of some of the writers quoted, their "ruthless logic," or their obscurity; the inculpated passages are but few and scattered in proportion to their context; they are harsh, but sound worse than they mean; they are hardly interpreted and pressed. He reminds Dr. Pusey that there is not much to choose between the Oriental Churches and Rome on this point, and that of the two the language of the Eastern is the most florid, luxuriant, and unguarded. But, after all, the true feeling comes out at last, "And now, at length," he says, "coming to the statements, not English, but foreign, which offend you, I will frankly say that I read some of those which you quote with grief and almost anger." They are "perverse sayings," which he hates. He fills a page and a half with a number of them, and then deliberately pronounces his rejection of them.

After such explanations, and with such authorities to clear my path, I put away from me as you would wish, without any hesitation, as matters in which my heart and reason have no part (when taken in their literal and absolute sense, as any Protestant would naturally take them, and as the writers doubtless did not use them), such sentences and phrases as these :—that the mercy of Mary is infinite, that God has resigned into her hands His omnipotence, that (unconditionally) it is safer to seek her than her Son, that the Blessed Virgin is superior to God, that He is (simply) subject to her command, that our Lord is now of the same disposition as His Father towards sinners—viz. a disposition to reject them, while Mary takes His place as an Advocate with the Father and Son; that the Saints are more ready to intercede with Jesus than Jesus with the Father, that Mary is the only refuge of those with whom God is angry; that Mary alone can obtain a Protestant's conversion; that it would have sufficed for the salvation of men if our Lord had died, not to obey His Father, but to defer to the decree of His Mother, that she rivals our Lord in being God's daughter, not by adoption, but by a kind of nature; that Christ fulfilled the office of Saviour by imitating her virtues; that, as the Incarnate God bore the image of His Father, so He bore the image of His Mother; that redemption derived from Christ indeed its sufficiency, but from Mary its beauty and loveliness; that as we are clothed with the merits of Christ so we are clothed with the merits of Mary; that, as He is Priest, in like manner is she Priestess; that His body and blood in the Eucharist are truly hers, and appertain to her; that as He is present and received therein, so is she present and received therein; that Priests are ministers as of Christ, so of Mary; that elect souls are born of God and Mary; that the Holy Ghost brings into fruitfulness His action by her, producing in her and by her Jesus Christ in His members; that the kingdom of God in our souls, as our Lord speaks, is really the kingdom of Mary in the soul —and she and the Holy Ghost produce in the soul extraordinary things—and when the Holy Ghost finds Mary in a soul He flies there.

Sentiments such as these I never knew of till I read your book, nor, as I think, do the vast majority of English Catholics know them. They seem to me like a bad dream. I could not have conceived them to be said. I know not to what authority to go for them, to Scripture, or to the Fathers, or to the decrees of Councils, or to the consent of schools, or to the tradition of the faithful, or to the Holy See, or to Reason. They defy all the *loci theologici*. There is nothing of them in the Missal, in the Roman Catechism, in the Roman *Raccolta*, in the Imitation of Christ, in Gother, Challoner, Milner, or Wiseman, so far as I am aware. They do but scare and confuse me. I should not be holier, more spiritual, more sure of perseverance, if I twisted my moral being into the reception of them; I should but be guilty of fulsome frigid flattery towards the most upright and noble of God's creatures if I professed them—and of stupid flattery too; for it would be like the compliment of painting up a young and beautiful princess with the brow of a Plato and the muscle of an Achilles. And I should expect her to tell one of her people in waiting to turn me off her service without warning. Whether thus to feel be the *scandalum parvulorum* in my case, or the *scandalum Pharisaeorum*, I leave others to decide; but I will say plainly that I had rather believe (which is impossible) that there is no God at all, than that Mary is greater than God. I will have nothing to do with statements, which can only be explained by being explained away. I do not, however, speak of these statements, as they are found in their authors, for I know nothing of the originals, and cannot believe that they have meant what you say; but I take them as they lie in your pages. Were any of them the sayings of Saints in ecstasy, I should know they had a good meaning; still I should not repeat them myself; but I am looking at them, not as spoken by the tongues of Angels, but according to that literal sense which they bear in the mouths of English men and

English women. And, as spoken by man to man in England in the nineteenth century, I consider them calculated to prejudice inquirers, to frighten the unlearned, to unsettle consciences, to provoke blasphemy, and to work the loss of souls.

Of course; it is what might be expected of him. But Dr. Newman has often told us that we must take the consequences of our principles and theories, and here are some of the consequences which meet him; and, as he says, they "scare and confuse him." He boldly disavows them with no doubtful indignation. But what other voice but his, of equal authority and weight, has been lifted up to speak the plain truth about them? Why, if they are wrong, extravagant, dangerous, is his protest solitary? His communion has never been wanting in jealousy of dangerous doctrines, and it is vain to urge that these things and things like them have been said in a corner. The Holy Office is apt to detect mischief in small writers as well as great, even if these teachers were as insignificant as Dr. Newman would gladly make them. Taken as a whole, and in connection with notorious facts, these statements are fair examples of manifest tendencies, which certainly are not on the decline. And if a great and spreading popular *cultus*, encouraged and urged on beyond all former precedent, is in danger of being developed by its warmest and most confident advocates into something of which unreason is the lightest fault, is there not ground for interfering? Doubtless Roman writers may be quoted by Dr. Newman, who felt that there was a danger, and we are vaguely told about some checks given to one or two isolated extravagances, which, however, in spite of the checks, do not seem to be yet extinct. But Allocutions and Encyclicals are not for errors of this kind. Dr. Newman says that "it is wiser for the most part to leave these excesses to the gradual operation of public opinion,—that is, to the opinion of educated and sober Catholics; and this seems to me the healthiest way of putting them down." We quite agree with him; but his own Church does not think so; and we want to see some evidence of a public opinion in it capable of putting them down. As it is, he is reduced to say that "the line cannot be logically drawn between the teaching of the Fathers on the subject and our own;" an assertion which, if it were true, would be more likely to drag down one teaching than to prop up the other; he has to find reasons, and doubtless they are to be found thick as blackberries, for accounting for one extravagance, softening down another, declining to judge a third. But in the meantime the "devotion" in its extreme form, far beyond what he would call the teaching of his Church, has its way; it maintains its ground; it becomes the mark of the bold, the advanced, the refined, as well as of the submissive and the crowd; it roots itself under the shelter of an authority which would stop it if it was wrong; it becomes "dominant"; it becomes at length part of that "mind of the living Church" which, we are told, it is heresy to impugn, treason to appeal from, and the extravagance of impertinent folly to talk of reforming.

It is very little use, then, for Dr. Newman to tell Dr. Pusey or any one else, "You may safely trust us English Catholics as to this devotion." "English Catholics," as such,—it is the strength and the weakness of their system,—have really the least to say in the matter. The question is not about trusting "us English Catholics," but the Pope, and the Roman Congregation, and those to whom the Roman authorities delegate their sanction and give their countenance. If Dr. Newman is able, as we doubt not he is desirous, to elevate the tone of his own communion and put to shame some of its fashionable excesses, he will do a great work, in which we wish him every success, though the result of it might not really be to bring the body of his countrymen nearer to it. But the substance of Dr. Pusey's charges remain after all unanswered, and there is no getting over them while they remain. They are of that broad, palpable kind against which the refinements of argumentative apology play in vain. They can only be met by those who feel their force, on some principle equally broad. Dr. Newman suggests such a ground in the following remarks, which, much as they want qualification and precision, have a basis of reality in them :—

It is impossible, I say, in a doctrine like this, to draw the line cleanly between truth and error, right and wrong.

This is ever the case in concrete matters which have life. Life in this world is motion, and involves a continual process of change. Living things grow into their perfection, into their decline, into their death. No rule of art will suffice to stop the operation of this natural law, whether in the material world or in the human mind. . . . What has power to stir holy and refined souls is potent also with the multitude, and the religion of the multitude is ever vulgar and abnormal; it ever will be tinctured with fanaticism and superstition while men are what they are. A people's religion is ever a corrupt religion. If you are to have a Catholic Church you must put up with fish of every kind, guests good and bad, vessels of gold, vessels of earth. You may beat religion out of men, if you will, and then their excesses will take a different direction; but if you make use of religion to improve them, they will make use of religion to corrupt it. And then you will have effected that compromise of which our countrymen report so unfavourably from abroad,—a high grand faith and worship which compels their admiration, and puerile absurdities among the people which excite their contempt.

It is like Dr. Newman to put his case in this broad way, making large admissions, allowing for much inevitable failure. That is, he defends his Church as he would defend Christianity generally, taking it as a great practical system must be in this world, working with human nature as it is. His reflection is, no doubt, one suggested by a survey of the cause of all religion. The coming short of the greatest promises, the debasement of the noblest ideals, are among the commonplaces of history. Christianity cannot be maintained without ample admissions of failure and perversion. But it is one thing to make this admission for Christianity generally, an admission which the New Testament in foretelling its fortunes gives us abundant ground for making; and quite another for those who maintain the superiority of one form of Christianity above all others, to claim that they may leave out of the account its characteristic faults. It is quite true that all sides abundantly need to appeal for considerate judgment to the known infirmity of human nature; but amid the conflicting pretensions which divide Christendom no one side can ask to have for itself the exclusive advantage of this plea. All may claim the benefit of it, but if it is denied to any it must be denied to all. In this confused and imperfect world other great popular systems of religion besides the Roman may use it in behalf of shortcomings, which, though perhaps very different, are yet not worse. It is obvious that the theory of great and living ideas, working with a double edge, and working for mischief at last, holds good for other things besides the special instance on which Dr. Newman comments. It is to be further observed that to claim the benefit of this plea is to make the admission that you come under the common law of human nature as to mistake, perversion, and miscarriage, and this in the matter of religious guidance the Roman theory refuses to do. It claims for its communion as its special privilege an exemption from those causes of corruption of which history is the inexorable witness, and to which others admit themselves to be liable; an immunity from going wrong, a supernatural exception from the common tendency of mankind to be led astray, from the common necessity to correct and reform themselves when they are proved wrong. How far this is realised, not on paper and in argument, but in fact, is indeed one of the most important questions for the world, and it is one to which the world will pay more heed than to the best writing about it. There are not wanting signs, among others of a very different character, of an honest and philosophical recognition of this by some of the ablest writers of the Roman communion. The day on which the Roman Church ceases to maintain that what it holds must be truth because it holds it, and admits itself subject to the common condition by which God has given truth to men, will be the first hopeful day for the reunion of Christendom.

XXVIII

NEWMAN'S PAROCHIAL SERMONS [1]

Dr. Newman's Sermons stand by themselves in modern English literature; it might be said, in English literature generally. There have been equally great masterpieces of English writing in this form of composition, and there have been preachers whose theological depth, acquaintance with the heart, earnestness, tenderness, and power have not been inferior to his. But the great writers do not touch, pierce, and get hold of minds as he does, and those who are famous for the power and results of their preaching do not write as he does. His sermons have done more perhaps than any one thing to mould and quicken and brace the religious temper of our time; they have acted with equal force on those who were nearest and on those who were farthest from him in theological opinion. They have altered the whole manner of feeling towards religious subjects. We

---

[1] *Parochial and Plain Sermons.* By John Henry Newman, B.D., formerly Vicar of St. Mary's, Oxford. Edited by W. J. Copeland, B.D. *Saturday Review*, 5th June 1869.

know now that they were the beginning, the signal and first heave, of a vast change that was to come over the subject; of a demand from religion of a thoroughgoing reality of meaning and fulfilment, which is familiar to us, but was new when it was first made. And, being this, these sermons are also among the very finest examples of what the English language of our day has done in the hands of a master. Sermons of such intense conviction and directness of purpose, combined with such originality and perfection on their purely literary side, are rare everywhere. Remarkable instances, of course, will occur to every one of the occasional exhibition of this combination, but not in so sustained and varied and unfailing a way. Between Dr. Newman and the great French school there is this difference—that they are orators, and he is as far as anything can be in a great preacher from an orator. Those who remember the tones and the voice in which the sermons were heard at St. Mary's—we may refer to Professor Shairp's striking account in his volume on Keble, and to a recent article in the *Dublin Review*—can remember how utterly unlike an orator in all outward ways was the speaker who so strangely moved them. The notion of judging of Dr. Newman as an orator never crossed their minds. And this puts a difference between him and a remarkable person whose name has sometimes been joined with his—Mr. F. Robertson. Mr. Robertson was a great preacher, but he was not a writer.

It is difficult to realise at present the effect produced originally by these sermons. The first feeling was that of their difference in manner from the customary sermon. People knew what an eloquent sermon was, or a learned sermon, or a philosophical sermon, or a sermon full of doctrine or pious unction. Chalmers and Edward Irving and Robert Hall were familiar names; the University pulpit and some of the London churches had produced examples of forcible argument and severe and finished composition; and of course instances were abundant everywhere of the good, sensible, commonplace discourse; of all that was heavy, dull, and dry, and of all that was ignorant, wild, fanatical, and irrational. But no one seemed to be able, or to be expected, unless he avowedly took the buffoonery line which some of the Evangelical preachers affected, to speak in the pulpit with the directness and straightforward unconventionality with which men speak on the practical business of life. With all the thought and vigour and many beauties which were in the best sermons, there was always something forced, formal, artificial about them; something akin to that mild pomp which usually attended their delivery, with beadles in gowns ushering the preacher to the carpeted pulpit steps, with velvet cushions, and with the rustle and fulness of his robes. No one seemed to think of writing a sermon as he would write an earnest letter. A preacher must approach his subject in a kind of roundabout make-believe of preliminary and preparatory steps, as if he was introducing his hearers to what they had never heard of; make-believe difficulties and objections were overthrown by make-believe answers; an unnatural position both in speaker and hearers, an unreal state of feeling and view of facts, a systematic conventional exaggeration, seemed almost impossible to be avoided; and those who tried to escape being laboured and grandiloquent only escaped it, for the most part, by being vulgar or slovenly. The strong severe thinkers, jealous for accuracy, and loathing clap-trap as they loathed loose argument, addressed and influenced intelligence; but sermons are meant for heart and souls as well as minds, and to the heart, with its trials and its burdens, men like Whately never found their way. Those who remember the preaching of those days, before it began to be influenced by the sermons at St. Mary's, will call to mind much that was interesting, much that was ingenious, much correction of inaccurate and confused views, much manly encouragement to high principle and duty, much of refined and scholarlike writing. But for soul and warmth, and the imaginative and poetical side of the religious life, you had to go where thought and good sense were not likely to be satisfied.

The contrast of Mr. Newman's preaching was not obvious at first. The outside form and look was very much that of the regular best Oxford type—calm, clear, and lucid in expression, strong in its grasp, measured in statement, and far too serious to think of rhetorical ornament. But by degrees much more opened. The range of experience from which the preacher drew his materials, and to which he appealed, was something wider, subtler, and more delicate than had been commonly dealt with in sermons. With his strong, easy, exact, elastic language, the instrument of a powerful and argumentative mind, he plunged into the deep realities of the inmost spiritual life, of which cultivated preachers had been shy. He preached so that he made you feel without doubt that it was the most real of worlds to him; he made you feel in time, in spite of yourself, that it was a real world with which you too had concern. He made you feel that he knew what he was speaking about; that his reasonings and appeals, whether you agreed with them or not, were not the language of that heated enthusiasm with which the world is so familiar; that he was speaking words which were the result of intellectual scrutiny, balancings, and decisions, as well as of moral trials, of conflicts and suffering within; words of the utmost soberness belonging to deeply gauged and earnestly formed purposes. The effect of his sermons, as compared with the common run at the time, was something like what happens when in a company you have a number of people giving their views and answers about some question before them. You have opinions given of various worth and expressed with varying power, precision, and distinctness, some clever enough, some clumsy enough, but all more or less imperfect and unattractive in tone, and more or less falling short of their aim; and then, after it all, comes a voice, very grave, very sweet, very sure and clear, under whose words the discussion springs up at once to a higher level, and in which we recognise at once a mind, face to face with realities, and able to seize them and hold them fast.

The first notable feature in the external form of this preaching was its terse unceremonious directness. Putting aside the verbiage and dulled circumlocution and stiff hazy phraseology of pulpit etiquette and dignity, it went straight to its point. There was no waste of time about customary formalities. The preacher had something to say, and with a kind of austere severity he proceeded to say it. This, for instance, is the sort of way in which a sermon would begin:—

Hypocrisy is a serious word. We are accustomed to consider the hypocrite as a hateful, despicable character, and an uncommon one. How is it, then, that our Blessed Lord, when surrounded by an innumerable multitude, began, *first of all*, to warn His disciples against hypocrisy, as though they were in especial danger of becoming like those base deceivers the Pharisees? Thus an instructive subject is opened to our consideration, which I will now pursue.—Vol. I. Serm. X.

The next thing was that, instead of rambling and straggling over a large subject, each sermon seized a single thought, or definite view, or real difficulty or objection, and kept closely and distinctly to it; and at the same time treated it with a largeness and grasp and ease which only a full command over much beyond it could give. Every sermon had a purpose and an end which no one could misunderstand. Singularly devoid of anything like excitement—calm, even, self-controlled—there was something in the preacher's resolute concentrated way of getting hold of a single defined object which reminded you of the rapid spring or unerring swoop of some strong-limbed or swift-winged creature on its quarry. Whatever you might think that he did with it, or even if it seemed to escape from him, you could have no doubt what he sought to do; there was no wavering, confused, uncertain bungling in that powerful and steady hand. Another feature was the character of the writer's English. We have learned to look upon Dr. Newman as one of the half-dozen or so of the innumerable good writers of the time who have fairly left their mark as masters on the language. Little, assuredly, as the writer originally thought of such a result, the sermons have proved a permanent gift to our literature, of the purest English, full of spring, clearness, and force. A hasty reader would perhaps at first only notice a very light, strong, easy touch, and might think, too, that it was a negligent one. But it was not negligence; real negligence means at bottom bad work, and bad work will not stand the trial of time. There are two great styles—the self-conscious, like that of Gibbon or Macaulay, where great success in expression is accompanied by an unceasing and manifest vigilance that expression shall succeed, and where you see at each step that there is or has been much care and work in the mind, if not on the paper; and the unconscious, like that of Pascal or Swift or Hume, where nothing suggests at the moment that the writer is thinking of anything but his subject, and where the power of being able to say just what he wants to say seems to come at the writer's command, without effort, and without his troubling himself more about it than about the way in which he holds his pen. But both are equally the fruit of hard labour and honest persevering self-correction; and it is soon found out whether the apparent negligence comes of loose and slovenly habits of mind, or whether it marks the confidence of one who has mastered his instrument, and can forget himself and let himself go in using it. The free unconstrained movement of Dr. Newman's style tells any one who knows what writing is of a very keen and exact knowledge of the subtle and refined secrets of language. With all that uncared-for play and simplicity, there was a fulness, a richness, a curious delicate music, quite instinctive and unsought for; above all, a precision and sureness of expression which people soon began to find were not within the power of most of those who tried to use language. Such English, graceful with the grace of nerve, flexibility, and power, must always have attracted attention; but it had also an ethical element which was almost inseparable from its literary characteristics. Two things powerfully determined the style of these sermons. One was the intense hold which the vast realities of religion had gained on the writer's mind, and the perfect truth with which his personality sank and faded away before their overwhelming presence; the other was the strong instinctive shrinking, which was one of the most remarkable and certain marks of the beginners of the Oxford movement, from anything like personal display, any conscious aiming at the ornamental and brilliant, any show of gifts or courting of popular applause. Morbid and excessive or not, there can be no doubt of the stern self-containing severity which made them turn away, not only with fear, but with distaste and repugnance, from all that implied distinction or seemed to lead to honour; and the control of this austere spirit is visible, in language as well as matter, in every page of Dr. Newman's sermons.

Indeed, form and matter are closely connected in the sermons, and depend one on another, as they probably do in all work of a high order. The matter makes and shapes the form with which it clothes itself. The obvious thing which presents itself in reading them is that, from first to last, they are a great systematic attempt to raise the whole level of religious thought and religious life. They carry in them the evidence of a great reaction and a scornful indignant rising up against what were going about and were currently received as adequate ideas of religion. The dryness and primness and meagreness of the common Church preaching, correct as it was in its outlines of doctrine, and sober and temperate in tone, struck cold on a mind which had caught sight, in the New Testament, of the spirit and life of its words. The recoil was even stronger from the shallowness and pretentiousness and self-display of what was popularly accepted as earnest religion; morally the preacher was revolted at its unctuous boasts and pitiful performance, and intellectually by its narrowness and meanness of thought and its thinness of colour in all its pictures of the spiritual life. From first to last, in all manner of ways, the sermons are a protest, first against coldness, but even still more against meanness, in religion. With coldness they have no sympathy, yet coldness may be broad and large and lofty in its aspects; but they have no tolerance for what makes religion little and poor and superficial, for what contracts its horizon and dwarfs its infinite greatness and vulgarises its mystery. Open the sermons where we will, different readers will rise from them with very different results; there will be among many the strongest and most decisive disagreement; there may be impatience at dogmatic harshness, indignation at what seems overstatement and injustice, rejection of arguments and conclusions; but there will always be the sense of an unfailing nobleness in the way in which the writer thinks and speaks. It is not only that he is in earnest; it is that he has something which really is worth being in earnest for. He placed the heights of religion very high. If you have a religion like Christianity—this is the pervading note—think of it, and have it, worthily. People will differ from the preacher endlessly as to how this is to be secured. But that they will learn this lesson from the sermons, with a force with which few other writers have taught it, and that this lesson has produced its effect in our time, there can be no doubt. The only reason why it may not perhaps seem so striking to readers of this day is that the sermons have done their work, and we do not feel what they had to counteract, because they have succeeded in great measure in counteracting it. It is not too much to say that they have done more than anything else to revolutionise the whole idea of preaching in the English Church. Mr. Robertson, in spite of himself, was as much the pupil of their school as Mr. Liddon, though both are so widely different from their master.

The theology of these sermons is a remarkable feature about them. It is remarkable in this way, that, coming from a teacher like Dr. Newman, it is nevertheless a theology which most religious readers, except the Evangelicals and some of the more extreme Liberal thinkers, can either accept heartily or be content with, as they would be content with St. Augustine or Thomas à Kempis—content, not because they go along with it always, but because it is large and untechnical, just and well-measured in the proportions and relative importance of its parts. People of very different opinions turn to them, as being on the whole the fullest, deepest, most comprehensive approximation they can find to representing Christianity in a practical form. Their theology is nothing new; nor does it essentially change, though one may observe differences, and some important ones, in the course of the volumes, which embrace a period from 1825 to 1842. It is curious, indeed, to observe how early the general character of the sermons was determined, and how in the main it continues the same. Some of the first in point of date are among the "Plain Sermons"; and though they may have been subsequently retouched, yet there the keynote is plainly struck of that severe and solemn minor which reigns throughout. Their theology is throughout the accepted English theology of the Prayer-book and the great Church divines—a theology fundamentally dogmatic and sacramental, but jealously keeping the balance between obedience and faith; learned, exact, and measured, but definite and decided. The novelty was in the application of it, in the new life breathed into it, in the profound and intense feelings called forth by its ideas and objects, in the air of vastness and awe thrown about it, in the unexpected connection of its creeds and mysteries with practical life, in the new meaning given to the old and familiar, in the acceptance in thorough earnest, and with keen purpose to call it into action, of what had been guarded and laid by with dull reverence. Dr. Newman can hardly be called in these sermons an innovator on the understood and recognised standard of Anglican doctrine; he accepted its outlines as Bishop Wilson, for instance, might have traced them. What he did was first to call forth from it what it really meant, the awful heights and depths of its current words and forms; and next, to put beside them human character and its trials, not as they were conventionally represented and written about, but as a piercing eye and sympathising spirit saw them in the light of our nineteenth century, and in the contradictory and complicated movements, the efforts and failures, of real life. He took theology for granted, as a Christian preacher has a right to do; he does not prove it, and only occasionally meets difficulties, or explains; but, taking it for granted, he took it at its word, in its relation to the world of actual experience.

Utterly dissatisfied with what he found current as religion, Dr. Newman sought, without leaving the old paths, to put before people a strong and energetic religion based, not on feeling or custom, but on reason and conscience, and answering, in the vastness of its range, to the mysteries of human nature, and in its power to man's capacities and aims. The Liberal religion of that day, with its ideas of natural theology or of a cold critical Unitarianism, was a very shallow one; the Evangelical, trusting to excitement, had worn out its excitement and had reached the stage when its formulas, poor ones at the best, had become words without meaning. Such views might do in quiet, easy-going times, if religion were an exercise at will of imagination or thought, an indulgence, an ornament, an understanding, a fashion; not if it corresponded to such a state of things as is implied in the Bible, or to man's many-sided nature as it is shown in Shakspeare. The sermons reflect with merciless force the popular, superficial, comfortable thing called religion which the writer saw before him wherever he looked, and from which his mind recoiled. Such sermons as those on the "Self-wise Enquirer" and the "Religion of the Day," with its famous passage about the age not being sufficiently "gloomy and fierce in its religion," have the one-sided and unmeasured exaggeration which seems inseparable from all strong expressions of conviction, and from all deep and vehement protests against general faults; but, qualify and limit them as we may, their pictures were not imaginary ones, and there was, and is, but too much to justify them. From all this trifling with religion the sermons called on men to look into themselves. They appealed to conscience; and they appealed equally to reason and thought, to recognise what conscience is, and to deal honestly with it. They viewed religion as if projected on a background of natural and moral mystery, and surrounded by it—an infinite scene, in which our knowledge is like the Andes and Himalayas in comparison with the mass of the earth, and in which conscience is our final guide and arbiter. No one ever brought out so impressively the sense of the impenetrable and tremendous vastness of that amid which man plays his part. In such sermons as those on the "Intermediate State," the "Invisible World," the "Greatness and Littleness of

Human Life," the "Individuality of the Soul," the "Mysteriousness of our Present Being," we may see exemplified the enormous irruption into the world of modern thought of the unknown and the unknowable, as much as in the writers who, with far different objects, set against it the clearness and certainty of what we do know. But, beyond all, the sermons appealed to men to go back into their own thoughts and feelings, and there challenged them; were not the preacher's words the echoes and interpreting images of their own deepest, possibly most perplexing and baffling, experience? From first to last this was his great engine and power; from first to last he boldly used it. He claimed to read their hearts; and people felt that he did read them, their follies and their aspirations, the blended and tangled web of earnestness and dishonesty, of wishes for the best and truest, and acquiescence in makeshifts; understating what ordinary preachers make much of, bringing into prominence what they pass by without being able to see or to speak of it; keeping before his hearers the risk of mismanaging their hearts, of "all kinds of unlawful treatment of the soul." What a contrast to ordinary ways of speaking on a familiar theological doctrine is this way of bringing it into immediate relation to real feeling:—

It is easy to speak of human nature as corrupt in the general, to admit it in the general, and then get quit of the subject; as if, the doctrine being once admitted, there was nothing more to be done with it. But, in truth, we can have no real apprehension of the doctrine of our corruption till we view the structure of our minds, part by part; and dwell upon and draw out the signs of our weakness, inconsistency, and ungodliness, which are such as can arise from nothing but some strange original defect in our original nature. . . . We are in the dark about ourselves. When we act, we are groping in the dark, and may meet with a fall any moment. Here and there, perhaps, we see a little; or in our attempts to influence and move our minds, we are making experiments (as it were) with some delicate and dangerous instrument, which works we do not know how, and may produce unexpected and disastrous effects. The management of our hearts is quite above us. Under these circumstances it becomes our comfort to look up to God. "Thou, God, seest me." Such was the consolation of the forlorn Hagar in the wilderness. He knoweth whereof we are made, and He alone can uphold us. He sees with most appalling distinctness all our sins, all the windings and recesses of evil within us; yet it is our only comfort to know this, and to trust Him for help against ourselves.—Vol. I. Serm. XIII.

The preacher contemplates human nature, not in the stiff formal language in which it had become conventional with divines to set out its shortcomings and dangers, but as a great novelist contemplates and tries to describe it; taking in all its real contradictions and anomalies, its subtle and delicate shades; fixing upon the things which strike us in ourselves or our neighbours as ways of acting and marks of character; following it through its wide and varying range, its diversified and hidden folds and subtle self-involving realities of feeling and shiftiness; touching it in all its complex sensibilities, anticipating its dim consciousnesses, half-raising veils which hide what it instinctively shrinks from, sending through it unexpected thrills and shocks; large-hearted in indulgence, yet exacting; most tender, yet most severe. And against all this real play of nature he sets in their full force and depth the great ideas of God, of sin, and of the Cross; and, appealing not to the intelligence of an aristocracy of choice natures, but to the needs and troubles and longings which make all men one, he claimed men's common sympathy for the heroic in purpose and standard. He warned them against being fastidious, where they should be hardy. He spoke in a way that all could understand of brave ventures, of resolutely committing themselves to truth and duty.

The most practical of sermons, the most real and natural in their way of dealing with life and conduct, they are also intensely dogmatic. The writer's whole teaching presupposes, as we all know, a dogmatic religion; and these sermons are perhaps the best vindication of it which our time, disposed to think of dogmas with suspicion, has seen. For they show, on a large scale and in actual working instances, how what is noblest, most elevated, most poetical, most free and searching in a thinker's way of regarding the wonderful scene of life, falls in naturally, and without strain, with a great dogmatic system like that of the

Church. Such an example does not prove that system to be true, but it proves that a dogmatic system, as such, is not the cast-iron, arbitrary, artificial thing which it is often assumed to be. It is, indeed, the most shallow of all commonplaces, intelligible in ordinary minds, but unaccountable in those of high power and range, whether they believe or not, that a dogmatic religion is of course a hard, dry, narrow, unreal religion, without any affinities to poetry or the truth of things, or to the deeper and more sacred and powerful of human thoughts. If dogmas are not true, that is another matter; but it is the fashion to imply that dogmas are worthless, mere things of the past, without sense or substance or interest, because they are dogmas. As if Dante was not dogmatic in form and essence; as if the grandest and worthiest religious prose in the English language was not that of Hooker, nourished up amid the subtleties, but also amid the vast horizons and solemn heights, of scholastic divinity. A dogmatic system is hard in hard hands, and shallow in shallow minds, and barren in dull ones, and unreal and empty to preoccupied and unsympathising ones; we dwarf and distort ideas that we do not like, and when we have put them in our own shapes and in our own connection, we call them unmeaning or impossible. Dogmas are but expedients, common to all great departments of human thought, and felt in all to be necessary, for representing what are believed as truths, for exhibiting their order and consequences, for expressing the meaning of terms, and the relations of thought. If they are wrong, they are, like everything else in the world, open to be proved wrong; if they are inadequate, they are open to correction; but it is idle to sneer at them for being what they must be, if religious facts and truths are to be followed out by the thoughts and expressed by the language of man. And what dogmas are in unfriendly and incapable hands is no proof of what they may be when they are approached as things instinct with truth and life; it is no measure of the way in which they may be inextricably interwoven with the most unquestionably living thought and feeling, as in these sermons. Jealous, too, as the preacher is for Church doctrines as the springs of Christian life, no writer of our time perhaps has so emphatically and impressively recalled the narrow limits within which human language can represent Divine realities. No one that we know of shows that he has before his mind with such intense force and distinctness the idea of God; and in proportion as a mind takes in and submits itself to the impression of that awful vision, the gulf widens between all possible human words and that which they attempt to express :—

When we have deduced what we deduce by our reason from the study of visible nature, and then read what we read in His inspired word, and find the two apparently discordant, *this* is the feeling I think we ought to have on our minds ;—not an impatience to do what is beyond our powers, to weigh evidence, sum up, balance, decide, reconcile, to arbitrate between the two voices of God,—but a sense of the utter nothingness of worms such as we are; of our plain and absolute incapacity to contemplate things *as they really are;* a perception of our emptiness before the great Vision of God; of our "comeliness being turned into corruption, and our retaining no strength"; a conviction that what is put before us, whether in nature or in grace, is but an intimation, useful for particular purposes, useful for practice, useful in its department, "until the day break and the shadows flee away"; useful in such a way that both the one and the other representation may at once be used, as two languages, as two separate approximations towards the Awful Unknown Truth, such as will not mislead us in their respective provinces.—Vol. II. Serm. XVIII.

"I cannot persuade myself," he says, commenting on a mysterious text of Scripture, "thus to dismiss so solemn a passage" (*i.e.* by saying that it is "all figurative"). "It seems a presumption to say of dim notices about the unseen world, 'they only mean this or that,' as if one had ascended into the third heaven, or had stood before the throne of God. No; I see herein a deep mystery, a hidden truth, which I cannot handle or define, shining 'as jewels at the bottom of the great deep,' darkly and tremulously, yet really there. And for this very reason, while it is neither pious nor thankful to explain away the words which convey it, while it is a duty to use them, not less a duty is it to use them humbly, diffidently, and teachably, with the thought of God before us, and of our own nothingness."—Vol. III. Serm. XXV.

There are two great requisites for treating properly

the momentous questions and issues which have been brought before our generation. The first is accuracy—accuracy of facts, of terms, of reasoning; plain close dealing with questions in their real and actual conditions; clear, simple, honest, measured statements about things as we find them. The other is elevation, breadth, range of thought; a due sense of what these questions mean and involve; a power of looking at things from a height; a sufficient taking into account of possibilities, of our ignorance, of the real proportions of things. We have plenty of the first; we are for the most part lamentably deficient in the second. And of this, these sermons are, to those who have studied them, almost unequalled examples. Many people, no doubt, would rise from their perusal profoundly disagreeing with their teaching; but no one, it seems to us, could rise from them—with their strong effortless freedom, their lofty purpose, their generous standard, their deep and governing appreciation of divine things, their thoroughness, their unselfishness, their purity, their austere yet piercing sympathy—and not feel his whole ways of thinking about religion permanently enlarged and raised. He will feel that he has been with one who "told him what he knew about himself and what he did not know; has read to him his wants or feelings, and comforted him by the very reading; has made him feel that there was a higher life than this life, and a brighter world than we can see; has encouraged him, or sobered him, or opened a way to the inquiring, or soothed the perplexed." They show a man who saw very deeply into the thought of his time, and who, if he partly recoiled from it and put it back, at least equally shared it. Dr. Newman has been accused of being out of sympathy with his age, and of disparaging it. In reality, no one has proved himself more keenly sensitive to its greatness and its wonders; only he believed that he saw something greater still. We are not of those who can accept the solution which he has accepted of the great problems which haunt our society; but he saw better than most men what those problems demand, and the variety of their often conflicting conditions. Other men, perhaps, have succeeded better in what they aimed at; but no one has attempted more, with powers and disinterestedness which justified him in attempting it. The movement which he led, and of which these sermons are the characteristic monument, is said to be a failure; but there are failures, and even mistakes, which are worth many successes of other sorts, and which are more fruitful and permanent in their effects.

XXIX

CARDINAL NEWMAN[1]

It is not wonderful that people should be impressed by the vicissitudes and surprises and dramatic completeness of Cardinal Newman's career. It is not wonderful that he should be impressed by this himself. That he who left us in despair and indignation in 1845 should have passed through a course of things which has made him, Roman Catholic as he is, a man of whom Englishmen are so proud in 1879, is even more extraordinary than that the former Fellow of Oriel should now be surrounded with the pomp and state of a Cardinal. There is only one other career in our time which, with the greatest possible contrasts in other points, suggests in its strangeness and antecedent improbabilities something of a parallel. It is the train of events which has made "Disraeli the Younger" the most powerful Minister whom England has seen in recent years. But Lord Beaconsfield has aimed at what he has attained to, and has fought his way to it through the

[1] *Guardian*, 21st May 1879.

chances and struggles of a stirring public life. Cardinal Newman's life has been from first to last the life of the student and recluse. He has lived in the shade. He has sought nothing for himself. He has shrunk from the thought of advancement. The steps to the high places of the world have not offered themselves to him, and he has been content to be let alone. Early in his course his rare gifts of mind, his force of character, his power over hearts and sympathies, made him for a while a prominent person. Then came a series of events which seemed to throw him out of harmony with the great mass of his countrymen. He appeared to be, if not forgotten, yet not thought of, except by a small number of friends —old friends who had known him too well and too closely ever to forget, and new friends gathered round him by the later circumstances of his life and work. People spoke of him as a man who had made a great mistake and failed; who had thrown up influence and usefulness here, and had not found it there; too subtle, too imaginative for England, too independent for Rome. He seemed to have so sunk out of interest and account that off-hand critics, in the easy gaiety of their heart, might take liberties with his name.

Then came the first surprise. The *Apologia* was read with the keenest interest by those who most differed from the writer's practical conclusions; twenty years had elapsed since he had taken the unpopular step which seemed to condemn him to obscurity;

and now he emerged from it, challenging not in vain the sympathy of his countrymen. They awoke, it may be said—at least the younger generation of them—to what he really was; the old jars and bitternesses had passed out of remembrance; they only felt that they had one among them who could write—for few of them ever heard his wonderful voice—in a way which made English hearts respond quickly and warmly. And the strange thing was that the professed, the persistent denouncer of Liberalism, was welcomed back to his rightful place among Englishmen by none more warmly than by many Liberals. Still, though his name was growing more familiar year by year, the world did not see much more of him. The head of a religious company, of an educational institution at Birmingham, he lived in unpretending and quiet simplicity, occupied with the daily business of his house, with his books, with his correspondence, with finishing off his many literary and theological undertakings. Except in some chance reference in a book or newspaper which implied how considerable a person the world thought him, he was not heard of. People asked about him, but there was nothing to tell. Then at last, neglected by Pius IX., he was remembered by Leo XIII. The Pope offered him the Cardinalship, he said, because he thought it would be "grateful to the Catholics of England, and to England itself." And he was not mistaken. Probably there is not a single thing that the Pope could do which would be so heartily welcomed.

After breaking with England and all things English in wrath and sorrow, nearly thirty-five years ago, after a long life of modest retirement, unmarked by any public honours, at length before he dies Dr. Newman is recognised by Protestant England as one of its greatest men. It watches with interest his journey to Rome, his proceedings at Rome. In a crowd of new Cardinals—men of eminence in their own communion—he is the only one about whom Englishmen know or care anything. His words, when he speaks, pass *verbatim* along the telegraph wires, like the words of the men who sway the world. We read of the quiet Oxford scholar's arms emblazoned on vestment and furniture as those of a Prince of the Church, and of his motto—*Cor ad cor loquitur*. In that motto is the secret of all that he is to his countrymen. For that skill of which he is such a master, in the use of his and their "sweet mother tongue," is something much more than literary accomplishment and power. It means that he has the key to what is deepest in their nature and most characteristic in them of feeling and conviction—to what is deeper than opinions and theories and party divisions; to what in their most solemn moments they most value and most believe in.

His profound sympathy with the religiousness which still, with all the variations and all the immense shortcomings of English religion, marks England above all cultivated Christian nations, is really the bond between him and his countrymen, who yet for the most part think so differently from him, both about the speculative grounds and many of the practical details of religion. But it was natural for him, on an occasion like this, reviewing the past and connecting it with the present, to dwell on these differences. He repeated once more, and made it the keynote of his address, his old protest against "Liberalism in religion," the "doctrine that there is no positive truth in religion, but one creed is as good as another." He lamented the decay of the power of authority, the disappearance of religion from the sphere of political influence, from education, from legislation. He deplored the increasing impossibility of getting men to work together on a common religious basis. He pointed out the increasing seriousness and earnestness of the attempts to "supersede, to block out religion," by an imposing and high morality, claiming to dispense with it.

He dwelt on the mischief and dangers; he expressed, as any Christian would, his fearlessness and faith in spite of them; but do we gather, even from such a speaker, and on such an occasion, anything of the remedy? The principle of authority is shaken, he tells us; what can he suggest to restore it? He under-estimates, probably, the part which authority plays, implicitly yet very really, in English popular religion, much more in English Church religion; and authority, even in Rome, is not everything, and does not reach to every subject. But authority in our days can be nothing without real confidence in it; and where confidence in authority has been lost, it is idle to attempt to restore it by telling men that authority is a good and necessary thing. It must be won back, not simply claimed. It must be regained, when forfeited, by the means by which it was originally gained. And the strange phenomenon was obviously present to his clear and candid mind, though he treated it as one which is disappearing, and must at length pass away, that precisely here in England, where the only religious authority he recognises has been thrown off, the hold of religion on public interest is most effective and most obstinately tenacious.

What is the history of this? What is the explanation of it? Why is it that where "authority," as he understands it, has been longest paramount and undisputed, the public place and public force of religion have most disappeared; and that a "dozen men taken at random in the streets" of London find it easier, with all their various sects, to work together on a religious basis than a dozen men taken at random from the streets of Catholic Paris or Rome? Indeed, the public feeling towards himself, expressed in so many ways in the last few weeks, might suggest a question not undeserving of his thoughts. The mass of Englishmen are notoriously anti-Popish and anti-Roman. Their antipathies on this subject are profound, and not always reasonable. They certainly do not here halt between two opinions, or think that one creed is as good as another. What is it which has made so many of them, still retaining all their intense dislike to the system which Cardinal Newman has accepted, yet welcome so heartily his honours in it, notwithstanding that he has passed from England to Rome, and that he owes so much of what he is to England? Is it that they think it does not matter what a man believes, and whether a man turns Papist? Or is it not that, in spite of all that would repel and estrange, in spite of the oppositions of argument and the inconsistencies of speculation, they can afford to recognise in him, as in a high example, what they most sincerely believe in and most deeply prize, and can pay him the tribute of their gratitude and honour, even when unconvinced by his controversial reasonings, and unsatisfied by the theories which he has proposed to explain the perplexing and refractory anomalies of Church history? Is it not that with history, inexorable and unalterable behind them, condemning and justifying, supporting and warning all sides in turn, thoughtful men feel how much easier it is to point out and deplore our disasters than to see a way now to set them right? Is it not also that there are in the Christian Church bonds of affinity, subtler, more real and more prevailing than even the fatal legacies of the great schisms? Is it not that the sympathies which unite the author of the *Parochial Sermons* and the interpreter of St. Athanasius with the disciples of Andrewes, and Ken, and Bull, of Butler and Wilson, are as strong and natural as the barriers which outwardly keep them asunder are to human eyes hopelessly insurmountable?

XXX

CARDINAL NEWMAN'S COURSE[1]

THE long life is closed. And men, according to their knowledge and intelligence, turn to seek for some governing idea or aspect of things, by which to interpret the movements and changes of a course which, in spite of its great changes, is felt at bottom to have been a uniform and consistent one. For it seems that, at starting, he is at once intolerant, even to harshness, to the Roman Church, and tolerant, though not sympathetic, to the English; then the parts are reversed, and he is intolerant to the English and tolerant to the Roman; and then at last, when he finally anchored in the Roman Church, he is seen as—not tolerant, for that would involve dogmatic points on which he was most jealous, but—sympathetic in all that was of interest to England, and ready to recognise what was good and high in the English Church.

Is not the ultimate key to Newman's history his keen and profound sense of the life, society, and prin-

[1] *Guardian*, 13th August 1890.

ciples of action presented in the New Testament? To this New Testament life he saw, opposed and in contrast, the ways and assumptions of English life, religious as well as secular. He saw that the organisation of society had been carried, and was still being carried, to great and wonderful perfection; only it was the perfection of a society and way of life adapted to the present world, and having its ends here; only it was as different as anything can be from the picture which the writers of the New Testament, consciously and unconsciously, give of themselves and their friends. Here was a Church, a religion, a "Christian nation," professing to be identical in spirit and rules of faith and conduct with the Church and religion of the Gospels and Epistles; and what was the identity, beyond certain phrases and conventional suppositions? He could not see a trace in English society of that simple and severe hold of the unseen and the future which is the colour and breath, as well as the outward form, of the New Testament life. Nothing could be more perfect, nothing grander and nobler, than all the current arrangements for this life; its justice and order and increasing gentleness, its widening sympathies between men; but it was all for the perfection and improvement of this life; it would all go on, if what we experience now was our only scene and destiny. This perpetual antithesis haunted him, when he knew it, or when he did not. Against it the Church ought to be the perpetual protest, and the fearless challenge, as it was in the days of the New

Testament. But the English Church had drunk in, he held, too deeply the temper, ideas, and laws of an ambitious and advancing civilisation; so much so as to be unfaithful to its special charge and mission. The prophet had ceased to rebuke, warn, and suffer; he had thrown in his lot with those who had ceased to be cruel and inhuman, but who thought only of making their dwelling-place as secure and happy as they could. The Church had become respectable, comfortable, sensible, temperate, liberal; jealous about the forms of its creeds, equally jealous of its secular rights, interested in the discussion of subordinate questions, and becoming more and more tolerant of differences; ready for works of benevolence and large charity, in sympathy with the agricultural poor, open-handed in its gifts; a willing fellow-worker with society in kindly deeds, and its accomplice in secularity. All this was admirable, but it was not the life of the New Testament, and it was *that* which filled his thoughts. The English Church had exchanged religion for civilisation, the first century for the nineteenth, the New Testament as it is written, for a counterfeit of it interpreted by Paley or Mr. Simeon; and it seemed to have betrayed its trust.

Form after form was tried by him, the Christianity of Evangelicalism, the Christianity of Whately, the Christianity of Hawkins, the Christianity of Keble and Pusey; it was all very well, but it was not the Christianity of the New Testament and of the first ages. He wrote the *Church of the Fathers* to show they were not merely evidences of religion, but really living men; that they could and did live as they taught, and what was there like the New Testament or even the first ages now? Alas! there was nothing completely like them; but of all unlike things, the Church of England with its "smug parsons," and pony-carriages for their wives and daughters, seemed to him the most unlike: more unlike than the great unreformed Roman Church, with its strange, unscriptural doctrines and its undeniable crimes, and its alliance, wherever it could, with the world. But at least the Roman Church had not only preserved, but maintained at full strength through the centuries to our day two things of which the New Testament was full, and which are characteristic of it—devotion and self-sacrifice. The crowds at a pilgrimage, a shrine, or a "pardon" were much more like the multitudes who followed our Lord about the hills of Galilee—like them probably in that imperfect faith which we call superstition—than anything that could be seen in the English Church, even if the Salvation Army were one of its instruments. And the spirit which governed the Roman Church had prevailed on men to make the sacrifice of celibacy a matter of course, as a condition of ministering in a regular and systematic way not only to the souls, but to the bodies of men, not only for the Priesthood, but for educational Brotherhoods, and Sisters of the poor and of hospitals. Devotion and sacrifice, prayer and self-denying charity, in one word sanctity, are at once on the surface of the New Testament and interwoven with all its substance. He recoiled from a representation of the religion of the New Testament which to his eye was without them. He turned to where, in spite of every other disadvantage, he thought he found them. In S. Filippo Neri he could find a link between the New Testament and progressive civilisation. He could find no S. Filippo—so modern and yet so Scriptural—when he sought at home.

His mind, naturally alive to all greatness, had early been impressed with the greatness of the Church of Rome. But in his early days it was the greatness of Anti-Christ. Then came the change, and his sense of greatness was satisfied by the commanding and undoubting attitude of the Roman system, by the completeness of its theory, by the sweep of its claims and its rule, by the even march of its vast administration. It could not and it did not escape him, that the Roman Church, with all the good things which it had, was, as a whole, as unlike the Church of the New Testament and of the first ages as the English. He recognised it frankly, and built up a great theory to account for the fact, incorporating and modernising great portions of the received Roman explanations of the fact. But what won his heart and his enthusiasm was one thing; what justified itself to his intellect was another. And it was the reproduction, partial, as it might be, yet real and characteristic, in the Roman Church of the life and ways of the New Testament, which was the irresistible attraction that tore him from the associations and the affections of half a lifetime.

The final break with the English Church was with much heat and bitterness; and both sides knew too much each of the other to warrant the language used on each side. The English Church had received too much loyal and invaluable service from him in teaching and example to have insulted him, as many of its chief authorities did, with the charges of dishonesty and bad faith; his persecutors forgot that a little effort on his part might, if he had been what they called him, and had really been a traitor, have formed a large and compact party, whose secession might have caused fatal damage. And he, too, knew too much of the better side of English religious life to justify the fierce invective and sarcasm with which he assailed for a time the English Church as a mere system of comfortable and self-deceiving worldliness.

But as time went over him in his new position two things made themselves felt. One was, that though there was a New Testament life, lived in the Roman Church with conspicuous truth and reality, yet the Roman Church, like the English, was administered and governed by men—men with passions and faults, men of mixed characters—who had, like their English contemporaries and rivals, ends and rules of action not exactly like those of the New Testament. The Roman Church had to accept, as much as the English, the modern conditions of social and political life, however different in outward look from those of the Sermon on the Mount. The other was the increasing sense that the civilisation of the West was as a whole, and notwithstanding grievous drawbacks, part of God's providential government, a noble and beneficent thing, ministering graciously to man's peace and order, which Christians ought to recognise as a blessing of their times such as their fathers had not, for which they ought to be thankful, and which, if they were wise, they would put to what, in his phrase, was an "Apostolical" use. In one of the angelical hymns in the *Dream of Gerontius*, he dwells on the Divine goodness which led men to found "a household and a fatherland, a city and a state" with an earnestness of sympathy, recalling the enumeration of the achievements of human thought and hand, and the arts of civil and social life—καὶ φθέγμα καὶ ἠνεμόεν φρόνημα καὶ ἀστυνόμους ὀργάς—dwelt on so fondly by Aeschylus and Sophocles.

The force with which these two things made themselves felt as age came on—the disappointments attending his service to the Church, and the grandeur of the physical and social order of the world and its Divine sanction in spite of all that is evil and all that is so shortlived in it—produced a softening in his ways of thought and speech. Never for a moment did his loyalty and obedience to his Church, even when most tried, waver and falter. The thing is inconceivable to any one who ever knew him, and the mere suggestion would be enough to make him blaze forth in all his old fierceness and power. But perfectly satisfied of his position, and with his duties clearly defined, he could allow large and increasing play, in the leisure of advancing age, to his natural sympathies, and to the effect of the wonderful spectacle of the world around him. He was, after all, an Englishman; and with all his quickness to detect and denounce what was selfish and poor in English ideas and action, and with all the strength of his deep antipathies, his chief interests were for things English — English literature, English social life, English politics, English religion. He liked to identify himself, as far as it was possible, with things English, even with things that belonged to his own first days. He republished his Oxford sermons and treatises. He prized his honorary fellowship at Trinity; he enjoyed his visit to Oxford, and the welcome which he met there. He discerned how much the English Church counted for in the fight going on in England for the faith in Christ. There was in all that he said and did a gentleness, a forbearance, a kindly friendliness, a warm recognition of the honour paid him by his countrymen, ever since the *Apologia* had broken down the prejudices which had prevented Englishmen from doing him justice. As with his chief antagonist at Oxford, Dr. Hawkins, advancing years brought with them increasing gentleness, and generosity, and courtesy. But through all this there was perceptible to those who watched a pathetic yearning for something which was not to be had: a sense, resigned—for so it was ordered—but deep and piercing, how far, not some of us, but all of us, are from the life of the New Testament: how much there is for religion to do, and how little there seems to be to do it.

XXXI

CARDINAL NEWMAN'S NATURALNESS[1]

EVERY one feels what is meant when we speak of a person's ways being "natural," in contrast to being artificial, or overstrained, or studied, or affected. But it is easier to feel what is meant than to explain and define it. We sometimes speak as if it were a mere quality of manner; as if it belonged to the outside show of things, and denoted the atmosphere, clear and transparent, through which they are viewed. It corresponds to what is lucid in talk and style, and what ethically is straightforward and unpretentious. But it is something much more than a mere surface quality. When it is real and part of the whole character, and not put on from time to time for effect, it reaches a long way down to what is deepest and most significant in a man's moral nature. It is connected with the sense of truth, with honest self-judgment, with habits of self-discipline, with the repression of vanity, pride, egotism. It has no doubt to do with good taste and good manners, but it has as much

[1] *Guardian*, 20th August 1890.

to do with good morals—with the resolute habit of veracity with oneself—with the obstinate preference for reality over show, however tempting—with the wholesome power of being able to think little about oneself.

It is common to speak of the naturalness and ease of Cardinal Newman's style in writing. It is, of course, the first thing that attracts notice when we open one of his books; and there are people who think it bald and thin and dry. They look out for longer words, and grander phrases, and more involved constructions, and neater epigrams. They expect a great theme to be treated with more pomp and majesty, and they are disappointed. But the majority of English readers seem to be agreed in recognising the beauty and transparent flow of his language, which matches the best French writing in rendering with sureness and without effort the thought of the writer. But what is more interesting than even the formation of such a style—a work, we may be sure, not accomplished without much labour—is the man behind the style. For the man and the style are one in this perfect naturalness and ease. Any one who has watched at all carefully the Cardinal's career, whether in old days or later, must have been struck with this feature of his character, his naturalness, the freshness and freedom with which he addressed a friend or expressed an opinion, the absence of all mannerism and formality; and, where he had to keep his dignity, both his loyal obedience to the authority which enjoined it and the half-amused, half-bored impatience that he should be the person round whom all these grand doings centred. It made the greatest difference in his friendships whether his friends met him on equal terms, or whether they brought with them too great conventional deference or solemnity of manner. "So and so is a very good fellow, but he is not a man to talk to in your shirt sleeves," was his phrase about an over-logical and over-literal friend. Quite aware of what he was to his friends and to the things with which he was connected, and ready with a certain quickness of temper which marked him in old days to resent anything unbecoming done to his cause or those connected with it, he would not allow any homage to be paid to himself. He was by no means disposed to allow liberties to be taken or to put up with impertinence; for all that bordered on the unreal, for all that was pompous, conceited, affected, he had little patience; but almost beyond all these was his disgust at being made the object of foolish admiration. He protested with whimsical fierceness against being made a hero or a sage; he was what he was, he said, and nothing more; and he was inclined to be rude when people tried to force him into an eminence which he refused. With his profound sense of the incomplete and the ridiculous in this world, and with a humour in which the grotesque and the pathetic sides of life were together recognised at every moment, he never hesitated to admit his own mistakes—his "floors" as he called them. All this ease and frankness with those whom he trusted, which was one of the lessons which he learnt from Hurrell Froude, an intercourse which implied a good deal of give and take—all this satisfied his love of freedom, his sense of the real. It was his delight to give himself free play with those whom he could trust; to feel that he could talk with "open heart," understood without explaining, appealing for a response which would not fail, though it was not heard. He could be stiff enough with those who he thought were acting a part, or pretending to more than they could perform. But he believed—what was not very easy to believe beforehand—that he could win the sympathy of his countrymen, though not their agreement with him; and so, with characteristic naturalness and freshness, he wrote the *Apologia*.

XXXII

LORD BLACHFORD[1]

LORD BLACHFORD, whose death was announced last week, belonged to a generation of Oxford men of whom few now survive, and who, of very different characters and with very different careers and histories, had more in common than any set of contemporaries at Oxford since their time. Speaking roughly, they were almost the last product of the old training at public school and at college, before the new reforms set in; of a training confessedly imperfect and in some ways deplorably defective, but with considerable elements in it of strength and manliness, with keen instincts of contempt for all that savoured of affectation and hollowness, and with a sort of largeness and freedom about it, both in its outlook and its discipline, which suited vigorous and self-reliant natures in an exciting time, when debate ran high and the gravest issues seemed to be presenting themselves to English society. The reformed system which has

[1] *Guardian*, 27th Nov. 1889.

taken its place at Oxford criticises, not without some justice, the limitations of the older one; the narrow range of its interests, the few books which men read, and the minuteness with which they were "got up." But if these men did not learn all that a University ought to teach its students, they at least learned two things. They learned to work hard, and they learned to make full use of what they knew. They framed an ideal of practical life, which was very variously acted upon, but which at any rate aimed at breadth of grasp and generosity of purpose, and at being thorough. This knot of men, who lived a good deal together, were recognised at the time as young men of much promise, and they looked forward to life with eagerness and high aspiration. They have fulfilled their promise; their names are mixed up with all the recent history of England; they have filled its great places and governed its policy during a large part of the Queen's long reign. Their names are now for the most part things of the past—Sidney Herbert, Lord Canning, Lord Dalhousie, Lord Elgin, Lord Cardwell, the Wilberforces, Mr. Hope Scott, Archbishop Tait. But they still have their representatives among us — Mr. Gladstone, Lord Selborne, Lord Sherbrooke, Sir Thomas Acland, Cardinal Manning. It is not often that a University generation or two can produce such a list of names of statesmen and rulers; and the list might easily be enlarged.

To this generation Frederic Rogers belonged, not the least distinguished among his contemporaries;

and he was early brought under an influence likely to stimulate in a high degree whatever powers a man possessed, and to impress a strong character with elevated and enduring ideas of life and duty. Mr. Newman, with Mr. Hurrell Froude and Mr. Robert Wilberforce, had recently been appointed tutors of their college by Dr. Copleston. They were in the first eagerness of their enthusiasm to do great things with the college, and the story goes that Mr. Newman, on the look-out for promising pupils, wrote to an Eton friend, asking him to recommend some good Eton men for admission at Oriel. Frederic Rogers, so the story goes, was one of those mentioned; at any rate, he entered at Oriel, and became acquainted with Mr. Newman as a tutor, and the admiration and attachment of the undergraduate ripened into the most unreserved and affectionate friendship of the grown man—a friendship which has lasted through all storms and difficulties, and through strong differences of opinion, till death only has ended it. From Mr. Newman his pupil caught that earnest devotion to the cause of the Church which was supreme with him through life. He entered heartily into Mr. Newman's purpose to lift the level of the English Church and its clergy. While Mr. Newman at Oxford was fighting the battle of the English Church, there was no one who was a closer friend than Rogers, no one in whom Mr. Newman had such trust, none whose judgment he so valued, no one in whose companionship he so delighted; and the master's friendship was returned by the disciple with a noble and tender, and yet manly honesty. There came, as we know, times which strained even that friendship; when the disciple, just at the moment when the master most needed and longed for sympathy and counsel, had to choose between his duty to his Church and the claims and ties of friendship. He could not follow in the course which his master and friend had found inevitable; and that deepest and most delightful friendship had to be given up. But it was given up, not indeed without great suffering on both sides, but without bitterness or unworthy thoughts. The friend had seen too closely the greatness and purity of his master's character to fail in tenderness and loyalty, even when he thought his master going most wrong. He recognised that the error, deplorable as he thought it, was the mistake of a lofty and unselfish soul; and in the height of the popular outcry against him he came forward, with a distant and touching reverence, to take his old friend's part and rebuke the clamour. And at length the time came when disagreements were left long behind and each person had finally taken his recognised place; and then the old ties were knit up again. It could not be the former friendship of every day and of absolute and unreserved confidence. But it was the old friendship of affection and respect renewed, and pleasure in the interchange of thoughts. It was a friendship of the antique type, more common, perhaps, even in the last century than with us, but enriched with Christian hopes and Christian convictions.

Lord Blachford, in spite of his brilliant Oxford reputation, and though he was a singularly vigorous writer, with wide interests and very independent thought, has left nothing behind him in the way of literature. This was partly because he very early became a man of affairs; partly that his health interfered with habits of study. It used to be told at Oxford that when he was working for his Double First he could scarcely use his eyes, and had to learn much of his work by being read to. The result was that he was not a great reader; and a man ought to be a reader who is to be a writer. But, besides this, there was a strongly marked feature in his character which told in the same direction. There was a curious modesty about him which formed a contrast with other points; with a readiness and even eagerness to put forth and develop his thoughts on matters that interested him, with a perfect consciousness of his remarkable powers of statement and argument, with a constitutional impetuosity blended with caution which showed itself when anything appealed to his deeper feelings or called for his help; yet with all these impelling elements, his instinct was always to shrink from putting himself forward, except when it was a matter of duty. He accepted recognition when it came, but he never claimed it. And this reserve, which marked his social life, kept him back from saying in a permanent form much that he had to say, and that was really worth saying. Like many of the distinguished men of his day, he was occasionally a journalist. We have been reminded by the *Times* that he at one time wrote for that paper. And he was one of the men to whose confidence and hope in the English Church the *Guardian* owes its existence.

His life was the uneventful one of a diligent and laborious public servant, and then of a landlord keenly alive to the responsibilities of his position. He passed through various subordinate public employments, and finally succeeded Mr. Herman Merivale as permanent Under-Secretary for the Colonies. It is a great post, but one of which the work is done for the most part out of sight. Colonial Secretaries in Parliament come and go, and have the credit, often quite justly, of this or that policy. But the public know little of the permanent official who keeps the traditions and experience of the department, whose judgment is always an element, often a preponderating element, in eventful decisions, and whose pen drafts the despatches which go forth in the name of the Government. Sir Frederic Rogers, as he became in time, had to deal with some of the most serious colonial questions which arose and were settled while he was at the Colonial Office. He took great pains, among other things, to remove, or at least diminish, the difficulties which beset the *status* of the Colonial Church and clergy, and to put its relations to the Church at home on a just and reasonable footing. There is a general agreement as to the industry and conspicuous ability with which his part of the work was done. Mr. Gladstone set an admirable example in recognising in an unexpected way faithful but unnoticed services, and at the same time paid a merited honour to the permanent staff of the public offices, when he named Sir Frederic Rogers for a peerage.

Lord Blachford, for so he became on his retirement from the Colonial Office, cannot be said to have quitted entirely public life, as he always, while his strength lasted, acknowledged public claims on his time and industry. He took his part in two or three laborious Commissions, doing the same kind of valuable yet unseen work which he had done in office, guarding against blunders, or retrieving them, giving direction and purpose to inquiries, suggesting expedients. But his main employment was now at his own home. He came late in life to the position of a landed proprietor, and he at once set before himself as his object the endeavour to make his estate as perfect as it could be made—perfect in the way in which a naturally beautiful country and his own good taste invited him to make it, but beyond all, as perfect as might be, viewed as the dwelling-place of his tenants and the labouring poor. A keen and admiring student of political economy, his sympathies were always with the poor. He was always ready to challenge assumptions, such as are often loosely made for the convenience of the well-to-do. The solicitude which always pursued him was the thought of his cottages, and it was not satisfied till the last had been put in good order. The same spirit prompted him to allow labourers who could manage the undertaking to rent pasture for a few cows; and the experiment, he thought, had succeeded. The idea of justice and the general welfare had too strong a hold on his mind to allow him to be sentimental in dealing with the difficult questions connected with land. But if his labourers found him thoughtful of their comfort his farmers found him a good landlord—strict where he met with dishonesty and carelessness, but openminded and reasonable in understanding their points of view, and frank, equitable, and liberal in meeting their wishes. Disclaiming all experience of country matters, and not minding if he fell into some mistakes, he made his care of his estate a model of the way in which a good man should discharge his duties to the land.

His was one of those natures which have the gift of inspiring confidence in all who come near him; all who had to do with him felt that they could absolutely trust him. The quality which was at the bottom of his character as a man was his unswerving truthfulness; but upon this was built up a singularly varied combination of elements not often brought together, and seldom in such vigour and activity. Keen, rapid, penetrating, he was quick in detecting anything that rung hollow in language or feeling; and he did not care to conceal his dislike and contempt. But no one threw himself with more genuine sympathy into the real interests of other people. No matter what it was, ethical or political theory, the course of a controversy, the arrangement of a trust-deed, the oddities of a character, the marvels of natural science, he was always ready to go with his companion as far as he chose to go, and to take as much trouble as if the question started had been his own. Where his sense of truth was not wounded he was most considerate and indulgent; he seemed to keep through life his schoolboy's amused tolerance for mischief that was not vicious. No one entered more heartily into the absurdities of a grotesque situation; of no one could his friends be so sure that he would miss no point of a good story; and no one took in at once more completely or with deeper feeling the full significance of some dangerous incident in public affairs, or discerned more clearly the real drift of confused and ambiguous tendencies. He was conscious of the power of his intellect, and he liked to bring it to bear on what was before him; he liked to probe things to the bottom, and see how far his companion in conversation was able to go; but ready as he was with either argument or banter he never, unless provoked, forced the proof of his power on others. For others, indeed, of all classes and characters, so that they were true, he had nothing but kindness, geniality, forbearance, the ready willingness to meet them on equal terms. Those who had the privilege of his friendship remember how they were kept up in their standard and measure of duty by the consciousness of his opinion, his judgment, his eagerness to feel with them, his fearless, though it might be reluctant, expression of disagreement. It was, indeed, that very marked yet most harmonious combination of severity and tenderness which gave such interest to his character. A strong love of justice, a deep and unselfish and affectionate gentleness and patience, are happily qualities not too rare. But to have known one at once so severely just and so indulgently tender and affectionate makes a mark in a man's life which he forgets at his peril.

THE END

Printed by R. & R. CLARK, LIMITED, *Edinburgh.*

www.ingramcontent.com/pod-product-compliance
Lightning Source LLC
Chambersburg PA
CBHW051201300426
44116CB00006B/399